Post-2015 UN Development

Making change happen

Edited by
Stephen Browne and Thomas G. Weiss

Routledge
Taylor & Francis Group

LONDON AND NEW YORK

First published 2014
by Routledge
2 Park Square, Milton Park, Abingdon, Oxon OX14 4RN

and by Routledge
711 Third Avenue, New York, NY 10017

*Routledge is an imprint of the Taylor & Francis Group, an informa
business*

British Library Cataloguing in Publication Data
A catalogue record for this book is available from the British
Library

Library of Congress Cataloging in Publication Data
  Post-2015 UN development : making change happen? / edited by
Stephen Browne and Thomas G Weiss.
    pages cm. – (Routledge global institutions ; 87)
    Includes bibliographical references and index.
    1. United Nations Development Group. 2. Economic
development projects. 3. United Nations–Economic assistance. 4.
United Nations–Technical assistance. I. Browne, Stephen, author,
editor of compilation. II. Weiss, Thomas George, author, editor of
compilation.
    JZ4972.P67 2014
    354'.2113–dc23
                  2014007888

ISBN: 978-0-415-85662-1 (hbk)
ISBN: 978-0-415-85663-8 (pbk)
ISBN: 978-0-203-72408-8 (ebk)

Typeset in Times New Roman
by Taylor & Francis Books

Contents

List of illustrations

Figures

Tables

Boxes

Notes on contributors

Roberto Bissio is Executive Director of the Third World Institute and coordinates the secretariat of Social Watch. During 2005 he was co-chair of the policy working group of the Global Call to Action against Poverty. He is a member of the UNDP's Civil Society Advisory Group and has served on the board of the Women's Environment and Development Organization and the Montreal International Forum. As a journalist and columnist, he has written extensively about a range of development issues.

Stephen Browne is Co-Director of the Future of the UN Development System (FUNDS) Project and Senior Fellow at the Ralph Bunche Institute for International Studies at The CUNY Graduate Center. He worked for more than 30 years in different organizations of the UN development system, sharing his time almost equally between agency headquarters and country assignments. He has written books and articles on aid and development throughout his career, his most recent being *The United Nations Development Programme and System* (2011), *The International Trade Centre* (2011), and *The United Nations Industrial Development Organization* (2012).

Graciana del Castillo is the author of *Rebuilding War-Torn States: The Challenges to Post-Conflict Reconstruction* (2008) and the forthcoming *Guilty Party: The International Community in Afghanistan* (2014). She was Senior Research Scholar, Adjunct Professor of Economics, and Associate Director of the Center of Capitalism and Society at Columbia University. She first worked with war-torn countries as the senior economist in the Office of the UN Secretary-General in the early 1990s and then at the International Monetary Fund.

Richard Golding is an independent management consultant specializing in governance, oversight, and risk management in the international development sector. After 25 years of service, in 2012 he retired from PricewaterhouseCoopers, where he was a partner in the International Consulting Division with global responsibility services delivered to the UN system and worked alongside teams for all other major multilateral and bilateral clients, including the World Bank, European Commission, USAID, UK DFID, the regional development banks, and The Global Fund. His early career was as a UK public sector chartered accountant and financial systems specialist in both the UK retail and financial services sector.

David Hulme is Professor of Development Studies and Executive Director of the Brooks World Poverty Institute, University of Manchester. He is Chief Executive Officer for the Effective States and Inclusive Development Research Centre, a consortium of African, Asian, European and US research institutes promoting social justice in poorer countries (www.effective-states.org). His recent books include *The Millennium Development Goals and Beyond*, with Rorden Wilkinson (2012) and *Global Poverty: How Global Governance Is Failing the Poor* (2010).

W. Andy Knight is Director of the Institute of International Relations (IIR) at the University of the West Indies and Professor and former Chair of the Department of Political Science at the University of Alberta; he is a Fellow of the Royal Society of Canada. He serves as Advisory Board Member of the World Economic Forum's Global Agenda Council on the Welfare of Children, and was a Governor of the International Development Research Centre (IDRC) from 2007 to 2012. He co-edited *Global Governance* from 2000 to 2005. Knight has written about various aspects of multilateralism, global governance, peace, and UN reform. His recent books include: *The Routledge Handbook of the Responsibility to Protect*, edited with Frazer Egerton (2012); *Towards the Dignity of Difference? Neither "End of History" Nor "Clash of Civilizations"* edited with Mojtaba Mahdavi (2012); and *Global Politics*, with Tom Keating (2010).

Cécile Molinier joined the UNDP in 1992 from the UN Secretariat. Earlier she lectured in French at Smith College in Massachusetts and taught English in France. Her first UNDP assignment was as Deputy Resident Representative in Tunisia, followed by Resident Coordinator/Resident Representative assignments in Sao Tomé and Principe, Togo, and Mauritania. She directed the UNDP Office in Geneva from 2007 until her retirement in 2012.

Craig N. Murphy teaches at Wellesley College and the McCormack Graduate School of Global and Policy Studies at the University of

Massachusetts–Boston. He is past president of the International Studies Association and past chair of the Academic Council on the UN System. His books include *International Organization and Industrial Change: Global Governance since 1850* (1994) and *The UN Development Program: A Better Way?* (2006) He has held visiting appointments at Wesleyan, Johns Hopkins, Harvard, and Brown Universities, and at Stanford's Center for Advanced Study in the Behavioral Sciences; he has worked for the United Nations and been a Fellow of the Radcliffe Institute of Advanced Study.

Richard O'Brien is an international economist and futurist who spent 20 years in international banking, with Rothschild's and as Chief Economist of American Express Bank, pioneering country risk analysis, as Editor of *The AMEX Bank Review* and as consultant to the World Bank for the *World Development Report*. As co-founder of Outsights, he led the development of the UK government's online database of future drivers of change and developed scenarios for the "world's very poorest." He has served on many boards including Chatham House, the Royal Economic Society and the Economic and Social Research Council, and chaired the BBC World Challenge competition on grass-roots innovation. He is the author of *Global Financial Integration: The End of Geography* (1992) and has co-written/edited more than a dozen books on international finance and economics.

Robert Picciotto is Visiting Professor, King's College, London. Previously at the World Bank, he held several senior management positions including Director, Projects Department in three regional offices; Vice-President, Corporate Planning and Budgeting; and Director-General, Independent Evaluation Group. For the past 10 years he has provided independent evaluation advice to several UN organizations, the Rockefeller Foundation, the North–South Institute, and Wilton Park. He serves on the boards of the UK Evaluation Society and the European Evaluation Society.

Michael von der Schulenburg was Executive Representative of the Secretary-General in Sierra Leone until April 2012, and previously had 30 years of experience with the United Nations and 4 years with the OSCE including assignments in Afghanistan, Iran, Iraq, Syria, and Somalia. He has written about UN reform, peacebuilding, and UN approaches in countries in conflict or emerging from conflict. He has also spearheaded comprehensive IT-based management reforms for management in countries emerging from conflicts.

Bjørn Skogmo was the Norwegian Ambassador who led the "UN-2015" project in the Ministry of Foreign Affairs and earlier held numerous senior positions: Ambassador to Paris, Deputy Secretary-General for Development, Permanent Representative to the UN in Geneva, Ambassador for Peacekeeping, Special Advisor and Ambassador in the Office of the Prime Minister, Deputy Director-General, Policy Planning Department, Counsellor at the UN Mission, New York, Head of Cabinet of Foreign Minister, Attaché and Chargé D'affaires in Ankara. He is author of *UNIFIL, International Peacekeeping in Lebanon 1978–88* (1990) and numerous articles on UN issues.

Silke Weinlich is a political scientist specializing in international relations and with a focus on international organizations and the United Nations (including peacekeeping, peacebuilding, development, and reform). In 2012 she joined the Centre for Global Co-operation Research at the University of Duisburg-Essen, Germany, where she heads the research unit on the (im)possibility of cooperation. Previously, she worked at the German Development Institute in Bonn on the reform of the UN development system.

Thomas G. Weiss is Presidential Professor of Political Science and Director Emeritus of the Ralph Bunche Institute for International Studies at The CUNY Graduate Center. He is past president of the International Studies Association and past chair of the Academic Council on the UN System. His most recent single-authored books include *Governing the World? Addressing "Problems without Passports"* (2014); *Global Governance: Why? What? Whither?* (2013); *Humanitarian Business* (2013); *What's Wrong with the United Nations and How to Fix It* (2012); and *Humanitarian Intervention: Ideas in Action* (2012). He is co-editor of the Routledge "Global Institutions Series" and co-director of the Wartime History and the Future United Nations Project and of the Future UN Development System Project.

Rorden Wilkinson is Professor of International Political Economy in the School of Social Sciences, and Research Director of the Brooks World Poverty Institute, at the University of Manchester. His recent books include *What's Wrong with the WTO and How to Fix It* (2014); *The Millennium Development Goals and Beyond* (2012); *Trade, Poverty, Development* (2012); *Global Governance Poverty and Inequality* (2010); and *The WTO: Crisis and the Governance of Global Trade* (2006). He is co-editor of the Routledge "Global Institutions Series."

Foreword

Mark Malloch-Brown

Talk about reform of the United Nations is incessant, both inside and outside the world organization. It has always been so. The original organizational architecture has been added to continuously over the last seven decades; member states have agreed to adapt its main pillars of activity to changing demands. As an organization designed to maintain international peace among states, it is now called upon to create and maintain peace within them. The composition and working methods of the Security Council are a constant topic of debate while the unwieldy General Assembly, with all its warts, remains the closest thing we have to a world parliament. The world organization is also the custodian of the Universal Declaration of Human Rights and a forum for conceiving and agreeing numerous standards, norms, and conventions. From its activities of postwar humanitarian relief, the UN is now the safe harbor for tens of millions of forcibly displaced persons and the coordinator of relief for numerous natural and human-made disasters.

The UN also has a fourth pillar—support for medium- and long-term development—which has seen enormous growth but little real adaptation. It remains less than the sum of its numerous parts. In fact, its role has arguably become weaker, not stronger over time. Whether in the area of development research, norm-setting, or technical assistance, the UN system is being increasingly outgunned not only by long-existing multilateral and bilateral development agencies but also by the many new privately supported initiatives that often have proved to be more nimble and better able to address emerging problems. When it comes to galvanizing world leaders, the decisions of other gatherings like the World Economic Forum, the Group of 20, and regional organizations now appear more relevant than the debates that churn long-windedly in the UN.

What is to be done? Stephen Browne and Thomas G. Weiss have assembled a strong team of authors in this extremely timely book that provides answers. There is no better compilation of insights about the UN's lack of cohesion, growing turf battles, declining capacity, clumsy implementation, and cooptation by bilateral and private interests of the family of organizations that calls itself—somewhat awkwardly—"the UN development system." For the many of us who consider the UN to possess a unique set of values and approaches to offer in the field of development, there is an ominous sense of urgency about the need for radical reform. The need for greater cohesion was recognized in the early stages of the world organization, but it has never been realized along the dimensions required.

Browne and Weiss established the Future UN Development System (FUNDS) Project, of which this edited volume is part. They aim to construct "the UN we want for the world we want." They aim to make change happen. To do so, the arguments here and elsewhere must appeal to all three UNs. The first consists of its most influential member states, which are growing in number as more of them emerge as economic powers. The second is composed of UN staff members who—more than many of them realize—are in a position to take the decisions on which the future relevance of the UN development system depends. And the third UN consists of those whose well-being is ultimately the target of all UN development cooperation: civil society and the global public at large. If the results of independent surveys by FUNDS on the future UN development system are any pointer, the UN's development shortcomings and necessary reforms have gained worldwide recognition.

The time to act was yesterday.

London, February 2014

Acknowledgments

This book grows from two factors: our own practical and analytical experiences with the United Nations development system (UNDS) coupled with our conviction that it is in crisis and requires substantial change and even transformation. Both led us to establish the "Future UN Development System" Project at the Ralph Bunche Institute for International Studies (www.FutureUN.org), and for the governments of Denmark, Sweden, Switzerland, and Norway to finance this volume and several other activities since 2011. We are immensely grateful.

As in many such undertakings, the list of persons to whom the editors owe an intellectual debt is lengthy. More people than we can possibly mention here contributed to this timely multicultural and multi-disciplinary conversation. The result was to bring together a dozen authors from different nationalities and disciplines. We cannot mention all the generous colleagues who attended seminars, conferences, and other gatherings during the two-year duration of this project; it will have to suffice to name those to whom we owe the most.

Some of the themes of this book were first presented and discussed at an authors' workshop in Geneva in February 2013. We are grateful to PricewaterhouseCoopers for having facilitated that conversation and to individuals who generously participated with comments and suggestions.

Closer to home at the Ralph Bunche Institute for International Studies at The Graduate Center of The City University of New York, where the project was based, Paul Alois provided thoughtful administrative support throughout, while Nancy Okada with the able assistance of Eli Karetny ensured that we both spent and conserved our funds judiciously. Danielle Zach patiently helped to edit and shape the texts.

This support and background was especially in evidence during a second workshop in November 2013 to solicit comments from outsiders (knowledgeable experts from the United Nations, nongovernmental organizations, and universities) on the penultimate drafts of the chapters.

The input from discussants at those sessions was especially important, and so we and the authors would like to thank: Barbara Adams, Simon Adams, Kwame Akonor, Barbara Crossette, Susan Eckey, John Hendra, Barry Herman, Bruce Jenks, James O. C. Jonah, Deborah Landey, Magnus Lennartson, Vikas Nath, Ejeviome Eloho Otobo, Sarah Papineau, Minh-Thu Pham, Geir Pederson, Ib Peterson, Gert Rosenthal, Mia Stennige, John Torpey, and Pio Wennubst.

We express our appreciation to our contributors not only for their insights and evident commitment but also for the collective journey of learning through their respective disciplines and life experiences. Despite both geographic, disciplinary, and personal diversities and logistic challenges, the project was truly a team effort and a pleasure for the editors.

Finally, we are indebted to our friend and colleague Mark Malloch-Brown for gracing these pages with a substantive foreword that reflects his knowledge and insights from many years as a practitioner of and commentator on the problems and prospects of UN development. His willingness to call into question organizational shibboleths and his commitment to multilateral cooperation have been an inspiration.

Stephen Browne and Thomas G. Weiss
Geneva and New York
March 2014

Abbreviations

CSO	civil society organization
DA	Development Agenda
DAC	Development Assistance Committee (OECD)
DaO	Delivering as One
DDR	disarmament, demobilization, and reintegration
DESA	Department of Economic and Social Affairs (UN)
DFID	Department for International Development (UK)
DRC	Democratic Republic of the Congo
ECOSOC	Economic and Social Council
EPTA	Expanded Programme for Technical Assistance
EU	European Union
FAO	Food and Agriculture Organization
FUNDS	Future UN Development System
GDP	gross domestic product
HDI	Human Development Index
HDR	Human Development Report
HLP	high-level panel
IFI	international financial institution
IGO	intergovernmental organization
IMF	International Monetary Fund
IPCC	Intergovernmental Panel on Climate Change
MDG	Millennium Development Goal
NGO	nongovernmental organization
ODA	official development assistance
OECD	Organisation for Economic Co-operation and Development
PBC	Peacebuilding Commission (UN)
PRSP	Poverty Reduction Strategy Paper
QCPR	Quadrennial Comprehensive Policy Review
SDG	sustainable development goal

TNC	transnational corporation
UNCTAD	UN Conference on Trade and Development
UNDG	UN Development Group
UNDG	UN Development Group
UNDP	UN Development Programme
UNDS	UN development system
UNEG	UN Evaluation Group
UNFPA	UN Population Fund
UNHCR	UN High Commissioner for Refugees
UNICEF	UN Children's Fund
WFP	World Food Programme
WHO	World Health Organization
WTO	World Trade Organization

Introduction

The UN we want for the world we want

Stephen Browne and Thomas G. Weiss

In spite of some early misgivings, the eight millennium development goals (MDGs), along with 21 separate targets and over 60 indicators, which emerged in 2000 from the United Nations Millennium Summit, have been widely praised as benchmarks for development progress. The accolades result not so much because they are new—some, like universal primary education, have been targets for many decades—but because they have been a basis for assiduous monitoring. In particular, they have acted as a clear metric for countries to assess their achievements and shortfalls.

It is commonplace but wrong to dismiss debate about naming and shaming—for development performance or anything else—because governments, like people, care about their reputations and image. Approval and disapproval often explain social behavior.[1] Why do powerful and less powerful states care? Ian Johnstone answers: "states care about collective judgment of their conduct because they have an interest in reciprocal compliance by and future cooperation with others, as well as a more long-term interest in predictability and stability."[2] States are not fond of being singled out for behavior that flaunts norms and agreements, nor for being laggards.

This book is mainly, but not exclusively, about the UN development system (UNDS). For many people's taste, "system" is too rigorous a word for a disparate and dysfunctional "family" (another favorite description) of more than 30 organizations, agencies, programs, and funds with a mandate to support medium- and longer-term development objectives. There are an almost equal number of smaller training and research institutions and functional commissions under this development umbrella. System is more of an aspirational term, and in that sense it has meaning: if everything that the UN does outside its other functions of international peace and security, human rights and social justice, and humanitarian action could be brought into self-reinforcing alignment, there is little doubt that the UNDS would be much more effective than it is today. This angle is, in fact, a central *leitmotif* of this book. Even more ambitiously, there are clearly circumstances of fragile statehood for which coherence across all parts of the UN system is desperately required. In short, more and more organizations that had been mainly involved in development are being pulled into fragile and war-torn states, and those organizations and parts of the UN that had mainly operated in a handful of war-torn states are now operating in countries that until recently had been peaceful.

Since 2000 the MDGs have provided the basis of a development agenda for the UN. With the fateful terminal year 2015 approaching, the development system has initiated an intensive process of determining the goals that might follow the MDGs. In June 2012, the Rio+20 conference called for new sustainable development goals (SDGs) and the secretary-general established a High-level Panel on the Post-2015 Development Agenda co-chaired by three serving heads of government, which reported in May 2013.[3] Many other parallel consultations have been taking place throughout the world, and the United Nations set in motion a global conversation online that brought over 1 million responses. A UN task force led by the Department of Economic and Social Affairs (DESA) has produced technical reports drawing on the work of agencies, and an Open Working Group of 30 government representatives in New York is charged with distilling a considerable body of recommendations into a set of proposed new goals for consideration by the 69th session of the General Assembly late in 2014.

If the UN is successful in agreeing to a new set of meaningful goals aimed at the elimination of global poverty and the advancement of human development by 2030, it will be an important achievement. But it will be incomplete if the UN does not think beyond that task and examine its own capacity to help countries to meet those goals. This edited volume pulls together wide-ranging essays that seek to establish the extent to which the UN development system is indeed fit for that purpose.

Before briefly spelling out the contents of this book and the logic behind individual chapters, this introduction examines two dimensions of reform and summarizes the changing awareness about the current system's shortcomings.

Two dimensions of reform: coherence and capacity

While the UN is driving the process—dubbed "The World We Want"— there has been very little introspection on its own organizational capacity to help countries to meet the new goals. There is no doubt that a strong, cohesive, and responsive UN system—less dispersed than the current one (see Figure I.1)—would be able to play an essential role in ensuring progress, and in particular the important task of monitoring it, a conclusion that was reinforced by a survey among an expert panel.[4] However, the UNDS suffers from two chronic weaknesses: it has become increasingly disjointed, and it has not adequately adapted to contemporary needs, being sidelined by other more effective development organizations and initiatives along with alternative sources of finance, expertise, and oversight.[5]

To address the first problem, a High-Level Panel on UN System-wide Coherence was established in 2006, chaired by three serving prime ministers. It examined the work of the United Nations in development, environment, and humanitarian assistance, and not surprisingly found "policy incoherence, duplication and operational ineffectiveness across the system."[6] Its solution was to "deliver as one" (DaO).

More coherence within the UN development system is crucial if the world organization is to fulfill the terms of its mandate—indeed, this is the point of departure and justification for the current phase of the Future UN Development System (FUNDS) Project that seeks to extend conclusions from earlier work. The prevailing atomization

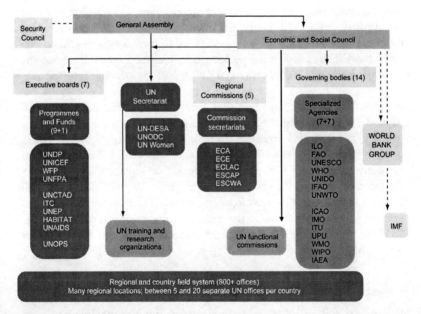

Figure I.1 UN development system

detracts from the UN's ability to react to local as well as global challenges. Moreover, coherence is also diminished by the substantial transaction costs associated with ever more elaborate mechanisms of coordination with, at most, questionable benefits. In the meantime, piecemeal changes have substituted for reform. As former UN deputy secretary-general Mark Malloch-Brown puts it: "a long period of tinkering with the UN machinery may actually allow the growing gap between performance and need to increase ... the call for reform is likely to grow steadily" and "the question remains when not if."[7]

But there are also concerns of relevance that go far deeper, the second problem. Are all parts and all activities of UN development organizations still needed? Are there new capacities which the UN should take on? Astonishingly, there has not been a serious debate on the system's capacity for some 45 years. The so-called Jackson report of 1969 contained many important recommendations which, if implemented, could have contributed to a stronger development system.[8] Indeed, Sir Robert Jackson undoubtedly turns in his grave with some regularity because he began his 1969 evaluation of the UNDS by writing that "the machine as a whole has become unmanageable in the strictest sense of the word. As a result, it is becoming slower and more unwieldy like some prehistoric monster." That lumbering dinosaur is now four-and-a-half decades older and certainly not better adapted to the climate of the twenty-first century. In reality, the intergovernmental deliberations that followed the publication of his report failed to forge a meaningful reform path. Nonetheless and in the period since, Jackson's concerns about the system's capacity to deliver have if anything only become more acute.

It is long beyond time to consider transforming the UN in the development domain, in these two critical dimensions: coherence and capacity. Promoting greater coherence across the system is an urgent priority, but it is also necessary to revisit the capacity of the system in order to determine, in a more fundamental sense, in what today's and certainly tomorrow's UN could and should be engaged. The FUNDS Project has been designed to examine critically both the roles and functioning of the UN development system. The main rationale for this book, and its timing, is the unusual opportunity provided by the 2015 threshold to rethink the UN development system and to empower it to support a new development agenda (see Figure I.2).

Changing awareness

If form is to follow function—to repeat a functionalist maxim about how best to structure multilateral cooperation—then "the UN we want"

Who should identify the new goals?

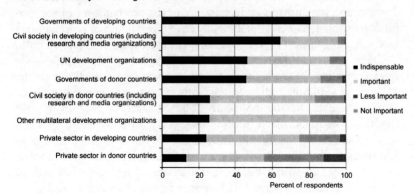

Who should ensure the goals are met?

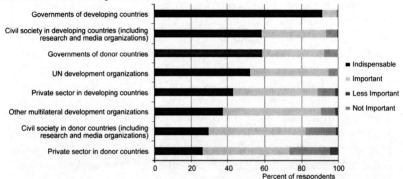

Who should monitor progress?

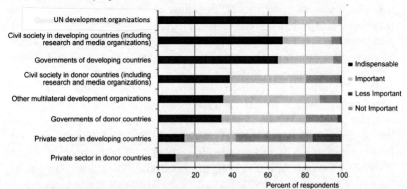

Figure I.2 New development goals: who does what?

will be the one that is best equipped to respond to emerging challenges. There is an ever-growing understanding of the prerequisites of successful development, as well as of a rapidly changing balance of power among UN member states. The UN development system must adjust to both.

General Assembly resolution 55/2 approved the *Millennium Declaration* in 2000, which contained many goals in addition to the MDGs, most in areas either too difficult to measure unambiguously or too sensitive to handle politically. The declaration contained eight chapters. The MDGs were substantially derived from Chapters III (on development and poverty eradication) and IV (on environment). But in addition to subscribing to basic values of freedom, equality, and tolerance (Chapter I), world leaders had also agreed to meet objectives of peace and security (Chapter II), human rights, democracy, and good governance (Chapter V), protecting the vulnerable (Chapter VI), as well as meeting the special needs of Africa (Chapter VII) and strengthening the United Nations (Chapter VIII). The next UN summit on the occasion of the world organization's 60th anniversary in autumn 2005 reaffirmed in its outcome document[9] a similar set of objectives and added landmark statements on the "responsibility to protect" and the creation of the Peacebuilding Commission and the Human Rights Council.[10] These two documents constitute to date the most elaborate agreed development agendas for the member states of the United Nations.

Thus, while the eight MDGs had value as surrogate benchmarks of progress toward human development, the Millennium Declaration was a more far-reaching and ambitious outline of "the world we want." What made the MDGs exceptional was the construction of, by UN standards at least, effective monitoring arrangements through country and global reports and conferences at regular intervals of five years to take stock and measure success or failure in reaching quantifiable and time-bound objectives. But for the other objectives of these summit declarations, there was insufficient concern about governments' compliance, particularly with respect to contested issues with a harsher ideological content and edge.

The MDGs were centered on poverty, health, education, and environment, which traced their pedigree to a series of UN global conferences of the 1990s. They usually had one or more UN sponsoring organizations: UNICEF for children (1990), the UN Environment Programme (UNEP) for sustainability (1992), UN Population Fund (UNFPA) for population (1994), the Food and Agriculture Organization (FAO) for food (1996), and so on.[11] Although the presence and influence of nongovernmental organizations (NGOs) and civil society organizations (CSOs) was very much increasingly in evidence,[12] the results reflected the rather more technocratic concerns that have been the focus of development since the birth of technical assistance.

Apart from the understandable desire to measure progress, the simple rationale behind the MDGs was that more development assistance to essential public services would accelerate development. The connection has been implicitly championed by most donor agencies and by strong aid proponents like Jeffrey Sachs.[13] As an advisor to the secretary-general, he formerly led the Millennium Project and promotes "millennium villages" designed to demonstrate how aid money can have a direct and beneficial impact on development goals.[14]

But we now know better and present the UNDS with two uncomfortable realities. First, the difference between progress and stagnation in the development arena is not primarily determined by technical parameters, nor by the quantity of money that is thrown at individual projects or collective programs, however well-conceived—and they are not always. Contemporary analysis about development stresses the paramount importance of sound institutions "that allow virtuous circles of innovation, economic expansion, more widely-held wealth, and peace"[15] and good governance. Angus Deaton has called the process of channeling aid money to fix world poverty, the "hydraulic" approach: "if water is poured in at one end, water must pour out of the other end."[16] One need not be a cynic or a fan of William Easterly or Dambisa Moyo to appreciate the shortcomings of traditional aid and the growing disenchantment with the legacies of failed experiments.[17]

The human development metrics featured in the MDGs are important symptoms of progress, and they will doubtless continue to be a key feature in future lists of goals. But they are insufficient as a UN agenda and ever more inadequate as the main rationale for more official development assistance. UN organizations have used the MDGs as targets to justify a continuing extension of ongoing technical assistance projects accompanied by a proliferation of new ones. But the claim of helping to eradicate poverty through mere delivery of more national public goods, while making no impact on inclusion and sustainability, is a hollow one. The future UN agenda will need to be much broader if the system is to be effective. Governance, institutions, and stability are part of the essential context for continuing development, and their importance has only increased with growing social upheaval within many developing countries whose economies are faltering or have actually collapsed. It is no surprise, therefore, that the high-level panel's proposed 12 goals include some controversial but essential undertakings, namely those falling under the heading of good governance and effective institutions in addition to peace and security. Whether or not the goals eventually agreed include metrics for measurement and monitoring in these areas, the United Nations must consider them part of its future agenda—that is, if it is to remain relevant, let alone effective. Indeed, the range of norms, operational competencies, and expertise provides the UNDS with a comparative advantage in pulling together responses to the myriad challenges facing the poorest countries, many of which are experiencing civil wars or rebounding from violent conflicts.

The second uncomfortable reality is the shift in the global economic balance of power. To speak of a rich North of donors and a poor South of aid recipients no longer has meaning, if it ever had. The notion of a center of industrialized countries with a periphery of undiffer-entiated developing countries in the global South is distinctly out-moded. The economic, political, military, and diplomatic milieu is far more dynamic and complex than the simple binary stereotype, especially the "us" versus "them" confrontational dimension. For the UN's development system, in particular, a growing number of countries are graduating from "developing" status. Three of the world's seven largest economies (China, India, and Brazil) were formerly—and in some minds are still—designated as "developing countries" but are now donors along with other rapidly growing countries. Indeed, South Korea, Mexico, and Chile are members of the "rich club," the Organisation for Economic Co-operation and Development (OECD).

The rise of the South's emerging powers will demand fundamental adjustments—"transformations" may not be too strong a term—in UN thinking and practice. The development debates in UN global con-ferences, the Economic and Social Council (ECOSOC), the General Assembly's Second Committee, and elsewhere have for decades suffered from the Manichean affliction of North–South confrontation and bar-gaining.[18] They invariably falter or are bailed out at the eleventh hour over questions of funding; and success and failure are measured by the extent to which the so-called developed countries have agreed to commit resources. But defining the global South or Third World or Group of 77 (G77) developing countries essentially in terms of aid-receivers because they have nothing else in common is not just ana-chronistic, it is a misguided notion driven by the indoctrinations of the aid industry. These ambiguities are well illustrated by the awkward alignment of one of the world's most dynamic economies, largest polluter, and foremost alternative-energy proponent, China, as part of a coalition with the G77 developing countries in calling for more aid from the "rich" countries for the development of renewable energy.

Moreover, "countries across the world have been converging toward higher levels of human development," the *Human Development Report*

2013 aptly concludes. "All groups and regions have seen notable improvement in all HDI [human development index] components ... On this basis, the world is becoming less unequal."[19] The result is, in the words of the Oxford Martin Commission for Future Generations, that "shared networks now transcend state boundaries and render distinctions between North, South, East and West increasingly redundant."[20]

The new alignments will manifest themselves in a variety of ways, some predictable and some not. In the UN's intergovernmental deliberations, there will be new and different voices. In the FUNDS survey of global experts in October 2013, for instance, respondents thought that emerging powers would be more likely to align with one another than with either the traditional donor countries or with poorer developing countries. New alignments will result in a less obsessive concentration on what the traditional donor countries can be expected to fund. The growth in bilateral (as opposed to third-party financed) South–South cooperation will create new geographical alignments, including more regional agreements. We have already seen increases in South–South trade, financing, and technological transfers. In part the growing role of foreign direct investment (FDI) by poorer to wealthier countries introduces yet another element into the dynamics that reverse or at least substantially alter many traditional roles and stereotypes. For the time being, all types of intergovernmental organizations in general and the structures of the UNDS in particular appear incapable of accommodating changing power relations.

In addition to the inertia of UN member states, the world body's country and regional presences have essentially not been altered let alone transformed. Until now, countries of the undifferentiated South—and many ex-socialist "transition economy" countries as well—have witnessed a rather uniform institutional development: hosting an ever-growing number of offices from organizations of the UN system, the main purpose of which has been to dispense technical assistance. For host governments, the high-level panel of 2006 spelled out the waste of redundant and essentially parallel presences and called for more unity within UN "country teams." The partial steps in this direction, with obvious benefits for host governments, have in fact incurred even higher transaction costs in the tasks of negotiating greater harmony among the UN system's organizations.[21]

To be clear, meaningful gains in coherence and resource savings will only come with comprehensive integration. But that pipe-dream of consolidation, the only sensible option in the field, cannot be achieved without much greater unity among the headquarters of UN organizations, starting with those which fall under the direct authority of the secretary-general. If there were a will, there would surely be a way. In a notable understatement, the *Human Development Report 2013* comments, "the principles that have driven post-Second World War institutions and guided policymakers need recalibration."[22]

There are prima facie avenues for potential savings that result from merely looking at some global statistics: over 1,000 UN field offices dispensing development assistance and a total of 1,400 offices for the system as a whole.[23] Do the various moving parts of the UN development system and its member states require so many offices? Is it not time to ask that question, especially because the numbers are still growing? Do Mexico and Thailand still each need the presence of more than 20 UN bodies in their capital cities? While a universal presence of the world organization may still be desirable for certain functions (including representation, information gathering, and norm dissemination), a more rational distribution would suggest a larger presence in the neediest countries and a dismantling of the heavy structures that are relics in better-off developing countries.

About this book

What about the UN's future agenda? This book deals primarily with the problems and prospects of the UN development system, which we have defined as the 30-plus UN organizations that have medium- and longer-term development objectives as part of their mandates. Almost all are members of the UN Development Group (UNDG), chaired by the administrator of the UN Development Programme (UNDP).

The book is divided into four parts, and the first, "The essence of contemporary UN multilateralism," establishes the context for the UNDS. In Chapter 1, "UN roles and principles governing multilateral assistance," Bjørn Skogmo describes the UN as the "nucleus of global international cooperation," but he warns that it needs to reinvent itself and focus on its roles as catalyst and actor in areas where it cannot easily be supplanted. In a fundamental sense, Craig Murphy's Chapter 2, "Evolution of the UN development system," does not perceive a big difference between the UNDS and the UN system as a whole, especially among clients. In looking at the various phases of the development system's evolution, he assesses where it has helped to influence the development process and where it stands today. From being at the center of the "global politics of development," the UNDS is in danger of fading or even disappearing from the development landscape, or at least being far more peripheral than it has been in the past. Richard O'Brien's Chapter 3 explores "Drivers of change for the UN's future role" and looks further ahead to scenarios spanning the expected 15-year lifespan of the next generation of development goals. His five "drivers" of change underlie shifts in the global landscape that will place new demands on global cooperation through the UN system.

"Grappling with the present and future: results, funding, management" is the second part, which is concerned with the development system's performance, now and in the future. More than ever, the UNDS is driven by the sources and direction of financial resources, and in Chapter 4, "Funding the UN system," Silke Weinlich reviews patterns, including the growing dominance of a limited number of donors through earmarking. She also examines new sources of funds from the global South and the impact of funding patterns on the nature and performance of today's UNDS and asks what this heralds for the future. In Chapter 5, Robert Picciotto's "Evaluating the UN development system" begins by describing as "woefully inadequate" the UN's current methods of performance evaluation. He suggests how they could be improved; and he recommends that the UN could be made more effective if it could more successfully bridge the development and security divide, foreshadowing a theme taken up in the next part of the book.

With funding go the responsibilities of accountability and transparency, an urgent priority for the UN, and the subject of Richard Golding's Chapter 6, "Making the UN more accountable and transparent." The last few years have seen an increase in oversight and transparency throughout the system, including the appearance of ethics offices, new systems of accounting, and results-based budgeting and management. The real test of openness, however, will go beyond the instigation of new processes and only come when staff are recognized and rewarded for their efforts to improve transparency and performance. There is a long way to travel yet on this unfinished itinerary.

The third part is concerned with the UN's role in addressing "The requirements of war-torn states." As anticipated in the early chapters, the precise frontiers of the UNDS are difficult to trace. This book recognizes that, where the development system could make the most impact—in situations of armed conflict and fragility—the prerequisites of stability are paramount. In war-torn states, therefore, the United Nations can show real strength if its efforts are upheld by operational inputs from all its pillars of peace operations, rights and justice, humanitarian relief, and development. But while a lot has been expected of the UN system in fragile and conflict-prone states, its performance has been patchy at best. The three chapters in Part III deal with the UN's role in peacebuilding, which should be able to combine the virtues of an organization that straddles development and security, but

depends on a full understanding of the process of transition from conflict to stable development. Andy Knight's Chapter 7, "Aligning UN
development efforts and peacebuilding," comprehensively reviews the
evolution of the security–development nexus and the attempts at
aligning the UN's various operational pillars. Several notable milestones (such as the Brahimi report of 2000) have been passed on the
way, but alignment has not been achieved in a sustainable manner. To
do so would require "considerable additional structural and institutional reforms" within the UN. And beyond greater internal coherence,
successful peacebuilding also requires successful engagement by the
UN with many state and non-state actors within crisis-prone countries.

His perspective provides a background for the following two chapters.
Graciana del Castillo's Chapter 8 asks: "The economics of peace: is the
UN system up to the challenge?" Her answer is ambiguous and not
always encouraging. She carefully analyzes the nature of the transition from
armed conflict to stability and determines that it has four dimensions—
security, political, social, and economic. Failure in one jeopardizes
success in the others. Transitions also have phases, passing from the
economics of war through the economics of peace to the economics of
development. It is particularly in the phase regarding the economics of
peace, where the UN is most ill-equipped institutionally. The UN
system needs to take a hard look at its capacity in this area and the use of
its resources. It also needs to develop a clearer idea of how to measure
successful peacebuilding. Michael von der Schulenburg's Chapter 9,
"Can peacebuilding drive the UN change agenda?" explores examples
of UN work in practice, which also helps to illustrate the strengths and
weaknesses of the system. His conclusion draws especially on his own work
in Sierra Leone. In more and more countries—and especially in those
in which the UN is considered the most effective partner—the need for
mere development coherence within the UNDS is overshadowed by the
urgency of getting all parts of the system to work together better.

Part IV reviews the prospects for meaningful change in "Toward a
reformed UN development system." The kind of challenges that confront the United Nations as a whole have changed radically since its
foundation and will continue to evolve, perhaps dramatically. Until
2015, the UN's focus remains on the MDGs, but different targets will
be needed beyond that date. In Chapter 10, "The UN and the post-
2015 Development Agenda," David Hulme and Rorden Wilkinson
review the elaborate process of developing a new agenda. While the
UN will provide the forum in which new goals will be decided, they
conclude that its role in shaping those goals will be diminished compared with the MDGs, especially given its "limited capacity to promote

ideas or take on leadership roles." Roberto Bissio's Chapter 11 places the emphasis elsewhere, on "'We the peoples' in the UN development system." He makes clear that the UN's relationship with civil society will also change. NGOs and CSOs have grown both in shaping UN agendas and in helping to implement the consequences. He sees the main challenge for the UN in transforming attitudes toward civil society from being merely an instrumental tool to being a genuine partner in building and sustaining open governance. He also underlines, as do many other critics, the need to distinguish clearly between the pluses and minuses of the non-profit and for-profit members that are often merged in some definitions of civil society and UN negotiations. In Chapter 12, "Revisiting UN development: the prospects for reform," Cécile Molinier and Stephen Browne review the long history of attempted reform in the UNDS, culminating in the 2006 *Delivering as One* report and subsequent ECOSOC deliberations around the periodic "comprehensive policy reviews" of UN operations. As indications of the desirable directions of reform, they highlight the findings of the global perception surveys conducted by the FUNDS project that provide insights about the strengths and weaknesses of the UN system, and how it needs to change. The imperatives facing today's UNDS demand the kind of changes that are reflected in global opinion.

The editors conclude with a set of practical proposals designed to enhance the UN's fitness for purpose as an effective instrument for development. We provide a modestly sanguine reply in the medium term to "Post-2015, can change happen?"

Notes

1 Jeffrey T. Checkel, "International Norms and Domestic Politics: Bridging the Rationalist-Constructivist Divide," *European Journal of International Relations* 3, no. 4 (1997): 473–95; and "Norms, Institutions, and National Identity in Contemporary Europe," *International Studies Quarterly* 43, no. 1 (1999): 83–114.
2 Ian Johnstone, "The Power of Interpretive Communities," in *Power in Global Governance*, ed. Michael Barnett and Raymond Duvall (Cambridge: Cambridge University Press, 2005), 187.
3 *Report of the High-Level Panel on the Post-2015 Development Agenda*, available at www.post2015hlp.org/the-report/.
4 Stephen Browne and Thomas G. Weiss, "New Development Goals: Plus Ça Change?" FUNDS Briefing no. 7, June 2013. www.futureun.org/en/Publications-Surveys/Article?newsid=13
5 FUNDS Project and World Federation of UN Associations (WFUNA), "Making Change Happen," 2012. www.wfuna.org/resource/making-change-happen-enhancing-the-un%E2%80%99s-contribution-to-development

 6 United Nations, *Delivering as One: Report of the Secretary-General's High-Level Panel on UN System-wide Coherence* (New York: UN, 2007), 2.
 7 Mark Malloch-Brown, *The Unfinished Global Revolution* (New York: Penguin Press, 2011), 190.
 8 UNDP, *A Study of the Capacity of the United Nations Development System* (Geneva: UN, 1969), document DP/5 (often referred to as the Jackson report after its main author).
 9 United Nations, *2005 World Summit Outcome Document*, UN document A/RES/60/1, 24 October 2005.
10 See Thomas G. Weiss and Barbara Crossette, "The United Nations: The Post-Summit Outlook," in *Great Decisions 2006* (New York: Foreign Policy Association, 2006), 9–20.
11 Michael G. Schechter, *United Nations Global Conferences* (London: Routledge, 2005).
12 See Nora McKeon, *The United Nations and Civil Society: Legitimating Global Governance—Whose Voice?* (London: Zed Books, 2009); and Kerstin Martens, *NGOs and the United Nations: Institutionalization, Professionalization and Adaptation* (Houndmills, Basingstoke: Palgrave Macmillan, 2005).
13 Jeffrey D. Sachs, *The End of Poverty* (New York: Penguin Press, 2005).
14 The impact of the Millennium Villages project in 10 African countries has been examined critically by researchers in the Overseas Development Institute in London, and the Center for Global Development in Washington, most recently in a paper by Michael Clemens and Gabriel Demombynes, "The New Transparency in Development Economics: Lessons from the Millennium Villages Controversy," available at http://international.cgdev.org/sites/default/files/Clemens-Demombynes-new-transparency_1.pdf
15 Daron Acemoglu and James A. Robinson, *Why Nations Fail: the Origins of Power, Prosperity and Poverty* (New York: Crown Business, 2012).
16 Angus Deaton, *The Great Escape: Health, Wealth, and the Origins of Inequality* (Princeton, N.J.: Princeton University Press, 2013), 272.
17 William Easterly, *The White Man's Burden* (Oxford: Oxford University Press, 2006), and Dambisa Moyo, *Dead Aid* (London: Allen Lane, 2009).
18 Thomas G. Weiss, "Moving Beyond North-South Theatre," *Third World Quarterly* 30, no. 2 (2009): 271–84.
19 UNDP, *Human Development Report 2013: The Rise of the South: Human Progress in a Diverse World* (New York: UNDP, 2013), 1.
20 Oxford Martin Commission for Future Generations, *Now for the Long Term* (Oxford: University of Oxford, Martin School, 2013), 17.
21 UN General Assembly, *Independent Evaluation of Delivering as One, Main Report* (New York: UN, 2012). Available at www.un.org/en/ga/deliveringas one/mainreport
22 UNDP, *Human Development Report 2013*, 2.
23 FUNDS Project, *Fact Book on the UN Development System* (Geneva: FUNDS, November 2010).

Part I
The essence of contemporary UN multilateralism

1   UN roles and principles governing multilateral assistance

Bjørn Skogmo

Rapid changes in the world economy are transforming the role of multilateral aid. The UN development system (UNDS)—the family of UN organizations, funds, programs, specialized agencies, and affiliated mechanisms charged to negotiate and implement international development objectives—is affected by these changes. The UN's global scope and universal intergovernmental membership are the basis for its unique legitimacy, but they can also be handicaps in a world economy increasingly driven by the private sector and by a civil society empowered by the digital revolution.

This chapter attempts to look at some of the changes now having a significant impact on the governance of the UNDS at three levels. It begins with the UNDS's relevance and ability to deliver on agreed international development objectives. Next the chapter explores the system's ability to support other core objectives of the UN such as international peace and security; its normative functions, including human rights and rights-based approaches; and the roles of specialized agencies in traditional public sector areas. And third, it looks at the ability of the UNDS to be a catalyst for partnerships with other global actors on key issues of global importance. The chapter is intentionally global in scope and does not examine country-level issues in detail or reforms of individual UN development funds, programs, or agencies.

The UN development system

The UN family of organizations—with its main organs, funds and programs, specialized agencies, commissions and committees, and its network of cooperation with other global actors—constitutes the nucleus of global intergovernmental cooperation. This means that there are linkages also to the wider debate about global governance, which was once but is no longer exclusively focused on traditional international organizations with the wider UN system at the center.[1] Global governance is now a much wider concept, in which inter-governmental cooperation will have to define its role and added value among a rising number of other actors. Efforts to strengthen regional and sub-regional organizations, inter-regional cooperation such as South–South networks, and more exclusive groupings such as the Group of 20, divert political energy and resources away from the global intergovernmental system, which is experiencing cutbacks in core budgets and reductions in voluntary contributions. Together, these other actors are growing much faster in number and in resources than global intergovernmental cooperation, however it is measured. The multilateral system, owned and governed by UN member states, is also evolving; but it is being pulled in various directions and has to determine its strategic role in an increasingly crowded and competitive institutional environment. To borrow an expression from a recent article, the world is becoming more "unruled," which raises new questions about the role of multilateral institutions in relation to global governance.[2]

The UNDS—alongside international peace and security and human rights—constitutes one of the three main pillars of the UN system. Inevitably, the UNDS is affected by rapid changes in the world economy and their impact at the country level. The discussion about the future of aid, the fragmentation of international development efforts, including multilateral aid, and the demand for more concrete results have exerted pressure on the UNDS to deliver more effectively at the country level, to report and to communicate better its achievements, and to continue its reform efforts. Some of the most lucid observers of the UN system argue that it presently seems "remarkably ill-adapted" to the challenges of the twenty-first century.[3] Others argue that the UNDS stands at a crossroads. It can "either embrace the deep reform required to remain relevant in today's global economy, or face the prospect of continued marginalization."[4]

The UN Development Group (UNDG), a formal coordinating group encompassing some 30 different entities, forms the nucleus of the UNDS and is an integral part of this wider UN system. The fact that most of these entities have autonomous governance mechanisms is both a source of fragmentation and a reason why consolidation and mergers are hard to achieve. The international financial institutions (IFIs)—the International Monetary Fund (IMF), the World Bank Group, and the regional banks—have special responsibilities within the system regarding monetary and financial issues, major investments in infrastructure, and systems development. For such key issues on the development agenda as providing capital for investment, economic growth, and job creation, the IFIs are the key players. They should be regarded as parts of the same global intergovernmental development system with largely the same owners, funders, and governors—that is, member states. The case for closer collaboration between the UN system and the IFIs is compelling,[5] and the new spirit of cooperation between these institutions initiated by the UN secretary-general and the World Bank president in 2013 could be an encouraging development.

Universal membership and the intergovernmental character of the UN system are important to understanding its role and limitations in relation to other global actors. In an international system built on Westphalian principles, viable and stable member states with democratic governments and the provision of basic public services are still the main building blocks, although they remain absent from a large number of UN member states. The resulting impediments from non-inclusive and non-democratic countries are limitations from the world organization, as is its intergovernmental character—despite such openings as the Global Compact, UN deliberations and operations often exclude or minimize participation by key actors from civil society, business, and the media. In the field of development, governments are still accountable for overall development policies, but most of the key tools—such as access to capital, technology, and investments—are now dominated by market-based actors and a variety of other instruments.

The effectiveness of the UN system remains dependent on the ability and political will among member states to agree on key objectives, priorities, reforms, and common actions. Setbacks and standstills in global negotiations are almost by definition due to the fact that member states continue to have different national interests and priorities and not due to an institutional failure of the UN system. In the governing bodies of most UN organizations, member states are able to reach consensual or compromise solutions on most ongoing issues, but often at the level of the least common denominator and sometimes by piling priorities on top of one other. The role of groups may be necessary for the management of negotiations, but they can, together with a strict interpretation of the rule of consensus, also reduce flexibility and possibilities for innovation. Linkages to other issues, such as the lack of progress in making the UN Security Council more representative of today's world, damages the legitimacy of the UN in the global South. Comprehensive reforms are clearly desirable, but until a critical mass of member states agrees on the direction and structures of a rejuvenated UNDS, reforms will continue on the step-by-step basis inherent in the very process of multilateralism.

One of the most challenging tasks in reforming the United Nations has been to find the proper balance between strengthening accountability within secretariats toward the executive boards, donors, and partners, on the one hand, and avoiding micromanagement, on the other hand. Member states have every right to hold UN secretariats accountable for the way money is spent, to insist that rules and regulations be respected, and to require that concrete development outcomes be identified and reported. But this balance may now have tipped too far toward micromanagement. Efforts to strengthen accountability systems have sometimes led to detailed and hierarchical operational rules and regulations, for instance on procurement and human resources, reducing the flexibility of program managers in the field to react quickly to changing situations. The major powers and developing countries often join forces in resisting strong mandates and organizational flexibility for executive bodies under the leadership of the secretary-general and agency heads.

Increased earmarking of funding to the UNDS by donors has also undermined core multilateral principles of shared goals, collective funding, and common action, further increasing fragmentation and reducing the flexibility of agency leaders.[6] Earmarking has increased significantly, accounting for 72 percent of total funding for operational activities for development in 2011.[7] Earmarking will not disappear, and "softer" earmarking to the main priorities of each agency can partly reduce fragmentation. A further transition to a more demand-driven approach will nevertheless diminish the UNDS's ability to implement common objectives and risk transforming it into a global contractor or consulting firm for member states.

If member states really wanted to reduce the fragmentation of the UNDS, they should restore the balance between regular budgets and voluntary contributions, and reverse the trends toward earmarking. They would also do more to abide by a guiding principle developed by the Development Assistance Committee (DAC) of the Organisation for Economic Co-operation and Development (OECD) to define the "good behavior" of donors in the multilateral system: "use and strengthen existing channels and think twice before establishing new ones."[8]

Development objectives in a rapidly changing world

The period since the first UN development decades in the 1960s and 1970s has witnessed profound and transformative changes. Shifts to market-based economies in developing countries, the end of the Cold War, the Internet revolution, and the rising importance of civil society have all affected the economic and political environment for development, both at the country level and globally. The financial crisis has further accelerated a shift in economic power and influence toward such emerging economies as China, India, Indonesia, Brazil, and South Africa.

Geopolitical changes inevitably affect the governance of UN development organizations, including the negotiations on institutional reform. Developing countries have demanded a larger say in the governance of the IFIs—particularly the World Bank and the IMF—for years. They are seeking new positions of power and influence in UN bodies. In principle, the UN system should be in a better position than other bodies to be an arena and a broker for the transition now taking place. Developing countries have often looked upon the UN—where they have a majority—as "their" organization in contrast to the international financial institutions where they have felt under-represented. If the ongoing transition in the paradigms of development continues to be seen through the lenses of North/South cleavages that are more and more irrelevant in today's world economy,[9] any transition will continue to be demanding, however, as many UN negotiations on development issues and on climate change are still dominated by an atmosphere of distrust.

In UNDS governing bodies, other conflicts have emerged. The UNDS has traditionally given priority to low-income countries considered to be most in need of aid. One of the thorniest issues in UNDS governing bodies has been to clarify the roles and responsibilities of middle-income countries (MICs), including the future of multilateral aid in them. There is a growing body of opinion, including a recent FUNDS survey, that the rise of emerging economies requires "major adjustments in the system including reducing the physical presence and program in middle-income and upper-middle-income countries where its traditional development cooperation services are becoming redundant."[10] The same survey indicates, however, that even the five countries in the BRICS (Brazil, Russia, India, China, South Africa) group are not unified in their views on UN reform issues. Traditional donors such as Norway argue that "scarce core resources of UN organizations should continue to be used primarily in low-income countries" while the MICs, and particularly the upper middle-income countries, "must be expected to take responsibility for poverty reduction within their borders by increasing tax revenues and implementing a social redistribution policy."[11] Some are increasingly in a position to shoulder more global responsibilities, such as increasing their contributions to UNDS core budgets. Emerging economies have indeed increased their core contributions, but the volume remains modest. At the same time, some MICs—led by a group of Latin American countries and supported by some Eastern European countries—have garnered support in, for instance, the governing bodies of the UN Development Programme (UNDP) and Population Fund (UNFPA) to defend their right to continue to receive multilateral aid through the UNDS.

The time when multilateral development is dominated and financed by the traditional 10–15 donors in the North is approaching its end. Traditional donor–recipient relationships are already being replaced by broader partnerships. There are still OECD member countries that could and should contribute more to multilateral development cooperation, but many of them are struggling with high levels of deficits and debt. There is a genuine risk that donor countries from the North may respond to the slowness and polarization of UN negotiations by giving further priority to bilateral programs or to other development channels more responsive to their own priorities, or by earmarking more UN funding.

The circle of donors must expand for multilateral development cooperation to be sustainable. There are some positive signs—efforts to increase the donor base for UN operational activities have reduced the dependency of funding from OECD/DAC countries from 71 percent in 1995 to 62 percent in 2010.[12] At present, there are many unknowns regarding how multilateral China and other emerging economies will be in their approaches to global development issues. In their cooperation with African countries, they have been much more bilateral than multilateral.

There are numerous examples of UN member states transcending narrow national interests and priorities and agreeing on global goals and common approaches. The contribution of the UNDS to the implementation and monitoring of the Millennium Development Goals (MDGs) has been vital. The process leading to the adoption of post-2015 sustainable development goals (SDGs) is a new test of whether the original multilateral idea—based on a sense of agreed goals and objectives, shared responsibilities, and common action—can be adapted to new realities.

Development approaches must above all take account of changes on the ground. The original objectives of development remain, but the functions of aid and the role of donors or foreign partners are changing rapidly. In Asia and in much of Latin America, aid has not played a major part in the impressive growth of emerging economies over the last decades—a fact that has revived debates in many donor countries on whether aid is necessary or really the best pathway to development.

Even in African countries, traditionally the largest recipients of aid, differentiation is growing. There are conflict, post-conflict, and fragile states that still need aid in its traditional sense: humanitarian relief;

reconstruction, rehabilitation, and development projects; and budgetary support. Some key UNDS functions—assistance to conflict, post-conflict, and fragile states and supporting poor countries that are still unable to benefit from globalization—will remain essential in coming years. Other African countries are experiencing sustained growth, however, and wish to be considered not as aid recipients, but as equal development partners. Bilateral aid agencies report a diminishing interest for traditional aid projects and a rising demand for investments, trade, and capacity building in key development sectors. Poverty and inequality levels remain very high, however, suggesting that broader development goals and strategies will continue to be necessary both at national and global levels. Capacity building will be needed to turn such strategies and future sustainable development goals into concrete results on the ground, but the role of traditional aid projects and programs by external actors will diminish. OECD/DAC statistics for 2013 indicate that aid to the neediest countries in Sub-Saharan Africa continues to fall, which is a serious concern.

The human and social dimensions of development retain their importance and relevance, even if in the wake of the financial crisis, there is a new emphasis on enhancing financial stability and stimulating growth. Economic and social development is not only about growth rates. The financial crisis has accentuated global concerns about rising unemployment, inequalities, and social justice, both from a macroeconomic, ethical, and political point of view. Such concerns now also pertain to countries in the North, particularly in Southern Europe, thereby also affecting the donor base for multilateral funding. The UNDS retains a key role in monitoring and documenting the inequities generated by economic development and in promoting human and social protection.

In the history of international development, the UNDS has made a major contribution by adding a human and social dimension to macroeconomic approaches. The human rights agenda, including economic, social, and cultural rights, is fundamental. UNICEF's landmark 1987 report, *Adjustment with a Human Face*, the UNDP's human development reports, the series of UN summits in the 1990s, and the MDGs drew attention to the need to eliminate absolute poverty and the importance of education and health, social issues, and women's rights. The FUNDS survey indicates that the UN has "become almost synonymous" with the MDGs, and that most of the current goals should be retained in the post-2015 development agenda.[13] Throughout its history, the UN system has been a key arena for negotiating and monitoring rights-based approaches to development, often in close interaction with civil society organizations.

The negotiations on the post-2015 development agenda have not been completed at the time of this writing. The emphasis on the human and social dimensions of globalization needs to be carried forward through the post-2015 agenda as important objectives. Convincing arguments have been made about why human development should be reaffirmed as the UNDP's core priority as well as for the other members of the UNDS.[14] Why? Because a more meaningful UN definition—that is, one that would receive enthusiastic backing by "we the peoples"—would need to encompass the adjective "human" in a different trio: namely *human* development, *human* rights, and *human* security.

In addition to its task of assisting developing countries at the national level, the UN system is charged with addressing a growing number of issues with truly global salience. Bridging the development and environmental agendas has proved to be extremely challenging. In spite of the Stockholm (1972) and Rio conferences (1992 and 2012) on environment and development and the growing number of UN environmental conventions, serious disconnects remain between the three main dimensions of sustainable development: economic growth, environmental protection, and social inclusion.

Nowhere are they more evident than in the inability of the international community of states to deal effectively with climate change. The Intergovernmental Panel on Climate Change—established by the UN Environment Programme (UNEP) and World Meteorological Organization and operating under UN auspices—has provided clear scientific knowledge about climate change and its socioeconomic impacts. In spite of protracted UN negotiations on global obligations to reduce emissions of greenhouse gases, governments are still unable to agree on key issues such as emission targets, burden-sharing, or funding to slow global warming. UN organizations have nevertheless important functions in areas such as data gathering, supporting intergovernmental decision making, coordinating finance, and implementing programs on the ground, as well as in agenda-setting, leadership, and norm creation.[15]

On the wider sustainable development issues, important steps forward were negotiated and adopted in 2013, including a strengthening of UNEP, the replacement of the former Commission on Sustainable Development with a new High-level Political Forum on Sustainable Development, and reforms in the working methods of the UN Economic and Social Council (ECOSOC). It remains to be seen how effective these reforms will be in overcoming cleavages between member states on the implementation of forthcoming SDGs, including burden-sharing of commitments and financing.

The size of and the nature of conditions attached to official development assistance (ODA) flows, debt relief, and rules and policies regarding foreign direct investment have long been crucial components of international debates. The financing for development agenda—as defined through the UN conferences in Monterrey (2002) and Doha (2008)—has expanded to focus on domestic resource mobilization, the fight against corruption, and the need to address illicit capital outflows from developing countries to tax havens. The sums involved in such capital flows are now dwarfing total ODA flows, confirming that aid is becoming more peripheral to development at the national level.

The UNDS, including the international financial institutions, can play supporting roles in assisting developing countries to mobilize national resources to reach their development goals. The IFIs will be the main contributor to efforts to stimulate sound financial management and generate economic growth, infrastructure, and jobs. But the rest of the UN system must find its added value in fields such as good governance policies and support for the consolidation of electoral systems and accountable administrations that will make it easier to generate economic growth and social justice. Better systems for collecting taxes, preventing illicit capital flight, and fighting corruption requires political will at the national level, but also requires know-how.

Supporting other UN roles and functions

The UNDS is not the only "system" within the broader family of UN institutions. The world organization is designed to promote at least three separate but closely interrelated functions: to help safeguard international peace and security; to negotiate and monitor international law and norms, including human rights and technical cooperation to implement these norms; and to promote economic, social, and human development. The UN development system underpins the world body's other functions. The further marginalization of the latter's development leg may, in turn, weaken the interest of developing countries in maintaining and strengthening the other functions of the United Nations.

In principle and often in practice, however, these functions and the UN's delivery systems overlap and are mutually reinforcing. But the individual parts of these systems tend to have separate lines of governance, linked to different ministries and constituencies in member states. This structure would not matter so much if member states were well coordinated in their approaches to global governance. But they too often work in a decentralized manner, which could be seen as a pragmatic, perhaps even inevitable, expression of pluralistic responses to the challenges of societies that are becoming increasingly complex.[16] At another level, this "pluralistic" approach may lead to a loss of strategic focus, further fragmentation, and a lack of synergies. The UN development system has to live with these contradictions, but they should not be used as excuses for not addressing more comprehensive reforms.

The maintenance of international peace and security is the primary objective of the United Nations as spelled out in the Preamble to the Charter. The UNDS has an essential role to play in supporting this objective—before, during, and after conflict. Economic and social development, including good governance policies and strengthening accountability within public institutions, is a critical contribution in strengthening the resilience of societies against the outbreak of war. The central parts of the UN's humanitarian machinery—the High Commissioner for Refugees, the World Food Programme, and UNICEF, with coordination provided by the Office for the Coordination of Humanitarian Affairs—are professional and well-resourced organizations that deliver relief and protection during and in the aftermath of war. The UNDS has a mandate to support post-conflict reconstruction and the strengthening of fragile states. Most of these activities come together under the concept of peacebuilding, which is increasingly recognized as a comparative advantage of the UN system.

The UN's normative system is based on the Charter, treaties and conventions, UN conferences, and the institutional mechanisms that monitor member-state compliance with agreed obligations. The UN's contribution to the world of ideas and normative development have been under-appreciated.[17] UN efforts form the backbone of international law and constitute an important part of the architecture of globalization. The UN normative system is equally central to the development of human rights and instruments to protect human security, including more recent additions such as the responsibility to protect (R2P). The prime responsibility for implementing existing norms and agreements as well as negotiating new instruments continues to rest with member states, but UN organizations possess a large number of mandates to monitor implementation and compliance.

Some of the specialized agencies and regional commissions may play minor roles from a development or even foreign policy perspective. They are, however, important arenas for technical cooperation and norm-setting for public sector ministries in member countries. The World Health Organization (WHO), which largely reflects the priorities of health ministries in member countries, has been less successful as a development agency than as a key global arena for international cooperation on medical and health issues. Less binding norms such as agreed "voluntary guidelines," which are more likely to include participation by non-state actors such as civil society organizations and businesses, have proved to be a very useful instrument for generating participation among non-state actors, and for establishing new partnerships to enhance the reach of global norms and values.

The UN system has by no means a monopoly on negotiating and determining global norms and standards. Important norms are being negotiated and managed outside the UN framework, particularly in the economic sphere. But in the efforts to promote international law and its incorporation and implementation at the country level, functioning political systems, governmental institutions, and intergovernmental cooperation remain indispensable.

The UNDS's fragmentation is often highlighted as a main reason for its relative ineffectiveness, particularly at the country level. The wider UN system is a loose, sector-defined structure; it was established to meet a wide variety of objectives with independent mandates and to accommodate autonomous governance mechanisms for each agency. It thus is too weak to ensure coherence. But fragmentation is not specific to the multilateral system. A large number of bilateral programs and an even larger number of civil society organizations add to this challenge.

One of the comparative advantages of the UN family is its potential to formulate and implement integrated, cross-sectoral approaches to complex challenges. Peacebuilding efforts in post-conflict countries and the involvement of many UN organizations in the fight against terrorism are only two of many examples in the UN system where broad inter-agency approaches have been negotiated and implemented with positive results. Nevertheless, this potential is far from being realized. There is still too much vertical thinking, too many turf battles, and too many gaps in mandates and resources for the system to live up to its potential. Integrated approaches and inter-agency cooperation should be more inclusive and open to non-UN partners.

Advances have nevertheless been made in inter-agency cooperation, and there has probably been more progress in the efforts to promote a system-wide approach over the last 15 years than previously. The establishment of the Chief Executives Board led by the secretary-general—which incorporates the UN Development Group and high-level committees on programs and on management—has yielded positive results.

Inter-agency efforts to overcome the challenge of fragmentation have centered on the promotion of system-wide coherence. The 2006 report of the secretary-general's High-level Panel on System-wide Coherence led to several partial reforms, including the establishment of UN Women, which is a merger of four previous UN entities dealing with women and gender.

At the country level, the establishment of the Delivering as One (DaO) principles and a new and more unified generation of UN Development Assistance Frameworks have led to positive results whose value should not be dismissed or underestimated. More than 30 developing countries have adopted the DaO model for UN agencies in their countries, and the number of countries that have adopted parts of the model now exceeds 70. The coherence agenda has contributed to a strengthening of country ownership of the development process and to better alignment of UNDS programs with national development plans. It continues to generate high transaction costs—involving too many internal meetings among UN organizations—and may be nearing the end of its potential without corresponding steps at headquarters. Given the challenges of fragmentation, the coherence agenda remains necessary but cannot be regarded as a reform end in itself. It should rather be considered as a vehicle to strengthen UNDS effectiveness and the ability of the UN to leverage partnerships both with national governments and other development actors.

Global challenges

Because of its universal membership and resulting normative legitimacy, the UN system is uniquely positioned to address emerging challenges that are truly global. The global public goods (GPG) agenda, presently grossly under-provided and under-financed, is rapidly becoming more pressing, particularly as regards climate change and sustainable development.

Presently the multilateral system does not have clear mandates for addressing the GPG agenda. Part of the reason may be a lack of an agreed definition and comprehension in UN circles about what such an agenda would really imply—should it be addressed as one comprehensive item or broken down into its individual parts as it has thus far? There has been resistance among developing countries to let the GPG agenda, which has been seen as largely caused and defined by industrialized countries, overshadow or divert funds away from core development issues.

Some parts of the global public goods agenda nevertheless constitute part of UN mandates and responsibilities. UN organizations play important roles as global safety nets that member states can mobilize for common action when needed. The Security Council remains crucial to determining whether emerging crises threaten international peace and security and agreeing on appropriate action when the politics are right. UN humanitarian agencies have mandates and resources to mobilize quickly to deliver relief and protection in natural and human-made emergencies. The WHO has established a worldwide network to prepare for pandemics or major outbreaks of communicable diseases. The IMF is a lender of last resort for countries facing financial crises. Numerous other examples could be mentioned.

There are, however, serious gaps in global response mechanisms to meet emerging challenges. For instance, it is harder to mobilize member states to agree on joint, preventive action than on joint measures to manage urgent crises. One area of rising importance is the threat from transnational organized crime, which threatens human, national, and regional security in parts of the world as well as undermining economic and social development. In areas important both for development and the GPG agenda such as sustainable energy, the role of the UN system has been largely limited to advocacy, without strong mandates or resources for effective action.

Innovative efforts to mobilize new financial resources for the fight against communicable diseases, climate change, and other grave concerns have been based on the necessity that the mobilization should be additional and separate from past ODA. As climate change becomes more pressing in the global South, these issues should be addressed by more comprehensive strategies and by common action.

Expanding partnerships with regional organizations, civil society, and the private sector is essential for the development agenda and for renewal of multilateralism in general. Partnerships will be absolutely crucial for the GPG agenda. The UN system can negotiate and monitor norms but will always depend on its owners and its partners to implement agreements. It could further expand its role as a convener and a catalyst to leverage cooperation with other partners to align key actors behind the provision of a specific global public good.[18] In many cases, the UN system will not be mandated or resourced to play the lead role in such global initiatives, but it could be a supporting and valuable partner for constructive initiatives coming from and led by other partners.

The UN Intellectual History Project has documented convincingly the extent of contacts and partnerships between the UN system and other non-state actors—to the extent that they have been labeled the "third UN."[19] Nongovernmental organizations play many roles in their interaction with the UNDS: as advisors and advocates, as watchdogs to ensure that member states and UN secretariats live up to their commitments, as implementing partners in humanitarian action, as rivals for new mandates and resources, as channels of communications to the general public, and as partners in global action.

Contacts between the UN and the private for-profit sector have been harder to achieve but have expanded rapidly in the last decade and a half. On normative issues, the Global Compact and initiatives such as the Business and Human Rights Initiative in the Council on Human Rights have successfully engaged business firms to commit themselves to respect fundamental global norms. On funding and operational issues, global health has been in the lead to explore new approaches through a significant number of global alliances and public–private partnerships such as the GAVI Alliance (formerly the Global Alliance for Vaccines and Immunisation), the Global Fund to Fight AIDS, Tuberculosis and Malaria, and UNITAID, where UN agencies such as WHO and UNICEF play important supporting roles. Secretary-General Ban Ki-moon has identified the expansion of partnerships as a priority for his second term and has launched important initiatives, for instance Every Woman Every Child, and Sustainable Energy for All. The arduous negotiations in the General Assembly about creating the Office for Partnerships in the regular UN budget indicate, however, a residual ideological resistance among developing countries to expand the public–private partnership agenda too rapidly.

One of the obstacles to further strengthening such partnerships has been the perceived need of many governments to maintain control of intergovernmental governance processes, and the accompanying unwillingness to involve new partners in UN governing bodies. For instance, civil society groups resist too close cooperation with for-profit corporations. Various models to strengthen such partnerships are being explored, for example by the establishment of "forums" open to both governments and non-state actors to bring relevant partners together for a more constructive dialogue on common challenges. The High-level Political Forum on Sustainable Development is the most recent example of partnership, and the UN Forum on Business and Human Rights is another. There are also examples, such as the Committee on Food Security, in which non-state actors are brought into regular UNDS structures while maintaining the integrity of the intergovernmental process.

Regional cooperation has long been a strategy for developing countries to meet the challenges of globalization; and recently there has been a strengthening of regional, sub-regional, and inter-regional cooperation in South–South groups to increase competitiveness in the global economy. The UN system has initiated strategic cooperation with regional organizations such as the African Union and the

Association of Southeast Asian Nations and is working to support South–South cooperation in several areas. Regionalization should not be seen as a rival but a complement to global cooperation.

Expanded partnerships with civil society, philanthropic, and business groups are vital not only to expand the funding base for the development agenda but as sources of innovation and partnerships for implementation. They are also important for maintaining public support for UN development. On this score, there are reasons for concern. Even in Norway, a country that has had a very positive attitude to multilateral aid and the UN as a key channel, critical voices have become stronger, perceptions of the UN as an ineffective bureaucracy more widespread, and traditional supporters more silent.

In the current financial environment of public poverty and private wealth, pressures to reduce ODA are increasing at the same time that insufficient public resources are available to finance the growing sustainable development agenda. There thus is a pressing need to strengthen new, additional, and innovative financing for this agenda and to strengthen multi-stakeholder partnerships at all levels. The UNDS should continue to use its catalytic capacity to convene and to support the establishment of such partnerships. In addition to the advances made in global health, innovative financing for climate change is being explored within UN entities, in bilateral cooperation projects, by sector groups, and by partnerships between different actors. An especially intriguing partnership is the Momentum for Change: Innovative Financing for Climate-friendly Investment, which was set up by the UN Climate Change Secretariat and World Economic Forum.

Conclusion

In a world of rapid change, there still remains much continuity in the mandates and functions that the UNDS is expected to fulfill. There are also increasing pressures from member states on UN organizations to set clearer priorities, become less bureaucratic, and be more effective and results-oriented at the operational level. The ongoing process to set the post-2015 development agenda is a prime occasion for a renewed focus on making the UNDS more relevant and effective with the aim of supporting and delivering the new agenda.

What about further reforms? The establishment of the High-level Forum for Sustainable Development and the strengthening of ECOSOC in 2013 hopefully signal that the "reform fatigue" that dominated UN circles in the 2009–12 period is receding. In spite of some encouraging steps, such as the UN Women reform and the abolition of the former

Commission on Sustainable Development, the risk remains of the default option for reform: setting up new institutional mechanisms inside or outside the UN system to meet new challenges while allowing existing institutions to linger on, supported by constituencies in member countries and other vested interests.

Strong leadership and new ideas from the secretary-general and other UN leaders are essential. But leadership is also required at the intergovernmental level, through new strategic alliances among a critical mass of countries from all regions that share a commitment to the common interest and to multilateralism. Such leadership will not come primarily from the major powers, which have other agendas and avenues for action. Traditional donors can still play a part, but such an alliance will clearly have to include key emerging economies as well as low-income countries and representatives from the traditional donor community.

Today the world is very far from having a global public sector to safeguard human security, shared functions, or common global needs. However, it does have a UN system that provides arenas for international cooperation on public sector functions, particularly in negotiating norms, rules, and global standards to facilitate cooperation between member states. At the national level, the provision of basic public services is indispensable for the maintenance of viable and stable states. This is one area in which the UNDS can continue to provide assistance to member states for the transfer of lessons learned to improve the quality and accountability of public services. Many of the operational aspects of technical assistance can be usefully left to other actors, such as bilateral agencies, international commercial actors, and civil society groups. But the ultimate responsibility for protection and the expansion of people's choices continues to lie with governments and democratic systems. A prerequisite is good governance in its broadest sense—strengthening openness, transparency, and accountability, facilitating strong citizenship and voice. These are issues already on the agenda of the UN development system and are still not getting enough attention. For the UNDS to maintain and strengthen its position in global development, it needs to reinvent itself and focus on its ability to catalyze strategic action in arenas where the UN cannot easily be replaced by other actors.

Finally, aid entails more than effectiveness. It is rooted in values of compassion and solidarity central to the UN's original vision. Multilateralism is more than an instrument for channeling assistance and safeguarding national interests. It is also about rediscovering common interests, about emphasizing inclusiveness, about mobilizing all countries for common action. It is hard to envisage tackling the challenges of the twenty-first century without effective multilateral cooperation at the global level, in which the UN development system will continue to play supportive and hopefully more catalytic roles.

Notes

1 Thomas G. Weiss, *Global Governance: Why? What? Whither?* (Cambridge: Polity Press, 2013).
2 Stewart Patrick, "The Unruled World: The Case for Good Enough Global Governance," *Foreign Affairs* 93, no. 1 (2014): 58–73.
3 Thomas G. Weiss, *What's Wrong with the United Nations and How to Fix It* (Cambridge: Polity Press, 2012).
4 Bruce Jenks and Bruce Jones, *United Nations Development at a Crossroads* (New York: Center on International Cooperation, New York University, 2013).
5 See Richard Jolly, "The UN and the World Bank: Time for Closer Relations," FUNDS Briefing no. 13, December 2013. www.futureun.org/en/Publications-Surveys/Article?newsid=29
6 United Nations, "Analysis of Funding of Operational Activities for Development of the United Nations System for the Year 2010," UN Department of Economic and Social Affairs, May 2012.
7 See Silke Weinlich, *Reforming Development Cooperation at the United Nations: An Analysis of Policy Position and Actions of Key States on Reform Options* (Bonn: German Development Institute, 2011), 36–77.
8 "2012 DAC Report on Multilateral Aid," OECD, February 2012. www.oecd.org/dac/aid-architecture/DCD_DAC(2012)33_FINAL.pdf
9 See David M. Malone and Lotta Hagman, "The North–South Divide at the United Nations: Fading at Last?" *Security Dialogue* 33, no. 4 (2002): 410–11; and Thomas G. Weiss, "Moving Beyond North-South Theatre," *Third World Quarterly* 30, no. 2 (2009): 271–84.
10 Stephen Browne and Thomas G. Weiss, "Emerging Economies and the UN Development System," FUNDS Briefing no. 10, September 2013. www.futureun.org/en/Publications-Surveys/Article?newsid=21
11 "Norway and the United Nations: Common Future, Common Solutions," Norwegian Ministry of Foreign Affairs, September 2012.
12 United Nations, "Analysis of Funding of Operational Activities for Development of the United Nations System for the Year 2010," UN Department of Economic and Social Affairs, May 2012.
13 Stephen Browne and Thomas G. Weiss, "New Development Goals: Plus Ça change?" FUNDS Briefing no. 7, June 2013. www.futureun.org/en/Publications-Surveys/Article?newsid=13
14 Craig N. Murphy and Stephen Browne, "UNDP: Reviving a Practical Human Development Organization," FUNDS Briefing no. 6, June 2013. www.futureun.org/en/Publications-Surveys/Article?newsid=12
15 See Alex Evans, "Sustainable Development," in Jenks and Jones, *United Nations Development at a Crossroads*, 64–68.
16 See for example the conference organized in Bonn, Germany, in October 2013 by the German Development Institute on "Fragmentation or Pluralism? The Organization of Development."

17 See Richard Jolly, Louis Emmerij, and Thomas G. Weiss, *UN Ideas That Changed the World* (Bloomington: Indiana University Press, 2009).
18 See the "Archimedes scenario" described by Jenks and Jones, *United Nations Development at a Crossroads*, vii.
19 Thomas G. Weiss, Tatiana Carayannis, and Richard Jolly, "The 'Third' United Nations," *Global Governance* 15, no. 1 (2009): 123–42.

2 Evolution of the UN development system

Craig N. Murphy

This short history of the UN development system begins with a brief discussion of how the system grew out of the work of the League of Nations and the wartime United Nations (the anti-fascist alliance in World War II). It then disaggregates the system's evolution into five periods—the last began with the global financial crisis of 2008 and triggered a new round of ongoing debate about UN reform.

At the outset it is important to understand that the UN development system and the UN system are often perceived as virtually identical. This conflation makes a great deal of sense, especially given that the UN's comparative advantage in grappling with the challenges of both insecurity and development increasingly appears to be in fragile and war-torn states and that the bulk of its staff and resources are devoted to assisting developing countries. Some 136,000 civilians work for the UN system in its country-level offices in about 160 countries or in the regional offices that serve them. Another 35,000 people work at the various headquarters, mostly in Europe and North America. There are also (as of January 2013) 93,000 uniformed peacekeepers seconded to the UN by national governments,[1] and almost all of them work in the global South; and more than 97 percent come from developing countries as well. All but two or three of the civilian regional and country offices are in the developing world or in the poorer countries of Eastern Europe,[2] and 81 percent of the UN system's civilian field staff are locally recruited. Staffs at the various headquarters include higher percentages of people from the global North. Nevertheless, most of the work at these headquarters involves overseeing activities in the field. Today, "the UN system" and "the UN *development* system" really connote virtually the same thing to many observers. Moreover, as the world organization attempts to make the most of limited resources in countries in distress, it makes little sense for the UN to separate the challenges of insecurity and underdevelopment into different administrative structures, one concerned with peacekeeping and humanitarian assistance, the other comprising the UN development system proper.

The UN development system before the UN Charter

The UN Charter refers to "development" only once. Placed last on the industrialized world's list of economic priorities, Article 55 called for "higher standards of living, full employment, and conditions of economic and social progress and development." This section provides the historical backdrop of the UN's development work, which has its roots in the League of Nations, the policies of colonial powers, and the wartime UN, which was heavily influenced by British and American staff.

During its existence, the League of Nations had experimented with giving people in colonies and in the less industrialized countries a stake in the world economic order. In what was a largely ineffective attempt at internationally monitored colonialism, the mandate system helped administer the colonies that had been stripped from Germany. More significantly, the League offered technical assistance to a few governments in the less industrialized world to encourage "development" even though, in those days, "development" was still understood as something that normally happened within the colonial world. Frederick Cooper and Randall Packard write, "What was new in the colonial world of the late 1930s and 1940s was that the concept of development became a framing device bringing together a range of interventionist policies and metropolitan finance with the explicit goal of raising colonial standards of living."[3] Embracing "development," Cooper and Packard argue, was a way for colonial governments to re-legitimize their rule in the face of challenges from local nationalists, labor movements, and the like.

The language used to describe the League's assistance is still used by the UN development system, and it reflected its origin in this colonial enterprise. The League sent an unprecedented technical assistance "mission" to China in 1931 to recommend reform of the country's entire educational system,[4] and in fact provided health assistance there during the 1930s. The League's field staff was part of the new religion of applying science to problems of government that had begun to supplant Protestant and Catholic missionary efforts. The League's technical assistance to an *independent* China became a model for a group of key Allied officials who moved directly from colonial administration in wartime Asia and Africa into the top economic positions within the UN Secretariat when the postwar organization opened shop in January 1946.

Perhaps the most important of these men was the British foreign ministry officer and protégé of John Maynard Keynes, David Owen, who had spent much of the war in the "Middle East Supply Centre" (MESC) in Cairo, a regional organization run by the United States and the United Kingdom. This office was tasked with creating more autarkic, but still prosperous, economies throughout the liberated colonies and dependent nations from Morocco eastward to India in order to free-up southern Mediterranean ports so that the southern front could be supplied through Italy. That ultimately successful scheme was the brainchild of a young Australian logistical genius, Robert Jackson, whom Owen worked under at the MESC.

Both would play central roles in the UN development system until they died (Owen in 1970, Jackson in 1991). Jackson went from the MESC to be the field commander of the UN Relief and Rehabilitation Administration (UNRRA), the first and the most robust civilian humanitarian and reconstruction operation of the war and immediate postwar era, which was much larger than anything that the UN has mounted since.[5] While Jackson went into the field with UNRRA, Owen went to New York to hire the other staff of the UN Secretariat and establish the UN development system.

Others who were there at the founding of the UN agree that Jackson's organization of the MESC, which was taken to UNRRA, then became the template for the organizational practices of the entire UN system. UNRRA staff, moreover, became the foundational workforce of the world body. Richard Symonds, who worked in the colonial government in India throughout the war and then went to the United Nations, explains:

> Working together in UNRRA were a number of people, particularly British and American, who were shortly afterwards to be appointed to key administrative posts in the United Nations and the specialized agencies. With this shared background of mistakes as well as achievements, they were able to agree on common personnel, salary, pension, and other arrangements which have been an important element in holding together the UN system.[6]

Richard and John Toye similarly argue that the unity of purpose in the early UN was a consequence of "patrimonial" hiring practices.

Owen, who initially served under the weak first secretary-general (Trygve Lie) and then under someone who saw his role as primarily external (Dag Hammarskjöld), was both willing and able to surround himself with like-minded people, albeit people from every continent and almost every UN member state.[7] These hiring practices contributed to a unified "culture" among United Nations Development Programme (UNDP) staff and the rest of the UN development system.[8]

Another important group shared much of this culture, namely US citizens involved with Roosevelt's Good Neighbor policy. For example, Harry Dexter White represented the United States at the 1944 Bretton Woods Conference where the majority of states taking part were Latin American members of the wartime United Nations. Eric Helleiner writes, "To be sure US officials supported international development in the 1940s for a number of strategic and economic reasons. But they were also influenced by the ideology of the New Deal with its interests in social justice, poverty alleviation, and interventionist economic policy."[9] In Robert Jackson's most famous policy document, he explains that White was the person who came up with the idea of the 1 percent of national income per year aid target. Ironically, this was the initial target that the noncombatant United Nations (mostly in Latin America) pledged to contribute to reconstruction in Europe and Japan—a down-payment of sorts for the postwar system that was supposed to continue to transfer a similar percentage of the national income of well-off countries to poorer ones in need of development.[10]

Humanitarian relief and technical assistance, 1946–60

With its early staff of anti-colonial Keynesians and New Dealers, the post-Charter United Nations quickly started backing into development. The UN gained organizational capacity in the field in part due to wrapping-up wartime agencies before the problems that they addressed had actually been solved. In 1946, the General Assembly passed on some of UNRRA's funding and one of its central problems (relief for children) to UNICEF.[11] The Food and Agriculture Organization (FAO) also received some of UNRRA's rump funding, and with it (and with the urging of the man closest to Owen in the UN Secretariat, economist Hans Singer) began to develop its connections to food surplus nations that would in 1961 result in the World Food Programme (WFP).[12] The continuing problem of providing humanitarian services to those displaced by war led to the creation of two other organizations, the Office of the UN High Commissioner for Refugees (UNHCR, in 1951) and the UN Relief and Works Agency for Palestinian Refugees (UNRWA, in 1949). Both were deeply influenced by the UNRRA model and both agencies provided training grounds for many later UN development system staffers.[13]

The most important cornerstone of the UN development system that was laid before the 1960s was the technical assistance network managed by the secretariat in New York, which in 1946 began offering such assistance to developing countries. It did not have the capacity to offer such assistance on its own, but acted as a middleman for such UN specialized agencies as the FAO, International Telecommunications Union (ITU), World Bank, International Monetary Fund (IMF), and even the International Trade Organization—the stillborn agency that had been intended to be the larger structure for the General Agreement on Tariffs and Trade (GATT), which continued to offer such assistance.[14]

UN technical assistance involved sending experts in every specialization in which national governments might be interested—from fish farming to public finance—on short-term "missions" to start programs and train local counterparts. There could be dozens of experts in one country at any time. Their work was coordinated by a representative of the secretary-general in the country's capital, originally called the "resident representative," appointed by the technical assistance section of the secretariat—the role that subsequently became the UNDP's resident representative and today's UN resident coordinator. Historians tend to attribute the structure of this entire program to David Owen, but his friendly competitor Robert Jackson disagreed on at least one point: "Resident Representatives, what were they? Nothing more than my country representatives of MESC. I mean, they're merely carrying on that concept."[15] Significantly, these in-country chiefs provided one of the few centers of coordination in the growing UN development system.

The UN's original program of technical assistance was given a major boost by US president Harry S. Truman's January 1949 "Point Four" pledge to assist the "underdeveloped countries" through "a cooperative enterprise in which all nations work together through the United Nations and its Specialized Agencies wherever practicable."[16] In 1949 the UN's program was given a new name, the Expanded Programme for Technical Assistance (EPTA), and a new system of central coordination. EPTA's Technical Assistance Board, which consisted of representatives of the secretary-general and of the executive heads of specialized agencies, vetted national requests, tried to match them with the programs that the agencies wanted to offer, and then made recommendations for the UN system's overall program to a Technical Assistance Committee of the Economic and Social Council (ECOSOC).

The significant new US funding—followed by smaller amounts from American allies, the Soviet Union and its allies, and neutrals such as Sweden—meant that the UN was able to expand its system of country offices from three in 1948 (Haiti, Iran, and Pakistan), to 15 in 1952, to 45 (almost all of the independent developing countries) in 1958. From then on, the UN as a matter of course added new country offices in every newly independent member state.[17]

Also in 1958, the General Assembly created a new agency, the UN Special Fund, to finance "pre-investment" technical assistance—the search for "bankable" projects to be funded by a new, as yet to be created, low-interest development facility, something fervently desired by the UN's growing majority of developing states. The developing countries wanted the facility to be placed under the UN Secretariat, but the United States, which had funded more than 60 percent of the UN system's development work through 1958 and had pledged to fund 50 percent thereafter, insisted the new facility be placed in the World Bank where Washington had an effective veto.[18]

Perhaps the most important characteristic of this period was the establishment of a radically decentralized UN development system, not only because the United States wanted to control the allocation of any significant amounts of money, but also because UN technical assistance was carried out by the specialized agencies (including the World Bank), leading to the proliferation of development activities throughout the UN system. Organizations originally cooperated for reasons of bureaucratic interest, not out of a concern for eliminating poverty or reducing global inequality; there is overwhelming evidence of a lack of interest in those issues among the early staff of every agency except UNICEF.[19] In fact, each was promised a minimum percentage share of the total technical assistance allocation. In the 1950s and 1960s, taking on technical assistance was the only way that most UN organizations and specialized agencies could grow. For every six or seven technical assistance experts that they placed in the field, secretariats in New York or Geneva or elsewhere could pay for one new professional position back at headquarters. As a result, by the mid-1960s, almost every organization within the UN system had a significant focus (at least in terms of its staff and funding) on the developing world, just as it does today.[20]

From the development decade to the North–South conflict, 1961–80

Historians of North–South relations are apt to look back upon the early 1960s as a moment when today's divisions between the global North and the global South first crystallized. The newly decolonized countries of Africa, Asia, and the Caribbean had become the UN's majority and, in 1964, they were joined by the original UN members in Latin America in the push for a permanent UN Conference on

Trade and Development (UNCTAD), and in a new alliance, the Group of 77 (G77). The G77, the argument goes, pressed its advantage in numbers over the former colonial powers to create not only UNCTAD, but also the UN Research Institute for Social Development (UNRISD) in 1963, the UN Industrial Development Organization (UNIDO) in 1965, and the unification of the UN's technical assistance, pre-investment, and coordination work under the UNDP in 1966.

All of that is true, but there was another, less confrontational side of the North–South story in the 1960s. This period was, after all, the "UN Development Decade," declared by President John F. Kennedy.[21] And almost until the end of the decade, the United States funded about half of the UN development system proper, the organizations under the secretary-general, not to mention its support to the World Bank. Moreover, until relatively late in the 1960s, there was a surprising level of agreement within the larger UN system about what development was and how it could be achieved. In those days, the Secretariat's Hans Singer as well as Amartya Sen and Mahbub ul Haq (developers of what many economists in the North would later consider the "subversive" UN concept of "human development") admired the modernization theory of W. W. Rostow that so influenced US policy toward develop-ing countries. Singer even argued to David Owen that each of Rostow's five stages of economic growth could be directly linked to one the key activities of the nascent UN development system.[22] Not surprisingly, therefore, in the late 1960s, the US-backed World Bank and UN development system proper collaborated in an extensive, reform-oriented evaluation of their joint work through the report of the Pearson Com-mission[23] and Robert Jackson's famous (or infamous) *Capacity Study*. That key study worried that the UN development system—with its scores of parts and lack of a central "brain"—had very little capacity.[24]

Nonetheless, by 1970 the development consensus had begun to fray. The World Bank's central role in development finance and the hege-mony of the economic orthodoxies preferred by national finance min-istries within it (in contrast to the growing dominance in New York of the more politically oriented ministries of development and foreign affairs of the G77) led to the ideological break between the Bretton Woods institutions and the UN development system proper.[25] More-over, new bilateral development agencies, rivals to the UN system, had sprung up throughout the North and thereby transformed the assumptions on which the Pearson Commission and Jackson reports were based. Finally, the vulnerability of the US and Western European economies in the early 1970s (and the exploitation of those vulner-abilities by Arab oil exporters during the 1973 war with Israel) triggered

a global conflict over the New International Economic Order (NIEO).
The global South hoped that the NIEO would replace the GATT and the
Bretton Woods institutions, which to many observers seemed to have
been irreparably damaged by the United States' unilateral decision in
1971 to remove its support of the fixed-rate exchange system. By 1976, in
Washington at least, the UN development system proper had become
identified with the NIEO and with opposition to the United States, thus
reversing the relationship that had existed from the 1940s until then.

While the conflict over the NIEO may have been the most obvious
manifestation of a crisis in the UN development system in the 1970s,
there was also a much deeper malaise. When the UN was young, and
even as late as the mid-1960s, the founders of the UN development
system believed that it would be quickly successful. Poverty would be
eliminated and much of the world would come to resemble the relatively
egalitarian, high-wage core of the global economy. That had not happened. Analysts and policymakers in the global South turned to theories
of neo-colonialism, dependency, and Northern opposition to NIEO to
explain why. Meanwhile, such Northern policymakers as Owen and
World Bank president Robert McNamara wondered if the problem
might be the rapid population growth in the global South, which has
undercut the impact of the historically unprecedented growth rates to which
the UN's and the World Bank's work may have contributed. Because
this worry was shared in parts of the global South, the development
system acquired another important organization, the UN Fund for
Population Activities (UNFPA, later Population Fund) in 1969, and
McNamara had tried to shift the World Bank's focus from achieving
growth to eliminating poverty. Both innovations would eventually have
a significant impact on the UN development system, but not until it
weathered the long ideological storm that had begun with the NIEO.

Structural adjustment versus human development, 1981–95

Ronald Reagan's inauguration in January 1981 marked the definitive
end of any remaining prospects for the NIEO. And the global economic shock that reverberated after the US central bank sent interest
rates above 20 percent in June pushed much of the developing world
into a period of economic stagnation that lasted until the mid-1990s.
Throughout this period, the Bretton Woods institutions turned most of
their attention from development per se (and from McNamara's anti-
poverty agenda) to structural adjustment. They repeatedly bailed out
near-bankrupt Third World governments (the IMF concentrating on
the richer states of Asia and Latin America, the World Bank on poorer

countries, especially in Africa) in exchange for the governments' commitment to draconian reductions in government spending and adoption of market-oriented domestic and international policies. The required spending cuts focused on social welfare activities and not on the security apparatus, thus enhancing the already powerful position of the military and police within many Third World countries. Meanwhile, leaders in the UN development system proper fought a rearguard action to try to moderate these seemingly anti-development policies. UNICEF officials argued for "adjustment with a human face."[26] The UNDP mounted an aggressive campaign of technical assistance to African governments that returned African neoclassical economists to their home countries to be interlocutors acceptable to the World Bank. These UNDP-sponsored economists were able to moderate some of the Bank's anti-welfare-oriented demands.[27] And analysts from both agencies joined those from the UN Educational, Social and Cultural Organization, the International Labour Organization, the World Health Organization, and the UN Secretariat to develop what Jean-Philippe Thérien calls "the UN paradigm" on global poverty—a view that the economic globalization that began in the 1980s had created losers in both the South and the North and that the macroeconomic policies of all countries needed to be changed in order to serve those individuals who had been disadvantaged.[28]

While some may remember this period as one of unproductive ideological contestation, it was also one in which the UN development system, very quietly, made a significant difference by contributing to state capacity in regions that were being drawn into the wave of economic and political globalization whose uneven consequences worried the developers of the UN paradigm. The UN helped train the exiled leadership who would eventually come to power in Namibia and South Africa,[29] created much of the administrative apparatus of the nascent Palestinian state in Gaza and the West Bank,[30] and helped Vietnam and China ease into their adoptions of market systems and their openings to the global economy.[31]

The last case is probably the most significant. Chinese leaders certainly attribute a great deal of their economic success to the UN's quiet help. In 2009, Khalid Malik, the Pakistani economist who served as UN resident coordinator in Beijing for many years, made a more global argument. Noting that China was taking on responsibilities for international finance, peacekeeping, and development assistance, Malik argued that the UN's long engagement had influenced the way that China has "become a full and active, concerned, global citizen," something that is good "not just for China, but globally as well."[32] The

UN's work may have helped transform Chinese leaders from being opponents of the liberal culture that underlies the UN development system, to being inquiring, relatively open-minded critics who have embraced the idea of a global community.

At the same time that the UN development system may have had some quiet impact in the 1980s and early 1990s, it is also clear that the system learned a great deal throughout the same period, perhaps some of it somewhat reluctantly. Women's movements throughout the world pressured UN organizations to put women more at the center of development analysis and programming, and significant progress has been made.[33] Even without such pressure, the culture of the UN development system led it to become an active supporter of the return of democracy in Latin America and Africa by providing critical institutional support to governments as they attempted to isolate or reform bureaucracies dominated by participants in the old military regimes.[34]

Yet perhaps the most significant institutional learning came through the establishment of the UNDP's Human Development Office, the producers since 1990 of the annual *Human Development Report* (HDR). Each year the office produces a single global HDR that focuses on a new dimension, a new side, of the wealth of relationships and current policy choices that determine the degree to which every human being can enjoy a full life. This refraction of the core concept into the entire spectrum of relevant policy realms has required the reports' authors constantly to expand the range of experts involved in their production. Each of the new dimensions has, in turn, helped maintain the vitality of the larger research program and of the concept itself. Amartya Sen summarizes Mahbub ul Haq's justification for this methodology:

> He wanted to build on agreement (what Cass Sunstein, the Chicago legal theorist, calls "an incompletely theorized agreement"). Such agreements may emerge pragmatically, on quite diverse grounds, after a general recognition that many things are important. Mahbub ... told the world: "Here we have a broad framework; you want something to be included in the list ... tell us what, and explain why. We will listen."[35]

Two of the reports that opened up especially significant debates were those in 1992, which first considered political freedom, and the 1995 report, *Gender and Human Development*.

The logic that led the Human Development Office in New York to include democratization, gender inequality, and cultural rights as issues central to development also implied that this office could never be the final word on what should be "included in the list" of human development concerns. For that reason, when James Gustave Speth was the UNDP administrator from 1993 to 1999, he instructed the heads of his country offices to encourage the production of national HDRs in every country in which the UNDP operated—that is, everywhere except Western Europe, the United States, Canada, Japan, Australia, and New Zealand.

Almost 700 of these reports have been published since 1992. Normally, they are completed by civil society teams approved by the national government, but the teams are assured the unusual freedom granted to ul Haq and his successors in the UNDP's global office: complete editorial control over the final report, which does not mean that governments do not intervene, only that they do so by making sure that a report is never started, or by trying to keep the number of reports in circulation within their own country quite low, not by censoring a report after it is completed. For example, Iran allowed the production of one report, in 1999, but the team that was to write the second report—which was to focus on the "dialogue of civilizations" within Iran—has never been appointed.

In some countries, the success of the national reports has led to the production of HDRs at the level of the province, city, or even neighborhood, all of which have focused on very different sets of variables than the income, health, and education measures that make up the global Human Development Index. In Brazil, where reports exist at all levels, they helped generate public demand for the relatively successful anti-poverty programs of the last decade. In Argentina, the first Buenos Aires city HDR shaped the public debate about responding to the financial collapse of 2001. At the same time, the 2002 report, which briefly became a national best-seller, played a significant role in the legislative debate over settling "the cultural deficit that accumulated during the military regime."[36]

In regions where national governments have been reluctant to have reports written on the topics that actually engage the public interest, the UNDP has supported the production of regional HDRs. Assuring equal opportunity, opening closed societies, and creating substantive democracy have been the themes of the HDRs that have received the most attention around the world: the successive volumes of the Arab HDR, first published in 2002. On the tenth anniversary of the 9/11 bombings, Fareed Zakaria called this first Arab HDR the most influential book to be published in the twenty-first century; it provided an explanation of the bombings and a rallying point for Arabs who wanted to pursue social transformation in a different way.[37]

In general, despite the culturally specific (liberal/social-democratic) origins of the human development concept, the HDRs collectively comprise a "dialogue of civilizations" because the process by which the many layers of HDRs have been produced reaches down into societies around the world. Although the civil society authors of the local HDRs come from national elites, the "broad framework" and the "incompletely theorized agreement" on which they are based have allowed many more issues to enter a global discussion on the nature of development.

Development begins to work, and becomes less important, 1996–2007

A cynic might argue that the UNDP's inclusive, open-ended HDR research program potentially served the UN development system well by giving it new goals during a period when its traditional goals—increasing per capita income and decreasing poverty—were particularly illusive. Of course, human development never really became the primary focus of most UN organizations involved in development, partially because in a competitive arena it was the UNDP's creation. And even if such a focus might once have seemed advantageous, the marked changes in the global political economy that seem to have begun in the mid-1990s may have taken away the need for a new paradigm. For most of the last two decades, poverty has been declining rapidly—very rapidly in China and the rest of East Asia, but significantly also in South Asia and Sub-Saharan Africa. At the same time, the middle class is growing, its percentage of the population more than doubling in developing Asia and quadrupling in China.[38] Half of the remaining poor are still in China and India, with the remainder almost entirely in Indonesia, Pakistan, Nigeria, and a relatively small number of "fragile states."[39]

Meanwhile, since the mid-1990s the significance of the financial flows into the developing world that come from the international development system as a whole (not just the UN) has diminished markedly. Before 1990, official development assistance (ODA) had always, since the end of World War II, been the largest flow of finance into the developing countries. Now portfolio equity investment (purchase of stocks and the like) is significantly larger. Remittances from nationals working abroad are three times greater. And foreign direct investment is almost five times greater. All the lines first crossed only after 1990.[40]

Arguably, the UN development system has yet to absorb the implication of any of these trends. When the lines first crossed, the primary concern of UN organizations was to deal with the almost flat line of

ODA relative to the income of developing countries as a whole, a line that extended back to the late 1960s. After the Cold War, UN organizations were expected to service a host of new activities with essentially the same funding—all the former communist countries that now sought development assistance to enter the global economy, and all the new places where the UN had taken on peacekeeping and humanitarian missions. Kofi Annan was the UN secretary-general most concerned about reforming the UN development system. He became convinced of the necessity for such reform while he was deputy and then head of peacekeeping in the early 1990s.[41]

Annan's predecessor and former boss, Boutros Boutros-Ghali, had tried an even more comprehensive rationalizing reform immediately after the end of the Cold War, only to be undercut by inter-agency politics that some even suggest were linked to Hillary Clinton's political ambitions. For instance, Carroll Bellamy, the powerful head of UNICEF who had been an even more powerful president of the New York City Council, certainly had Clinton's ear. Bellamy was worried about UNICEF's losing its autonomy under Boutros-Ghali's plan.[42] In any event, Bellamy, along with the head of the UNFPA, Nafis Sadik, and the head of the WFP, Catherine Bertini—all influential and politically connected in Washington—worked to undermine the comprehensive plan.[43]

Annan settled for an achievable system of coordinating the "the 32 UN funds, programmes, agencies, departments, and offices that play a role in development" through a single UN Development Group (UNDG) that also acts as the development arm of the UN system's Chief Executives Board (CEB), which includes the heads of all of the specialized agencies, including the IMF and World Bank, as well as what are officially called "Related Organizations"—the World Trade Organization and the International Atomic Energy Agency.[44] For the first time, there was something approaching a unified mechanism for coordinating the UN's development work from the top.

Further contributing to the centralized coordination was a push by the major bilateral donors, the World Bank, and the UNDP to create a set of global anti-poverty goals, which became the Millennium Development Goals (MDGs). At a global level, movement toward the goals was to be assessed by the UNDP, whose head also served as the head of the UNDG. Whereas at a national level, governments were supposed to create indicative plans, PRSPs (Poverty Reduction Strategy Papers) to be submitted to the IMF or the World Bank, more perhaps to be vetted for their economic orthodoxy than to be monitored for their success.[45] The collaboration between the Bretton Woods institutions, the UNDP, and the rest of the UN development system reflected a degree of ideological convergence that began in the mid-1990s. The World Bank embraced the UNDP's concept of human development—even if many in the Human Development Office wondered whether Bank staff actually understood it as an open-ended, democratically oriented research program. World Bank economists also moderated their belief in the free-market orthodoxy, sometimes called "the Washington Consensus," that they had embraced throughout the years of (largely unsuccessful) structural adjustment while UN analysts lost their aversion to some degree of economic laissez-faire. Jean-Philippe Thérien argues that, after 2000, the multilateral institutions all came to adopt global versions of Anthony Giddens's (and Tony Blair's) "Third Way"[46] between an inward-looking planned economy and the Washington Consensus, a policy of embracing globalization while maintaining a strong democratic state committed to social welfare.

At a national level, greater coordination was also attempted through strengthening the position of resident coordinator, which could in theory be held by an officer of any of the senior UN development organizations. Over time, these resident coordinators were supposed to lead in common premises shared by all UN organizations (including the World Bank and IMF) in each developing country's capital. By 2006, over one third of them actually did.[47] Annan also established an experimental program, "Delivering as One," in which eight selected country offices attempted to act as a single deliverer of UN services.[48]

Militating against all these attempts at rationalization and coordination were the centrifugal forces of the increasing demands on the UN system combined with its stagnant revenues. In every UN organization—in fact, probably in every twenty-first-century international development agency—local officers came to be judged by the degree to which they were able to create partnerships with national governments, private donors (global as well as local), private companies, bilateral donors, and almost any other legal source of additional funding. In 2005, Mark Malloch-Brown—Kofi Annan's close associate who served as his deputy secretary-general after being *primus inter pares* in the UN development system as UNDP administrator—complained, "In chasing after business of all sorts, UNDP had become a jack-of-all-trades but seemed the master of none. Any kind of development project in any sector you could imagine, UNDP was doing it somewhere in the world."[49] Something similar could probably have been said about almost every other UN organization at the time. The source of the problem was suggested by the answers that experienced senior staff members in over 30 UNDP offices gave during the previous year when asked, "What are the key factors you believe that UNDP headquarters uses in judging the performance of this office?" The most frequent answer was, "the volume of resources we raise," through all those myriad partnerships.[50] Malloch-Brown would probably say the number of those partnerships was a measure of the legitimacy that the UN was gaining in its primary mission to influence development policy to serve the MDGs or broader human development goals. But, to the country offices, that number just seemed to be an indicator of how well they could sell the UN brand to the largest number of the highest bidders.

Certainly the job of working for the UN development system became increasingly difficult over the last 20 years. Even if the real measure of one's success proved to be creating partnerships and bringing in the bucks, throughout the same period—and due to the same processes of reform initiated by Kofi Annan—a host of additional, often quite rational, indicators of performance were now also being used: results-based management instruments, incentives to find and stay with an organization's comparative advantage, and a strong or at least hortatory commitment to coherence.[51] At the same time, as in most large professional organizations in every part of the world, the neoliberal organizational ideology of the day meant that, for the men and women who started working in the UN development system in the 1990s or later, the old system of relatively permanent employment, guaranteed pensions, and a reliable sense that one would be treated with dignity by co-workers and superiors no longer existed. The UN development system was, perhaps, not as nice a place to work as it had once been, even though it still attracted some of the same kind of competent idealists who had followed David Owen through the door in 1946.

Conclusion: the UN development system today

Annan's reforms, those that were accomplished as well as those that were just attempted, were as much meant to keep that flow of competent idealists—people like himself—coming into the UN as they were to achieve their stated goals: eliminating poverty; expanding and maintaining freedom; strengthening the UN's increasingly effective system of peacemaking, peacekeeping, and peacebuilding; and re-embedding the global economy in larger social values. After the global financial crisis, the long-term significance of these reforms might be questioned. The differing experience of the crisis in different parts of the world—in particular, the relatively "good" crisis experienced in most of the rising economic powers—has created an important set of new players, including new providers of technical assistance, finance, and especially of effective models of development.[52] As one example, Brazil's cash-transfer programs, the world's largest program of this kind, have had remarkable success in reducing many of the indicators of extreme poverty.[53]

The remarkable economic success of Brazil, China, and other rapidly developing countries throughout the Great Recession has somewhat undermined the convergence on a socially oriented but still liberal "third way" development strategy that had dominated the professional discourse in the UN development agencies in the decade before the crisis. While Brazil might look like the model for a "third way" country, embracing globalization while strengthening a democratic welfare state, China's Communist Party–led development model, with its growing inequality and tight control of dissent, is something quite different. Moreover, China, Brazil, India, and the other rapidly growing countries are all exporting their own development models, along with a great deal of investment, throughout low- and middle-income countries. Despite the UN development system's history of being at the center of the global politics of development, it is now a less important part of the development landscape. Not only have other financial flows to developing countries outpaced ODA and continued to rise, but the overall amount of official development assistance itself has declined in response to the continuing crises, although the percentage directed through multilateral agencies (about 11 percent) has remained the same. The largest declines have been those of Spain, Italy, Greece, and Portugal. There has also been an odd shift away from the poorest countries, especially in Africa, toward middle-income countries in Asia, something that may reflect changing strategic priorities of the members of the Organisation for Economic Co-operation and Development (OECD), especially an increasing concern about the impact of China's rise on the rest of Asia.[54]

The Future UN Development System (FUNDS) project, of which this book is a part, is an element of the history of the UN development system in this most recent period, just as its immediate predecessor, the United Nations Intellectual History Project, shed light on earlier contributions.[55] Also pertinent for this short history are forward-looking studies by long-term headquarters executives (such as Bruce Jenks and Bruce Jones's *UN Development at a Crossroads*[56]) and pleas for the UN to reflect on its mistakes from former national staff members who have gone on to make major differences in their own countries (such as Fouzia Saeed's *Working with Sharks*[57]). Yet perhaps the greatest impact on the future of the UN development system will come from the leadership of the countries whose economies continue to rise— China, India, Brazil, and other emerging powers. While Khalid Malik may have exaggerated when he said that the ideas that the UN development system brought to China through its long and positive engagement may be good for the world as a whole, they are probably good for the future of the UN development system, whether or not that is good for the world.

Notes

1 All personnel statistics are rounded to the nearest 1,000. Statistics on peacekeepers as of 31 January 2013, "Rankings of Military and Police Contributions to UN Operations," www.un.org/en/peacekeeping/contributors/2013/jan13_1.pdf. Statistics on civilian field staff as of 31 December 2010, UN System Chief Executives Board for Coordination, High-level Committee on Management, "Head Count of Field Staff," CEB/2011/HLCM/HR/24/Rev.1, 12 December 2011, p. v including footnote e. Statistics on headquarters' staff as of 31 December 2010, UN System Chief Executives Board for Coordination, High-level Committee on Management, "Personnel Statistics," CEB/2011/HLCM/HR/13, p. 1, supplemented by overlooked data on the World Bank, from http://web.worldbank.org/WBSITE/EXTERNAL/EXTABOUTUS/0,contentMDK:20101240~menuPK:169705 2~pagePK:51123644~piPK:329829~theSitePK:29708,00.html and on the IMF from, www.imf.org/external/about/staff.htm. The current number of country offices is taken from www.undg.org/unct.cfm?module=CountryTeams& page=RcEmailReport (accessed 6 March 2013).
2 Those in Belgium, Turkey, and, possibly, Russia are the exceptions.
3 Frederick Cooper and Randall Packard, eds, "Introduction," in *International Development and the Social Sciences: Essays on the History and Politics of Knowledge* (Berkeley: University of California Press, 1997), 4.
4 League of Nations Mission of Educational Experts, *The Reorganization of Education in China* (Paris: League of Nations International Institute of Intellectual Cooperation, 1932).
5 Craig N. Murphy, *The UN Development Programme: A Better Way?* (Cambridge: Cambridge University Press, 2006), 37.
6 Richard Symonds, "Bliss Was It in That Dawn: Memoirs of an Early United Nations Career, 1946–79," Oxford, Bodleian Library, MS Eng. c. 4703, 26.
7 John Toye and Richard Toye, *The UN and the Global Political Economy* (Bloomington: Indiana University Press, 2004), 61.
8 Owen's impact on hiring remained almost 50 years later when I led a small research group that conducted hundreds of interviews with current and past staffers of the UNDP); we rarely met anyone whose personal connection to Owen was more than two degrees away. Murphy, *UNDP*, xvi–xvii lists those interviewed for the project.
9 Eric Helleiner, "Global Governance Meets Development: A Brief History of an Innovation in World Politics," in *Global Governance, Poverty, and Inequality*, ed. Rorden Wilkinson and Jennifer Clapp (London: Routledge, 2010), 42.
10 Robert G. A. Jackson, *A Study of the Capacity of the United Nations Development System*, vol. 2 (Geneva: UN, 1969), 4.

52   *Craig N. Murphy*

11 Maggie Black, *The Children and the Nations: The Story of UNICEF* (New York: UNICEF, 1986); see especially the "Foreword" by Robert G. A. Jackson.
12 D. John Shaw, *The UN World Food Programme and the Development of Food Aid* (Houndmills, Basingstoke: Palgrave, 2001), 17–36.
13 See Alexander Betts, Gil Loescher, and James Milner, *The United Nations High Commissioner for Refugees (UNHCR): The Politics and Practice of Refugee Protection*, 2nd edn. (London: Routledge, 2011); and Benjamin N. Schiff, *Refugees unto the Third Generation: UN Aid to Palestine* (Syracuse, NY: Syracuse University Press, 1995).
14 Murphy, *UNDP*, 53–54.
15 Robert G. A. Jackson, Transcripts of interviews, 1990, Oxford, Bodleian Library, MS Eng. c. 4678, fols. 58–59.
16 Sixten Heppling, *UNDP: From Agency Shares to Country Programmes, 1949–1975* (Stockholm: Ministry of Foreign Affairs, 1995), 23.
17 Adriano Garcia, *International Cooperation and Development: The United Nations Development Programme Resident Representative System* (Quezon City: University of the Philippines Law Center, 1982), 209; Yonah Alexander, *International Technical Assistance Experts: A Case Study in UN Experience* (New York: Praeger, 1966), 20.
18 Murphy, *UNDP*, 58, 68–69.
19 A point made throughout Jackson's "Foreword" to Black, *The Children and the Nations*.
20 This is the central theme (and central objection to the workings of the UN's development system) in Jackson, *Capacity of the UN Development System*.
21 UNICEF's 1996 annual report, *Fifty Years for Children: The State of the World's Children 1996*, includes an evocative discussion of the hopes of the early part of the decade, www.unicef.org/sowc96/1960s.htm
22 On Sen's and Haq's views see Murphy, *UNDP*, 241–42. "Subversive" is the adjective applied to the human development concept by former UNDP administator Mark Malloch-Brown. On Singer and Owen, see Murphy, *UNDP*, 64.
23 Lester B. Pearson, *Partners in Development: Report of the Commission on International Development* (New York: Praeger, 1969).
24 Jackson, *Capacity of the UN Development System*.
25 Stephen D. Krasner, *Structural Conflict: The Third World against Global Liberalism* (Berkeley: University of California Press, 1985) provides one of the most persuasive arguments about the domestic political sources of the Third World's position as presented at UN headquarters in New York or Geneva.
26 Giovanni Andrea Cornia, Richard Jolly, and Frances Stewart, eds, *Adjustment with a Human Face* (New York: Oxford University Press, 1987).
27 Murphy, *UNDP*, 224–31.
28 Jean-Philippe Thérien, "Beyond the North-South Divide: The Two Tales of Poverty," *Third World Quarterly* 20, no. 4 (1999): 723–42.
29 Ngila Mwase, "UNDP and the United Nations Institute for Namibia, 1976–90," and "Representation to the African Union and Liaison Office with the Economic Commission for Africa (RAULOE), 1977–2004," unpublished papers, UNDP Maputo, March 2005.
30 Work best summarized by the first head of the mission, John Olver, *Roadblocks and Mindblocks: Partnering with the PLO and Israel* (Rye, NY: self-published, 2002).

31 Murphy, *UNDP*, 177–81, 188–91.
32 UNDP in Europe and the Commonwealth of Independent States, "From across the Globe: Khalid Malik on China's Unprecedented Capacities to Tackle Poverty, Development Partnerships and the Financial Crisis – 14 April 2009," http://europeandcis.undp.org/cd/show/5428589E-F203-1EE9-BB06D9BC5D5E2F56
33 Murphy, *UNDP*, 206–11; Devaki Jain, *Women, Development, and the UN: A Sixty-Year Quest for Equality and Justice* (Bloomington: Indiana University Press, 2005).
34 Murphy, *UNDP*, 213–20.
35 Amartya Sen, "A Decade of Human Development," *Journal of Human Development* 1, no. 1 (2000): 22.
36 Murphy, *UNDP*, 251.
37 Fareed Zakaria, "A Decade after 9/11: Enduring Lessons for the Arab World," CNN, 12 September 2011, http://globalpublicsquare.blogs.cnn.com/2011/09/12/a-decade-after-911-enduring-lessons-for-the-arab-world
38 Bruce Jenks and Bruce Jones, *United Nations Development at a Crossroads* (New York: NYU Center on International Cooperation, 2013), 5.
39 Ibid., 6.
40 Ibid., 14.
41 Joshua S. Goldstein, *Winning the War on War: The Decline of Armed Conflict Worldwide* (New York: Dutton, 2011), 109–35.
42 "Move by UNICEF Chief to Dilute UN Reform Plan May Backfire," *Development Today: Nordic Outlook on Development Assistance, Business, and the Environment* 7, no. 11–12 (23 July 1997): 4.
43 Murphy, *UNDP*, 292–95.
44 UN Development Group, "About the UN Development Group," www.undg.org/content/about_the_undg_1
45 David Hulme, "The Millennium Development Goals (MDGs): A Short History of the World's Biggest Promise," University of Manchester, Brooks World Poverty Institute Working Paper 100, September 2009.
46 Jean-Philippe Thérien, "Multilateral Institutions and the Poverty Debate: Towards a Global Third Way?" *International Journal* 57, no. 2 (2002): 233–52.
47 "List of UN Houses by Region and Date Designated/Inaugurated May 2006," www.undg.org/content/common_premises_un_house/un_houses_by_region
48 The Coordination Officers from Albania, Cape Verde, Mozambique, Pakistan, Rwanda, Tanzania, Uruguay, and Vietnam, "Delivering as One: Lessons Learned from Pilot Countries," UNDG, June 2009, www.undg.org/docs/11117/091008-Lessons-Learned-from-Pilot-Countries.pdf
49 Mark Malloch-Brown, "UNDP 1999–2005: Accomplishments and Remaining Challenges," unpublished paper, p. 2.
50 Murphy, *UNDP*, 295.
51 Jenks and Jones, *UN Development at a Crossroads*, 28.
52 Craig N. Murphy, "Lessons of a 'Good' Crisis: Learning in and from the Third World," *Globalizations* 7, no. 1 (2010): 195–206.
53 Amie Shei, "Brazil's Conditional Cash Transfer Program Associated with Declines in Infant Mortality Rates," *Health Affairs* 32, no. 7 (2013): 1274–81.
54 Development Initiatives, "New Data Show International Aid Fell Again in 2012—and by More than in 2011," April 2013, www.devinit.org/wp-content/uploads/2013/08/DI-OECD-2012-data-briefing.pdf; data from the

OECD, "Query Wizard for International Development Statistics," http://stats.oecd.org/qwids/
55 See www.futureun.org/en/; and www.unhistory.org/
56 Jenks and Jones, *UN Development at a Crossroads.*
57 Fouzia Saeed, *Working with Sharks: A Pakistani Woman's Story of Sexual Harassment in the United Nations—From Personal Grievance to Public Law* (McLean, Va.: Advances Press, 2013).

3   Drivers of change for the UN's future role

Richard O'Brien

This chapter examines the changing context for future development, aid, and its governance, toward 2030 and beyond. After reviewing changes since the UN's foundation, it examines five key drivers of change: migration and mobility; political economy; security; the physical environment; and science and technology. These drivers can alter the context within which the primary challenges of the world—upholding the values and meeting the objectives identified in the Millennium Declaration, especially equality, eradicating poverty, and protecting the vulnerable—are tackled. After reference to the scenarios developed for an earlier Future of the UN Development System (FUNDS) workshop, the chapter considers how these changes may impact development and its governance, especially with regard to the United Nations.[1]

1945 to the present

Since World War II, we have witnessed major changes. World population has risen from just under 2.5 billion to over 7 billion—equivalent to discovering four nations with the population of today's India. Medicine has made remarkable strides in, for example, transplants and birth control although there has been nothing quite as revolutionary as penicillin. The next wave of advances is under way, in genetics and neuroscience. Some diseases—e.g., tuberculosis—have re-emerged from the brink of extinction. The computing and communications revolution has been a game changer. Transport has shrunk the planet through its reach and availability. Space is accessible to those with cash for the ticket. Today's world would not work without satellites. The Cold War is over, and we have avoided a World War III although we have many fragile states at war with themselves. The nuclear threat remains contained but still highly sensitive. The world's economic system has "globalized" around market capitalism. The number of independent countries has doubled. The survival of the planet and its ecosystem has become of increasing concern. Throughout, the global governance architecture of the UN has survived,[2] with almost universal state membership.

What have these changes meant for development? Despite averting world war, increasing global output ten times,[3] and almost quadrupling gross domestic product (GDP) per capita,[4] the rising tide has not lifted all boats. Measures of inequality—economic, social, political, environmental, technological—are widening. Gender discrimination remains the "single most widespread driver of inequalities" today.[5] Humankind has been successful at creating growth but not at sharing it—despite the rise of a large "middle" class in the developing world, projected to rise from 843 million to 3.9 billion between 2009 and 2030, an increase of more than 3 billion (see Figure 3.1). Some developing countries are richer, more powerful, graduating to join institutions such as the Organisation for Economic Co-operation and Development (OECD) and are no longer candidates for aid. Have the "graduates" achieved success as a result or perhaps in spite of aid? Aid and development are ever more closely linked to security. As private flows (corporate and

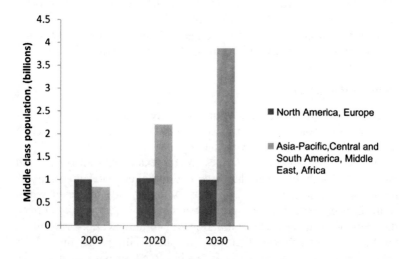

Figure 3.1 The rising middle class in the South
Source: Brookings Institution cited by the *UNDP Human Development Report 2013 The Rise of the South*, Figure 4.
Note: Middle class is defined as spending $10–100 per day (in 2005 PPP terms).

individual, legal and illegal) overtake government aid, should aid become history?

Five drivers of future change

Five drivers of future change will alter the context for development, aid, and its governance, requiring new thinking and action. Although not the only important drivers for change, the five discussed here—migration and mobility; political economy; security; the physical environment; and science and technology—combine a powerful mix of uncertainty from social, political, economic, environmental, and technological factors. The creation of gender equality alone, for example, would not only be a major leap forward for the Millennium Declaration's values of freedom, solidarity, tolerance, and justice and human rights; but it would also unleash, especially in poorer countries, the talent and value of human resources that growth needs to draw upon. Indeed, the drive toward equality in all its dimensions can be seen as a thread running throughout these changes, especially where access to resources, opportunities, security, and geographic space are under pressure.

Migration and mobility

Demography carries a seductive air of predictability and precision. By 2050 world population will rise from 7 billion to 8.3–10.9 billion—a "give or take a billion" range as the UN puts it.[6] We can perceive populations getting older or younger and track age cohorts over decades, such as baby boomers or the skewed gender pattern in China. Countries can plan for changed dependency ratios—funding pensions in ageing countries, creating jobs in younger countries—even if solutions are hard to execute. But while countries' future needs are shaped by their own demographics, the "third demographic dimension" of migration is critical, with tough governance challenges, within and between countries. Some call for migration to be part of the post-2015 development agenda.[7] With improved mobility, migration is likely to become a critical driver of change—as people "vote with their feet."

Migration within countries has seen urban population overtaking rural population worldwide, especially in developing economies. This could be an opportunity as well as a challenge if cities continue to be "the world's engines for business and innovation,"[8] providing the context for the provision of healthy living conditions (food, water, and healthcare) rather than repeating nineteenth-century European urban pollution and squalor.

International migration, however, is especially important for developing countries in seven ways. First, outward migration is an escape route for the poor and unemployed—a big "push" factor according to demographers. At the same time outflow can also decrease labor supply enough to improve job opportunities for those left behind. In some cases, this may also reduce populations dependent on the state. Second, migration may foster political stability by acting as a "safety valve" for countries that cannot create enough jobs in the short term.[9]

Third, while outward migration can reduce the pool of skilled labor at home, thereby hampering development—such as the outflow of nurses from Malawi or the Philippines—other developing countries may benefit as recipients. South Africa, for example, is the main beneficiary of healthcare workers from Malawi. Fourth, some countries actively devote resources to promote the training and "export" of skilled people as a foreign exchange earner; the Philippines government, for example, facilitates the emigration of nurses.

Fifth, outward migration has resulted in the boom in monetary remittances from rich to poor countries, now more than four times official aid flows. Migrants' remittances to developing countries may reach $540 billion by 2016, encouraging the view that official aid is becoming less critical. The largest flows in 2012 were to India ($69 billion) and China ($60 billion), but for some smaller countries remittances can be a quarter to a third of GDP. With the costs of transmitting remittances rising,[10] and new barriers being set up (often for fear of aiding money laundering), the UN General Assembly is considering the reduction of transaction costs as a possible post-2015 development goal.[11] Sixth, migrants can contribute to development through the transfer of non-financial capital, or "social remittances"—such as ideas, skills, social connections—acquired in host countries.[12] They or their children may even permanently return to their home countries, especially where opportunities are on the rise—as seen in Ghana, Vietnam, and India. Seventh, diasporas may also pressure host governments to support poorer home countries.

Migration also has an impact on rich and poor host countries, becoming one of the trickiest economic/political/social issues. How will attitudes to aid be affected in donor countries as they tackle sensitive immigration issues? As the political right gains from social fears over immigration, the United Kingdom's open philosophy, for instance, could weaken and change public attitudes to assistance overseas. The United States is already engaged in immigration reform, mixing pragmatic liberalism and a toughening of the process, seeking to legitimize 11 million existing "undocumented" immigrants whilst tightening border controls.[13] The number of migrants from the global South living in the North is over 80 million, which is now the number of migrants in the South born in the South each year (see Figure 3.2). These flows are likely to influence rich country attitudes toward development, including increasing calls for something to be done "at source" to slow the causes of economic migration.

Migration is part of the wider theme of mobility. Information technology (IT) is creating virtual mobility, allowing individuals to network for information and power, and governments and companies to gather information. We may be better informed in a more transparent world. Open source interaction can counterbalance centralized production, governance, and control. But Orwellian dystopias of surveillance and lack of privacy also result. Virtual mobility is powerful alongside increasing physical mobility, allowing cross-border communities and diaspora to communicate, and populations to appreciate opportunities elsewhere and react against conditions at home.

With technologies, the reordering of economies and societies may be only just starting: where will the jobs be in a world with three-dimensional printing or additive manufacturing? Increasing migration and virtual mobility alter perceptions of identity, as cultures mix and as more people have multiple loyalties, connections, homes, and passports. As participants

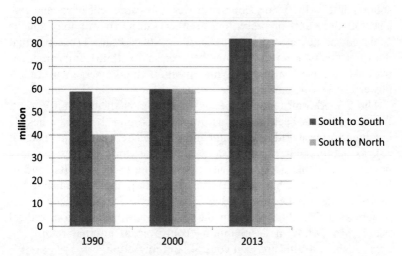

Figure 3.2 Number of migrants and origin
Source: UN Population Division, *International Migration 2013: Migration by Origin and Destination* (Population Facts No. 2013/3), September 2013.

in the 2010 FUNDS scenario workshop asked, "given that the UN is based around the state, how can it satisfy the needs of identities that cross borders, such as religion (and Islam in particular)?"

The cross-border movement of people is one of the five major globalization flows, alongside capital, goods, services, and information. New barriers to migration are just as possible as are new barriers to capital, to the flow of knowledge and intellectual property, and to goods and services. All these flows could be reversed. Where access to resources, jobs, opportunities, and to a way of life becomes harder, however, physical mobility will remain key to combating inequality of access.

Political economy: after the storm, the rise of the BRICS

The two biggest drivers of change in the arena of political economy may be the legacy of the biggest (peacetime) economic and financial crisis in most people's lifetimes (and the UN's), and the rise of the major emerging markets—Brazil, Russia, India, China, and South Africa (BRICS), among others. The first legacy of the crash may be states becoming more inward-looking and protective and less outward-looking and cooperative. The European Union (EU) may bear the most scars. The projected homogeneous, single market may develop at different speeds, new alliances, and even go into reverse. Some countries may splinter internally. If any country leaves, the game will have changed. The founding aim of preventing another European war may still be achieved, as acknowledged by the 2012 Nobel Peace Prize, but that does not preclude severe tensions between and within European countries. Alternatively, a new unifying ambition could emerge, ensuring a powerful EU voice on the global stage.

The United States may face a less existential challenge than Europe. Its recession has been neither as deep nor as long. It may be heavily indebted to the world (including China) but lenders can be as much at risk as debtors. The United States is still the world's largest military power even if this does not guarantee winning every war. Its "end of history" confidence has suffered from 9/11, Iraq, and Afghanistan; but its self-image may be stronger. Its global presence is undoubtedly under attack, as a front-line player in the "war on terror" and from radical Islam. Meanwhile, it is attempting controversial internal reforms in areas such as healthcare, gun control, and migration.

The crash has revived calls for alternatives to free-market capitalism, new regulations, and curbs on the "excesses" of globalization. The big loser so far has been "government," as the corporate world still shapes the market and as civil society seeks its own voice. The immediate legacy of the crash has been tighter public budgets and austerity, with corporate power shaken in reputation but hardly stirred.

The rise of the BRICS, now almost taken for granted, will reshape global power structures and could change the aid debate and the UN's structure. Hence, the FUNDS future scenarios have as one key dimension the changing governance structure for the world.[14] Rivalry and co-operation in the global arena is hardly new, even if the names change. But current and future uncertainties are undeniably huge. While China's economy may become the world's largest, it faces very real challenges: finding sufficient resources; internal security; environmental deterioration; and sustaining state-supported capitalism. India, soon to become the largest populated country, will still have low income per capita and high poverty like China. Thus, one of the biggest changes may be a world power structure comprising very rich developed countries alongside very large, but overall poor countries. As in the carbon debate, this makes it hard to find common ground.

Security: an ungovernable world?

Since World War II, a worldwide armed conflict has been avoided. The nuclear threat has been contained. But peace has not broken out, with at least four major threats to security that are especially relevant to development. First, there are many failed states, where the United Nations plays a varied role and where securing peace is a precursor to development. Second, there are the threats from non-state actors, including fundamentalists, gangs, terrorists, drug smugglers, and organized crime, in the physical and Internet world. Third, the major and emerging powers might come into direct conflict, with disputes over access to resources an obvious risk. Fourth, there arguably is the clash of cultures, beliefs, and civilizations along with rising fundamentalisms of various sorts.

Putting a damper on these threats would offer great benefits to security and thus development. How these threats are managed will be influenced by four aspects of governance: military power; regulation and control of cyberspace; the age-old competition between the state and the citizen (including privatization and the rise of civil society); and the form of governance, from democracy to dictatorship.

US military prominence may change, for example, as China further develops its capabilities, as nuclear proliferation is or is not constrained, and as the spread of small arms continues. Most countries will seek to develop new military capabilities from technology (e.g., robotics, drones, and other delivery systems) to counter the changing distribution of power.

Cyberspace is already a site for conflict and governance dilemmas, from cyber-attacks, to cyberspace regulation, and combating cyber-crime. Cyberspace overrides much of the traditional territorial basis of regulation, and there is already a clear difference of attitude to the use of cyberspace between the West and countries such as China. However, as the Wikileaks and Snowden phenomena have highlighted, any ethical high ground may not be very well populated for much longer.

The ability of "the state" to regulate is under considerable pressure, at home and abroad. Hence, we see largely failed efforts to control tax havens, regulate the Internet, and combat the drug trade. The challenge is not just one of combating illegal activities but of handling the shifting power from the state to civil society and business. In the postwar period, the annual business of corporations such as IBM and General Motors overtook the GDPs of many small countries. Now individual power is emerging, empowered by the Internet.

Alternatives to democracy may come from the peaceful commu-capitalism of China or belief-based fundamentalist movements with or without their more violent dimensions. Where failed states become more widespread and rip societies apart, democracy cannot offer quick results. The prospect of permanent failure for many people, with retrograde development and hopeless governance, becomes a threat to all. These trends will have a direct impact on the style of global governance. As the 2010 FUNDS participants observed: "the United States has reached its peak, which has implications for partnerships and the UN in its shaping of regulations and values."

The environment: saving the planet

Environmental change will have a big influence on developing countries (see Table 3.1). Poorer communities already suffer far greater loss of life from natural calamities due to weak infrastructure and protection. Developing countries are where the most visible environmental damage is being done—destruction of rainforests and the habitats of many species, damming of rivers for energy, and urban pollution. If developing countries bear a major share of the economic opportunity cost of "being green," how does this tally against efforts to transfer income to developing nations in the form of aid? Technology may offer new solutions but this environmental action is a running sore between developed and developing economies, where global governance may be needed to promote the global public good.

Developing countries are already the origin and destination of climate change migration as sea levels rise and as habitats become less

Table 3.1 IPCC projections for extreme weather events

Phenomenon (for which there is already an observed late twentieth-century trend)	Likelihood that trend occurred in late twentieth century (typically post-1960)	Likelihood of future trends based on projections for twenty-first century using SRES* scenarios
Warmer and fewer *cold* days and nights over most land areas	Very likely	Virtually certain
Warmer and fewer *hot* days and nights over most land areas	Very likely	Virtually certain
Warm spells/heat waves. Frequency increases over most land areas	Likely	Very likely
Heavy precipitation events. Frequency (or proportion of total rainfall from heavy falls) increases over most areas	Likely	Very likely
Area affected by droughts increases	Likely in many regions since 1970	Likely
Intense tropical cyclone activity increases	Likely in some regions since 1970	Likely
Increased incidence of extreme high sea level (excludes tsunamis)	Likely	Likely

Source: Intergovernmental Panel on Climate Change, *Summary for Policymakers in Climate Change 2007: The Physical Science Basis* (New York: UN, 2007).
Note: * SRES: IPCC Special Report on Emission Scenarios 2000.

tolerable. A particular downside may be the extent of "trapped" populations, poorer populations unable to move due to the high cost, whilst seeing their livelihoods destroyed.[15] If environmental change means a fall in the standard of living for all, will support for others' development decline, as opposed to favoring new sustainability goals?

Environmental challenges affect the availability of food, water, and energy and may create the "perfect storm" of rising demand overtaking dwindling supply. Food shortages and rising food prices hit the poor the hardest and hamper other development efforts; water shortages already are most acute in developing countries. The biggest rise in energy demand is already coming from the BRICS. An underlying factor in any country's development performance will be the distribution of and access to scarce resources. Hence, the second main dimension of the FUNDS scenarios was the availability of resources—the scarcity of which rendered the Millennium Development Goals (MDGs) very vulnerable.[16]

Environmental change also is driving significant spatial changes: the opening up of resources in warming polar regions and landmasses such as Siberia and Canada; and the flooding of such existing landmasses as Bangladesh. Governance of these emerging spaces is already a big agenda item for global cooperation and national ambitions.

Science and technology: new solutions

The fifth driver of change can yield solutions as well as challenges. It is hard to foresee, let alone set, the boundaries of possible changes. Biosciences are enhancing our ability to extend longevity and manipulate living organisms. The potential to create new materials is advancing rapidly, and so new forms of energy may not be far away. Our ability to network, communicate, and relate in novel and faster ways expands exponentially. Ray Kurzweil's moment of "singularity" when the brain is overtaken by computer power will not come tomorrow, but the speed at which computing has changed our understanding and our ways of life is a strong indicator of its power.[17] Probes into Space get closer to new discoveries, perhaps other life forms. Automation may be one of the more visible dimensions of change. Virtual arenas alter how we communicate and interact. Forms of military engagement are changing dramatically. The combination of the advances in different sciences will be increasingly powerful: nanoscience with computer science, material sciences with bioscience, engineering with computing.

These advances, often developed in the laboratories of industrialized countries, could be lifesavers if brought to bear in poor lands. Two obvious dimensions are in natural resources and in health. A new "green revolution" driven by genetic advances has to be on any list. Advances in creating new energy sources would ease some resource pressures, with uncertain impacts on oil and natural gas prices and on the earnings of commodity exporters. Advances in water management and in desalination could aid water-stressed areas. The possibilities fully validate the debate between the Malthusians and the techno-optimists.

How far will scientific healthcare advances help the poor? Every cutting edge advance in healthcare generates a new health cost and raises expectations for improved health. Many available solutions still need to be applied—as for malaria. It may well still be that public health management (from medicine to sanitation and clean water provision) is the best hope, short of the discovery of cheap miracle cures. That said, the more that is known about infectious diseases and causes of pandemics, the more developing nations may reap some of the benefits. And if developing countries can limit the growth in "diseases of affluence," that would be a great advance.

Indeed, health may represent one of the most important ways in which UN-supported collective action among national governments can promote development with knock-on benefits across the board. The recent Lancet Commission report put it succinctly:

> A unique characteristic of our generation is that collectively we have the financial and the ever-improving technical capacity to reduce infectious, child, and maternal mortality rates to low levels universally by 2035, to achieve a "grand convergence" in health. With enhanced investments to scale up health technologies and systems, these rates in most low-income and middle-income countries would fall to those presently seen in the best-performing middle-income countries.[18]

The report describes how these ambitions and global public goods can be achieved by international collective action—which could, almost, be taken as a model for the UN development system's ambitions (see Table 3.2).

Finally, the IT revolution has a long way to run. It underpins increasing interconnectivity, empowering people economically (the fishermen forecasting the weather with mobile devices), socially (social media in all its burgeoning dimensions), politically (the safe space of virtual networks for dissident voices). The surprises to date have been not just technological advances themselves but how people have adapted to and used them.

There are pluses and minuses concerning development prospects, as the 2010 FUNDS participants perceived: by 2025 technology "could, as in the case of mobile phones, allow Southern countries to overtake the more industrialized countries"[19]—the "leapfrog" effect. While there are now as many households in the developing world with access to the Internet (373 million) as in the developed (376 million), only 31 percent in the global South have access as opposed to 77 percent of the populations in the global North (see Figure 3.3). FUNDS participants noted technology's risks for governance: "there is a need to increase transparency and democracy and move away from a hierarchical approach to a more horizontal/networking approach to government. Information overload

Table 3.2 Four essential functions of international collective action

Function	Examples
Leadership and stewardship (core function)	Convening for negotiation and consensus building; consensus building on policy; cross-sectoral advocacy (e.g., on trade and health); agency for the dispossessed; advocating for sustainability and the environment
Ensuring provision of global public goods (core function)	Discovery, development, and delivery of new health tools; implementation research, extended cost-effective analyses, research priority-setting tools, and survey methodologies; knowledge generation and sharing; sharing of intellectual property (e.g., drug patent pools, technology transfer); harmonized norms, standards, and guidelines (e.g., quality assurance of medicines, WHO's vaccine position papers); market shaping (e.g., pooled procurement to reduce drug prices)
Management of externalities (core function)	Responding to global threats (e.g., pandemic influenza, antibiotic resistance, counterfeit drugs); surveillance and information sharing
Direct country assistance (supportive function)	Technical cooperation at national level; development assistance for health; emergency humanitarian assistance

Source: The Lancet Commission 2013: Dean T. Jamison, Lawrence H. Summers, George Alleyne, Kenneth J. Arrow, Seth Berkley, Agnes Binagwaho, Flavia Bustreo, David Evans, Richard G. A. Feachem, Julio Frenk, Gargee Ghosh, Sue J. Goldie, Yan Guo, Sanjeev Gupta, Richard Horton, Margaret E. Kruk, Adel Mahmoud, Linah K. Mohohlo, Mthuli Ncube, Ariel Pablos-Mendez, K. Srinath Reddy, Helen Saxenian, Agnes Soucat, Karene H. Ulltveit-Moe, and Gavin Yamey, "Global Health 2035: A World Converging Within a Generation," *The Lancet* 382, no. 9908 (2013): 1898–1955.

could distract from the main governance issues. More information does not mean more wisdom." Technology does not exist in a cultural vacuum, the participants noting the potential for "the clash of science/modern education/values and pluralism."

Implications for change: four future scenarios

The 2010 FUNDS workshop developed four alternative development scenarios, which are shaped by the availability of resources and changes in governance power worldwide (see Figure 3.4). The decline of the natural resource base was seen as "the highest [development] challenge ahead with the greatest certainty, against a backdrop of growing inequality beyond income (gender, spatial)."[20] The shift in governance

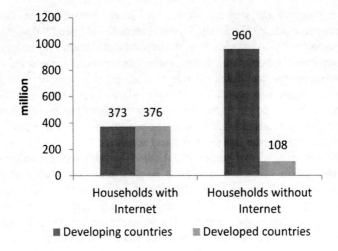

Figure 3.3 Households with Internet access, 2013
Source: International Telecommunication Union, *The World in 2013: ICT Facts and Figures*, February 2013, https://itunews.itu.int/En/3742-Highlights-from-The-World-in-2013-ICT-Facts-and-Figures.note.aspx

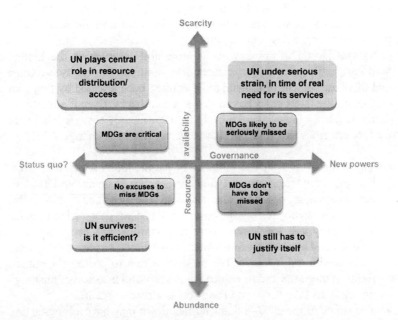

Figure 3.4 Alternative futures for 2025
Source: The Future of the UN Development System, *Conference Report*, November 2010

power reflected the highest impact and most certain of the various scenarios considered. Thus, the top right scenario, shaped by new powers and resource scarcity, is closest to the current world trajectory unless new resources are discovered and something arrests the shifting power balance.

The more that technology delivers solutions, the more likely resources will become less scarce or more abundant. This situation is represented in the scenarios below the horizontal axis of the matrix. Should the new powers stumble or incumbent powers recover their poise, the more possible are the figure's left hand scenarios.

Given current global trends, the United Nations will be under considerable strain just when it is most needed; and developmental goals will be missed, however restructured and reformed the world organization might be. In none of the scenarios can governance and reform afford to be seen to be wanting. The urgency for breaking out of any governance "inertia" could not be more clearly underlined.

Conclusion

So what are the prospects for change? Can these potentially momentous changes in the world environment trigger change in the UN development system? Will they alter development and aid needs? Will they catalyze organizational change?

Natural inertia in any system as large and complex as the United Nations usually relies on some shock or discontinuity to catalyze change and facilitate reform. Financial aid has often been affected by financial crises, and the latest crisis has caused some cutbacks. Even if a relatively declining role for financial aid is likely, there are already obvious candidates for UN priorities as a result of these various drivers of change.

- The physical and virtual mobility of people looks set to add stress between countries, cultures, and governance systems, and lead to new interactions, peaceably and otherwise. The speed and fluidity of this mobility is already testing the governance systems designed to manage it. Mobility will accelerate wherever environmental, economic, and political and security pressures intensify—wherever access to resources and a livelihood is scarce. The need for action to protect the human rights of migrants and to reduce the poverty and insecurity "pushing" migrants to take desperate measures is already urgent.
- The shock of the 2007–8 financial meltdown may have a long-lasting legacy, depending where it leaves the EU as a player and attitudes to capitalism and welfare thinking that underpin policies at home and development programs abroad. Financial crises facilitate

cutbacks but do not necessarily result in more efficient distribution of resources. Can markets rise to the challenge of efficient resource distribution alongside the guidance of government? Can UN institutions make a difference?

- If the rise of the BRICS and other emerging economies of the global South reshapes the world hierarchy of power, it surely will have a direct impact on UN governance structures. Shifts can change the primary actors in development, moving us toward a set of new alliances—within or outside multilateral approaches—perhaps with more power for the largest emerging economies and less power for the status quo. The changing list of actors—the rise of the illegal ones, the spread of civil society, the rise of the business sector—can in itself trigger changes and facilitate more multilateral reactions.

- Failed states, fundamentalism, cross-border crime, ongoing wars, and a host of security threats represent a disturbing set of fault lines. Insecurity will continue to be critical in governing access to scarce resources and reinforcing the links between development and security. While intra-state conflict may dominate the present agenda, can the United Nations also help avoid a return to interstate conflict?

- Climate change disrespects borders; it is driving migration and threatening livelihoods. In a more polluted world, scrambling for natural resources, our ability to deliver economic prosperity, human development, and well-being is under serious threat. Will the global governance system and UN institutions continue to fail to catalyze action by self-interested parties and widely differing constituencies— governments, the private sector, and civil society—to protect humankind's most precious public goods?

- In a more resource-constrained world, making enough scarce resources available will become much more difficult even with more efficient and fairer distribution. Competition for scarce goods threatens peace and security. Keeping the peace in the dash for resources may need more active UN governance.

- More positively, advances in science and technology offer the promise of new enablers for growth. The IT revolution already is altering daily lives, with costs and benefits as individuals endeavor to keep pace. IT access can and should be made more widely available. Technology may help avoid a Malthusian dystopia,[21] but it will require both massive advances in discovery and the smart application of those discoveries to succeed, such as providing effective public health systems for delivery of cures. Sharing progress is not easy. The application of new science is a major global public good that

will need to accommodate the narrower interests of its owners—
which could well benefit from UN involvement at various levels.

The 2010 FUNDS workshop identified interlinking vulnerabilities as
a key overriding global driver of change: "e.g. climate change leading to an
increase in natural disasters, in turn leading to migration—both internal
and international—which in turn breeds conflict—where the risk in turn
may be further heighted by natural resource scarcity." The concept of
human security developed in the early 1990s and requires continual
updating.[22] A robust strategy may require the UN system to be able to
anticipate and act early as needs alter over time. Part of this approach
may in fact be emerging, with a set of focused activities relevant to
failed states, a repositioning of emerging powers that no longer require
direct assistance, and debating the future role for those in the middle—
the economies with a growing middle class, but still with large numbers
of very poor people and where new emergencies still need relief.

A UN collective approach may become even more critical in a world in
which more cultures are interacting, and global public goods are in short
supply when they exist at all. In particular, the cross-cutting themes of
equality, a core Millennium Declaration value, may well be in the forefront
in a world in which access to scarce resources becomes more critical, and
different values collide as people move, as new power balances alter
ownership of assets, and as vulnerabilities increase. But there can be virtuous linkages. As mentioned, if gender discrimination is the most serious
cause of global inequalities, then successful advocacy and action on
women's rights and empowerment would bring widespread benefits and
could be the UN's single greatest contribution to global well-being. With
porous borders along with mobility and new conceptions of geography and
space, it may be the time to put greater focus on spatial differences and
inequalities between people—"poverty of access"—as opposed to just
between states. The threats ahead—massive migration, economic turbu-
lence, civil wars, climate change—should already be compelling
enough for the world not to wait for more shocks to trigger action.

Notes

1 "Scenarios for 2025," The Future of the UN Development System conference report, November 2010 (hereafter, "Scenarios for 2025"). www.
   futureun.org/media/archive1/reports/wp1033-report.pdf
2 Thomas G. Weiss and Ramesh Thakur, *Global Governance and the UN: An
   Unfinished Journey* (Bloomington: Indiana University Press, 2010).
3 Bradford DeLong, *Estimates of World GDP, One Million BC–Present*
   (1998), http://delong.typepad.com/print/20061012_LRWGDP.pdf

4 Jutta Bolt and Jan Luiten van Zanden, "The First Update of the Maddison Project; Re-Estimating Growth before 1820," Maddison Working Paper 4, January 2013. www.ggdc.net/maddison/maddison-project/publications/wp4.pdf

5 UNICEF and UN Women, *Addressing Inequalities: Synthesis Report of Global Thematic Consultation on Addressing Inequalities in the Post-2015 Development Agenda* (New York: UN, January 2013).

6 UN, Department of Economic and Social Affairs, Population Division, *World Population Prospects: The 2012 Revision, Highlights and Advance Tables* (New York: UN, 2013).

7 "Making Migration Work: An Eight Point Agenda for Action, Report of the Secretary-General," UN document A/68/190, 3 October 2013.

8 High-level Panel of Eminent Persons on the Post-2015 Development Agenda, *A New Global Partnership: Eradicate Poverty and Transform Economies through Sustainable Development* (New York: UN, 2013).

9 "Scenarios for the Poorest: The View from 2030," Outsights workshop, London, 2004, www.FutureUN.org

10 World Bank, "Migration and Development Brief," no. 21, 2 October 2013. http://siteresources.worldbank.org/INTPROSPECTS/Resources/334934-128899 0760745/MigrationandDevelopmentBrief21.pdf

11 "Making Migration Work: An Eight Point Agenda for Action, Report of the Secretary-General," UN document A/68/190, 3 October 2013.

12 Peggy Levitt and Deepak Lamba-Nieves, "Revisiting Social Remittances," *Journal of Ethnic and Migration Studies* 37, no. 1 (2011): 1–22.

13 World Bank, "Migration and Development Brief," no. 20, 19 April 2013. http://siteresources.worldbank.org/INTPROSPECTS/Resources/334934-128899 0760745/MigrationandDevelopmentBrief20.pdf

14 For a vision of the future implications of these power shifts for international governance, see "Scenarios for the Future International Environment 2010–20," Outsights, 2007, www.FutureUN.org

15 See UK Government Office for Science, *Foresight: Migration and Global Environmental Change* (London: Government Office for Science, 2011), www.gov.uk/government/uploads/system/uploads/attachment_data/file/2877 22/11-1115-migration-and-global-environmental-change-summary.pdf

16 "Scenarios for 2025."

17 Ray Kurzweil, *The Singularity Is Near* (New York: Penguin, 2006).

18 Dean T. Jamison, Lawrence H. Summers, George Alleyne, Kenneth J. Arrow, Seth Berkley, Agnes Binagwaho, Flavia Bustreo, David Evans, Richard G. A. Feachem, Julio Frenk, Gargee Ghosh, Sue J. Goldie, Yan Guo, Sanjeev Gupta, Richard Horton, Margaret E. Kruk, Adel Mahmoud, Linah K. Mohohlo, Mthuli Ncube, Ariel Pablos-Mendez, K. Srinath Reddy, Helen Saxenian, Agnes Soucat, Karene H. Ulltveit-Moe, and Gavin Yamey, "Global Health 2035: A World Converging Within a Generation," *The Lancet* 382, no. 9908 (2013): 1898–1955.

19 "Scenarios for 2025."

20 Ibid.

21 See Alasdair Keith, Richard O'Brien, and Michael Prest, "The Future of the Global Economy to 2030," Outsights, 2008, www.FutureUN.org

22 S. Neil MacFarlane and Yuen Foong Khong, *Human Security and the UN: A Critical History* (Bloomington: Indiana University Press, 2006).

Part II

Grappling with the present and future

Results, funding, management

4 Funding the UN system

Silke Weinlich

Money is not only relevant for realizing the UN's development-related activities, ranging from norm- and standard-setting to advocacy, knowledge production to technical assistance. It provides powerful incentives and consequently has a significant impact on the internal logic, functioning, and performance of the UN development system (UNDS). This chapter analyzes past and current trends as well as future prospects for funding the UNDS and discusses the consequences of the current funding system. At the moment, the UNDS relies foremost on supply-driven, headquarter-centered, and agency-oriented funding. The current funding system is fundamentally flawed and in need of reform, with significant consequences for UNDS effectiveness and efficiency as well as for its multilateral character.

The UNDS is a loosely coupled system that is made up of more than 30 organizations that significantly differ in terms of size, mandate, and functions. Specialized agencies such as the International Labour Organization (ILO) and the World Health Organization (WHO) are independent international organizations whose task is primarily to set standards; they also engage in technical assistance and tend to operate rather autonomously. Funds and programs such as the UN Development Programme (UNDP), the UN Children's Fund (UNICEF), and the World Food Programme (WFP) directly answer to the General Assembly and the secretary-general; they engage in operational development and humanitarian activities, while their development portfolio has been growing and also encompasses advocacy work, knowledge production, and other activities. UNDP, UNICEF, and WFP are the three largest UN organizations that have come to account for more than half of the funding. Several intergovernmental bodies form part of the UNDS. They perform oversight functions and serve as forums for global debates, consensus formation, and negotiations of universal norms. The General Assembly and the Economic and Social Council

(ECOSOC) and its committees are prominent examples, as is the recently established Development Cooperation Forum that brings together all development stakeholders. In formal terms, the World Bank Group is also *de jure* part of the UN system; but it is *de facto* separate and will not be further considered.

The chapter begins with an overview of the different types of funding, overall funding trends, and funding sources. It then discusses the impact of the current system on the efficiency, effectiveness, and the multi-lateral core of the UNDS. The chapter concludes by highlighting current reform proposals, discussing their potential for success, and proposing a way forward.

UNDS funding at a glance

In 2012, the UNDS received $23.9 billion for its operational activities—that is, for its humanitarian and development-related work.[1] The UNDS accounts for roughly 17 percent of the total official development assistance (ODA) of $150.9 billion in 2012 as reported by all donors to the Development Assistance Committee (DAC) of the Organisation for Economic Co-operation and Development (OECD). The UNDS is collectively a sizable player when compared with other multilateral development organizations such as the World Bank Group or the European Union (EU). If all contributions are taken in to account—including contributions from other multilateral sources—the UNDS becomes the biggest single multilateral channel for development assistance.[2] Considerable as it may be, the funding nevertheless cannot match the UNDS's potential tasks. Its overall mission is declared in Article 1 of the UN Charter: "to achieve international co-operation in solving international problems of an economic, social, cultural, or humanitarian character, and in promoting and encouraging respect for human rights and for fundamental freedoms for all." The various UN organizations have broad mandates in many policy areas, and the idea that all developing countries are eligible for UN assistance has led to a worldwide field presence.

The UNDS is funded from two different sources, namely assessed and voluntary contributions. Assessed contributions come from governments' financial membership obligations. They provide a regular and mostly reliable source of UN funding. Wealthier countries shoulder a greater burden; poorer countries make smaller contributions; and the poorest pay a symbolic price.[3] Assessed contributions are particularly relevant for UN peace operations and the UN's general budget, as well as for the general budgets of the specialized agencies. They play a small role for the UN's development activities. However, although often rather modest in size, general budgets ensure the functioning of the international administrations. They in turn support intergovernmental norm- and standard-setting activities and other work related to the provision of global public goods.

Voluntary contributions are the most important source of funding for the UNDS, and they are the sole source of income for the UN's funds and programs. Industrialized countries, mostly as part of their foreign aid policies, contribute to financing the work of individual organizations. Developing countries usually contribute financially or in kind to the assistance that they receive. In addition, many developing countries make a symbolic contribution to the UN's development work in general. Furthermore, during the last 15 years, voluntary contributions by non-state actors have gained considerable importance.

Voluntary contributions can come as core or non-core (in the form of earmarked, or "multi-bi") contributions. Contributions to core budgets lose their national identity and can be allocated as each organization sees fit in accordance with the priorities specified by the governing bodies. With earmarked funding, each donor individually specifies the purpose. Earmarking reflects a desire among donors for control, visibility, and flexibility. Such contributions can be focused on specific sectors, regions, or countries (including fragile states) where the bilateral donor may lack expertise, has no presence, or where its national strategy sets priorities. Earmarking makes contributions more visible as the funding "keeps its identity" by not being pooled; in addition, it enhances the influence and control of donors over UN organizations. Also, for some donor countries that take funding decisions locally in the program countries themselves, it is easier to contribute earmarked funds.[4] Non-core resources tend to focus on operational activities. Core resources in turn are used not only for program implementation, but up to one third is spent on in-house administration, knowledge management, and other non-program activities.

Even though there have been phases of decline or stagnation and even crises, the funding of the UNDS shows an impressive increase over the last six decades. Over the last two decades, total resources nearly doubled. There are, however, strong indications that the increase in funding will come to an end. ODA figures are expected to stagnate in the medium term.[5] In 2009, the worldwide decrease was also felt at the United Nations where for the first time since the 1990s, the total contributions for funding the UN's operational activities declined. Of course, the decline is felt differently across the system; some organizations continue to prosper while others suffer more acutely from financial losses.[6]

Four important trends can be observed in UNDS funding over time: a decentralization of funding structures; a decline in the share of the specialized agencies; an increase in non-core contributions; and an increase in nongovernment funding. The first two trends took place in the early years while the latter two are relatively recent.[7]

Early in the UN's history, a centralized funding model was put in place, however imperfect. The rather modest funds contributed to the Expanded Programme for Technical Assistance (EPTA) were distributed among the UN Secretariat and the specialized agencies in agreed and fixed proportions. The Food and Agriculture Organization (FAO), the WHO, UN Educational, Scientific and Cultural Organization, and the UN Secretariat received the biggest shares and used the money for technical assistance and a transfer of skills and knowledge to developing countries. When the Special Fund was created some years later, its resources were no longer distributed according to a fixed formula, but the specialized agencies still executed the majority of projects. In 1966 the Special Fund and EPTA were merged into the UNDP.

By that time, the WHO and others had already begun to finance parts of their technical assistance through their regular budgets. This decentralization continued, accelerated by the move toward national execution of programs that took away funds and decision-making authority from the specialized agencies. The agencies tried to compensate for these losses by finding alternative funding sources for their technical assistance activities. The UNDP, for its part, started to build up its own expertise to become more than just a funding mechanism. During the 1970s, around 75 percent of the total development funds were provided by the UNDP. In 1981, however, the UNDP accounted for only 11 percent of the total development expenditures.[8] From the late 1980s onward, the UNDP began to deliberately withhold funding from the specialized agencies and expanded its own delivery into areas already covered by other members of the UNDS. The specialized agencies lost importance for providing technical assistance, and the UNDP developed into the UN's most important operational development organization. The days of the centralized funding system were clearly over.

The end of the Cold War and increased globalization brought about transformations in the UNDS. Despite hopes for a peace dividend, the absence of the obvious foreign political rationales led to a decline in ODA, which was also felt at the United Nations. The downward trend was reversed with a reorientation of development policy toward thematic priorities.[9] In particular, the Millennium Development Goals (MDGs) succeeded in mobilizing resources; the focus on thematic priorities led to a significant increase in resources for the UNDS. Over the last two decades, donors nearly doubled their financial contributions. Funding for the UNDS expanded fast, often at an even faster pace than overall ODA.

This exponential increase in resources was paralleled by a qualitative change: the growth in non-core resources. Until the 1990s, the great majority of resources made available for the UNDS were core funds. After a peak in 1990–92, stagnation and sometimes a decline in core funding took place. More importantly, the ratio between core funding and earmarked contributions was basically reversed. As Figure 4.1 shows, in 1992 the share of core funding was still about 55 percent; with humanitarian assistance excluded, it came close to 70 percent. In 2012 the situation was the other way around. For the overall UNDS, the share of core funding was only 28 percent—32 percent without humanitarian assistance. For the entire UNDS, two-thirds of its funding came with strings attached. Other multilateral organizations also receive earmarked contributions. However, donors resort to non-core contributions with the UN in particular. The World Bank Group comes second, but only one third of its funding was earmarked in 2010.[10] In most UN organizations, the volume of earmarked contributions exceeds the funding made available for the core budget. There are only a few exceptions to this overall trend.[11] For the UNDP,

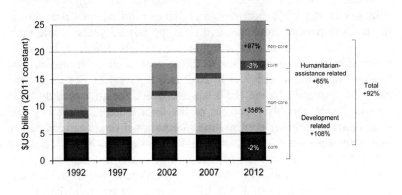

Figure 4.1 Real change over time of funding for UN operational activities for development, 1992–2012, constant US$ 2011 (percentage change relative to 1992)
Source: UN Department of Economic and Social Affairs, 2013

UNFPA, and UNICEF, for instance, the share of core funding in overall financing fell from nearly 80 percent in 1991 to roughly 30 percent in 2007.[12] The UNDP's core share went down even further and receded to 19 percent in 2012.[13]

Non-core resources come in different forms. Single-donor, project-, and program-specific funds make up roughly 80–90 percent of non-core budgets across the system. This share has been stable for several years. In general, this form of earmarking is said to be most at odds with the UN's multilateral character. In contrast, pooled non-core resources represent a better compromise between the wish of organizations for planning security, on the one hand, and donor wishes for greater flexibility and control, on the other. Another part of non-core resources is made up from so-called local or self-supporting resources—that is, resources that governments contribute to UN organizations for programming in the contributor's country.

Most funding for the UNDS is still contributed by industrialized countries, although in the last two decades there has been a growing diversification of the funding base. First, nongovernmental actors have become more important. Second, several developing countries either have turned into donors or act in a dual capacity as recipients and donors. However, the rise of the global South has not fully reached the UN, at least in terms of financial contributions.

Nongovernmental actors have developed into significant contributors to the UN's operational activities—indeed, this probably is the most important funding trend over the last 15 years. While their share of contributions was marginal in the late 1980s, it began to increase in the 1990s and grew to 22 percent of the overall contributions for operational activities in 2012 (see Figure 4.2). For some time now, the European Union (EU) has accounted for an especially large portion, being roughly 7 percent of the total amount; it thereby sets itself apart from other contributing international organizations. Other important actors are nongovernmental organizations (NGOs), notably the UNICEF national committees, which are independent, local NGOs that raise funds and advocate for children's rights in 36 countries. Nearly one third of UNICEF's revenues came from the private sector in 2012, and the national committees played a vital role.[14] For other UN organizations, more important contributions come from public–private partnership actors, philanthropic foundations, or other private sources. For the UNDP, for instance, there has been a sharp increase in resources contributed by the Global Fund to Fight HIV/AIDS, Malaria, and Tuberculosis, the Global Environment Facility (GEF), and the Multilateral Fund for the Implementation of the

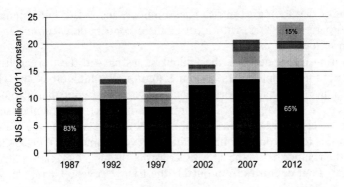

Figure 4.2 Main sources of funding, 1987–2012, UN operational activities for development

Source: UN Department for Economic and Social Affairs, 2013

Montreal Protocol. Together, the three global funds made up about 16 percent of total UNDP resources (2011).[15] Global funds brought a substantial increase in resources to the UNDS as a whole. Arguably, they were created because of disillusionment with the performance of the UNDS and its cumbersome intergovernmental bodies. Governments of industrialized countries, together with the private sector, created new financing institutions that would allow quick, efficient, and targeted support for specific challenges such as education, health, and the environment. It is somewhat ironic that the UNDS, especially the UNDP, turned into the largest implementing partner.

Not all contributions by nongovernmental actors are earmarked. UNICEF receives a substantial part of its core funding from the national committees. The World Intellectual Property Organization (WIPO) receives the large majority of its core funding from private corporations that pay fees for the services that WIPO provides. However, so far, for the most important bulk of nongovernmental contributions, a purpose is specified. This is especially true for the large sums contributed by the global funds and international organizations such as the EU.[16]

Governments remain the most important contributors of funds to the UNDS, although their share has gone down from about 94 percent in 1987 to roughly 77 percent in 2012. Industrialized countries continue to contribute the majority of funds—65 percent in 2012. The share of developing countries has nominally increased, but it remains at 10 percent in 2012, with most of these contributions coming in the form of local resources.

During recent decades, the United States has led the top ten list of contributing countries. In absolute figures, Washington is the clear leader in financing UN operational activities and contributes roughly 10 percent of total funds. Taken together, however, EU member states play an even larger role. Notably the United Kingdom, the Nordic countries (except for Denmark), and the Netherlands have been showing their support for the UN by consistently high financial contributions.[17] Four countries from outside the EU—Norway, Japan, Canada, and Australia—are also among the main contributors. Not surprisingly, the UNDS is most important for small countries since large and economically powerful countries tend to prefer bilateral over multilateral assistance, and increasingly so.[18]

A comparison with the assessment scale for the UN's regular budget shows that a number of countries are clearly below what they otherwise accept as their fair share. In return, others pay far more, in general such smaller countries as Sweden, Norway, Denmark, and Switzerland. These countries also shoulder a much greater burden in the area of core contributions.[19] Table 4.1 compiles financial information on UN contributions between 2009 and 2012 for the top five contributors. It displays their ranking in terms of absolute contributions, as well as in terms of the ratio between their contributions and gross national income (GNI). Not surprisingly, the Netherlands and Norway move up the ranks, whereas the United States and Japan move down.

Table 4.1 provides information on the contributions of four selected "emerging powers" that have gradually shifted from being recipients of development assistance to providers of aid and other forms of development assistance outside of the UN. Their successful development experiences have put them in a position to offer a wider range of technical expertise, goods, and services to other developing countries, although they still face significant development challenges within their own borders.[20] However, there are few signs thus far that these countries use the UN to realize their leadership aspirations. In 2012, the four together contributed $292 million to the UN's development-related operational activities, that is slightly less than 2 percent of the total. For the time being China, India, and South Africa prefer to remain recipient countries at the United Nations. If we exclude self-supporting contributions, between 2007 and 2012, none of the four countries provided more money to the UNDS than they received. For Brazil, this changed only in 2011.[21]

Table 4.1 Selected contributing governments to development-related activities, 2009–12

Contributor	Rank (amount)				Rank (percentage of GNI)				Local resources (mio. of current US $)				Country total excluding local resources (mio. of current US$)				Country share of UN total (in %)				Country share of UN general budget (in %)
	2009	2010	2011	2012	2009	2010	2011	2012	2009	2010	2011	2012	2009	2010	2011	2012	2009	2010	2011	2012	2011
USA	1	1	1	1	19	23	28	25	1	—	2	2	1305	1787	1499	1519	10	12.3	10.6	9.4	22
Japan	2	2	2	3	15	18	20	19	2	2	—	—	802	1048	1039	964	6.1	7.2	7.4	6.0	12.53
Netherlands	3	5	5	6	4	5	9	5	—	—	—	—	797	631	611	674	6.1	4.4	4.3	4.2	1.86
UK	4	3	3	2	12	11	11	9	—	—	1	—	744	836	1025	1216	5.7	5.8	7.3	7.5	6.60
Norway	5	4	4	4	1	1	1	1	—	—	—	—	694	748	805	763	5.3	5.2	5.7	4.7	0.87
China	21	18	19	20	43	44	50	48	16	22	33	22	61	70	64	70	0.5	0.5	0.5	0.4	3.189
India	25	28	30	27	37	41	49	—	5	9	5	8	33	26	30	30	0.3	0.2	0.2	0.2	0.53
Brazil	27	23	22	28	39	36	46	49	105	106	138	180	29	45	52	29	0.2	0.3	0.4	0.2	1.61
South Africa	37	33	36	36	28	29	41	—	3	5	1	6	11	13	11	12	0.1	0.1	0.1	0.1	0.38

Source: Statistical Annexes for 2009; 2010; 2012; Scale of Assessments for the appointment of expenses of the United Nations, UN document A/Res/64/248, 5 January 2010

However, also for the other three countries, there is some movement over time although their contributions to the UN still seem marginal when compared with the amounts spent on bilateral assistance. China has roughly tripled its contributions from $39 million in 2003 to $117 million in 2011, although in 2012 its contributions went down to $97 million. Both India and South Africa show a less steady increase over the years. Brazil is the outlier and has consistently provided larger contributions to the UNDS. However, in the past Brazil stood out mostly because the government supplemented its contributions with substantial payments for the delivery of services within Brazil itself.[22] The increase in contributions by the emerging powers seems to be taking place mostly in the area of humanitarian aid, with South–South cooperation being another focus area.[23]

Consequences of the current funding system

The decentralized funding structures, and especially the proliferation of non-core resources, have repercussions for how the UNDS works. The funds and programs do not dispose of a predictable and stable income; and for most of the specialized agencies, only a small part of assessed budgets can be used for operational activities.[24] UN agencies are faced with unpredictable contributions that are subject to considerable fluctuations. Despite pleas for multi-year pledges, many governments make their core contributions annually, allowing them to reduce funding when they feel the need to do so. This funding practice differs from what they do in most other multilateral organizations. The volatility is most pronounced in the area of non-core resources, since some 90 percent of the funds are contributed by single donors and are program- or project-specific. In addition to this erratic donor behavior, fluctuations in exchange rates complicate matters.[25] All this makes UN agencies particularly vulnerable to short-term, crisis-related cuts in contributions, as well as highly susceptible to political pressure since they depend on a handful of advanced industrialized states for the bulk of their resources.

Earmarked funds have several other disadvantages for UN organizations. They carry a significant workload since they come with additional administrative and reporting burdens that detract time, resources, and staff from actual development work. At the same time, the predominance of non-core funding has repercussions for the ability of the world body's organizations to plan ahead, set priorities, and follow through. Also, the staffing structures are affected and have become increasingly short-term and unstable, dependent on the continuation of projects and programs. Although many of them are multi-year, the insecurities involved create incentive structures for UN staff that may prove detrimental to actual development work. In addition, UN organizations complain that the administrative fees allowed by donors for implementing projects have not covered the actual costs. As a consequence, activities funded by earmarked contributions are subsidized by core contributions. If dwindling core resources are not sufficient to reproduce the normative and operative basis of the United Nations development system in the long term, the system's integrity will be seriously threatened.[26]

UN organizations have little choice but to actively mobilize resources, not only at headquarters but also within the countries in which they operate. Fund-raising consumes considerable time and effort—many argue to the detriment of actual development work. It is difficult for organizations to turn down offers of earmarked contributions that might not fit entirely with their mandate or priorities if they rely on that very donor for other resources. In addition, there are many other development agencies that compete for the same resources. Decentralized, competitive fund-raising reinforces the fragmented nature of the UN system. The UNDS with its various governing boards, accountability structures, and rules and regulations does not lend itself easily to cooperation among its agencies in the first place. Competition, as well as the individual reporting requirements that come with earmarked funds, makes it even more difficult to work closely and combine forces for greater impact.

Recent analysis shows that the UN's operational activities are spread too broadly and thinly; there exists a large number of small and scattered projects that are much less relevant to developing countries than what the UN could actually offer if it were to consolidate its activities.[27] While small projects can be appropriate in specific situations, it is a matter of debate whether, to what degree, and in which areas the UNDS should aim at delivering as one. However, the supply-driven and fragmented nature of the current funding system increases the difficulties of even trying to cooperate.[28] In addition, the great diversity of small projects is not free of duplication and overlap. And last but not least, one can argue that one of the potential benefits of multilateral development policy, cooperation among member states and others for a greater impact, is undermined. This harms the UNDS's reputation and credibility in the eyes of its stakeholders.

The current funding system also has repercussions for intergovernmental governance and oversight and, ultimately, for the multilateral core of the UNDS. The unique feature of the UNDS is its universal, multilateral character and equality of membership that sets it apart from bilateral development cooperation but also from other multilaterals such as the World Bank Group. All member states make financial contributions and jointly decide—with all states being formally equal—how and for what purposes the money is spent. This is the bedrock of the UN's legitimacy. It enables it to approach developing country governments, engage in technical cooperation activities, and advocate human rights and other universal norms. It also builds the foundation for the UN's convening power, its ability to act as an honest broker, and its normative work.

This bedrock, however, is being eroded; for some organizations, critics increasingly speak of a "bilateralization" of UN development policy.[29] When earmarked contributions are provided, bilateral agreements between donor governments and UN organizations are concluded that specify the particular requirements in terms of reporting, evaluation, or other administrative practices. An additional line of accountability is thereby created that circumvents the governing boards of UN organizations. In some cases, it can also mean that nongovernmental actors demand access to UN books, challenging the multilateral principle that UN agencies are solely accountable to member states.[30] Industrialized countries increasingly use bilateral and joint assessments of individual UN organizations to evaluate their performance and compare them with other multilateral organizations. The perspectives of developing countries (whose equal participation is ensured in formal UN governance structures) are largely absent; and a similar absence occurs within the informal structures set up by many Western countries to govern bilateral partnerships with individual UN organizations. Such agreements spell out priorities for the use of core and non-core contributions. While they can be beneficial to UN organizations in terms of providing more reliable and secure funding, they still represent an additional layer of bilateral governance that circumvents multilateral governing bodies.

The priorities that donors impose on the UNDS are not necessarily aligned with the mandates of UN organizations, and earmarked funding regularly provides incentives to expand their activities at the margins of their mandates. This view is challenged by voices from the field who claim that there is no big discrepancy between projects funded by core or non-core contributions. In addition, one could argue that a large amount of earmarked funding was and is directed toward reaching the MDGs and other multilaterally defined goals. Since the MDGs are part of an overall UN strategy, projects that aim at their fulfillment could be considered to be aligned with multilateral priorities. While there certainly is some truth in this argument, it cannot hide the fact that donors still pick and choose. Although there is a long tradition of influence by the advanced industrialized countries on the UNDS's overall direction, the disproportionate share of earmarked funds now provides them with an unprecedented power to set priorities that seems incongruent with multilateral principles. After all, it should not be forgotten that some topics or countries are always more "fashionable" among bilateral donors than others. The UNDS should be able to at least partially provide a corrective.

The disproportionate share of earmarking carries the risk of hollowing out the norms and values that the UNDS represents. Human rights, poverty reduction, and gender equality are core UNDP norms, but an evaluation of its projects financed by global funds and philanthropic foundations showed that some were overly narrow in purpose.[31] This conclusion undoubtedly also would apply to self-supporting contributions—that is, resources that governments of middle- and high-income countries provide for development services in their own country. There are indications that an actor such as the UNDP cannot properly be an advocate for global norms, and be a coordinator and capacity builder, if it acts as a development contractor.[32]

Remedies and cures?

Despite the increases over the last two decades, the current funding arrangements for the UNDS are unsustainable. For many years, states have been declaring their intentions to increase funding, especially core funding, and have pledged to make their contributions more reliable; but the results have so far not materialized. Many voices argue that the practice of earmarking will not go away, nor will the practice of vertical funding. Reverting to governmental sources exclusively or to a centralized funding system is neither likely nor practical. The UNDS must find ways of defending its multilateral integrity. In doing so, it will face a very different world. ODA flows are likely to stagnate and decrease in the longer term. At the same time, development challenges have changed since the MDGs were agreed upon and will do so to an even greater extent with the post-2015 agenda. Aid and poverty eradication will remain, but more important will be meeting the growing demand for global public goods that can only be provided through cooperation and an allocation of responsibilities. Today, envisaging sustainable development for what will soon be 9 billion people means thinking about how to achieve social equity and environmental sustainability within ecologically defined planetary boundaries.[33]

So far, reform attempts during the last decade have been piecemeal and have not yielded significant results. Most of them were in the category of technical fixes; some more ambitious proposals suffered from partial implementation.[34] The Quadrennial Comprehensive Policy Review (QCPR) resolution that provides policy guidance to the UNDS until 2016 dedicates four entire pages to the funding situation and provides the most recent attempt by member states and the UNDS to think seriously about reform.[35] In general, reform attempts fall under two broad strategies: to compensate for the lack of balance between core and non-core funding by increasing the core-like qualities of earmarked funds; and to tap into new funding sources.

In order to increase the core-like qualities of non-core funding, several proposals are currently under debate, or in a test phase. At the most basic level, contributors are asked to provide contributions that are as little earmarked as possible. One way to do so is by using system-wide funding instruments such as thematic or other multi-donor trust funds (MDTFs). MDTFs pool resources from more than one donor and thus possibly allow for economies of scale and a more flexible use by the UNDS. Their number exploded in the past few years from five UNDP-administered MDTFs in 2006 to 52 in 2012. But after a peak in 2009, the financial deposits are decreasing.[36] MDTFs provide opportunities for bilateral donors to make use of the UNDS in specific situations while avoiding overheads and support for what is perceived as an inefficient system. MDTFs have been used for such countries in crisis as Iraq, Sudan, and Sierra Leone. Yet they still constitute a small part of non-core funding, with complementary value to core funding at best. In contrast to humanitarian assistance, a serious pooling of resources aimed at development-related activities has not taken place. But MDTFs have added another layer to the institutional fragmentation of the UNDS and the international development system.

Another idea aims at firmly linking the multi-year programming strategies of individual organizations with actual and prospective core and non-core funds. Such strategic plans are agreed in governing bodies; in most cases, they have only been matched with a core budgetary framework and have left open opportunities for resource mobilization. Following the example of the WHO, which currently pioneers matching multilaterally agreed results and deliverables with resources, funding dialogues should take place also for the funds and programs and possibly other specialized agencies. Here, governments and private actors are asked to provide funding projections and assign them to thematic priorities contained in strategy documents. UN organizations in turn should remain within the thematic parameters of the approved framework without engaging in further resource mobilization. Ideally, this procedure enhances predictability, allows for a more flexible use of non-core funds, ensures more discipline in keeping with respective mandates and priorities, ensures that development demands are better met, creates greater trust in the UNDS, and gives meaning to multilateral priority-setting. It is a promising proposal that could bring improvements particularly for the UNDP, UNFPA, UNICEF, and UN Women, which are already working toward agency-specific budgets. However, it remains to be seen how far governments are willing and able to give up their funding flexibility, and if the program budget can establish itself as the main reference document. Stronger sticks and carrots might be needed to enforce a greater discipline among UN organizations and their partners. For instance, member states should explicitly request UN organizations to reject earmarked funding that is outside of their strategic focus. Naming and shaming of governments with good or bad multilateral "donorship" should be common practice. Governments should also be transparent about their funding practices, as should UN agencies.

The idea to align funding with UN development plans was also formulated at the country level. All available and projected financial contributions for operational activities should be consolidated within a common, system-wide budgetary framework that would be linked to the United Nations Development Assistance Framework (UNDAF), the UN's overarching programmatic document that is agreed with the host government. This proposal builds on previous reform attempts in the context of the Delivering as One (DaO) initiative that prioritized reforms at the country level and also attempted to better align UN programs and resources. To be successful, donors should refrain from straying outside of UNDAFs. Even more difficult may be to ensure cooperation by all UN organizations that in addition need to create strategic, results-oriented UNDAFs. In the mid-to-long term, the DaO initiative demonstrates that cooperation at the country level needs to be facilitated by administrative changes at headquarters.[37] Some changes, however, are already under way.

The integrated budgets at the headquarters and country levels provide an alternative to a third proposal that has been around for some years and is still debated. The suggestion was to define a certain "critical mass" of core resources that each agency needs to maintain its base structure and fulfill its core mandate. Although the General Assembly in 2010 asked the funds and programs to animate this proposal, there has been little progress. It is as difficult for UN organizations to formulate such a proposal as it is for governments to agree on the actual core mandates. Yet such a critical mass could then be coupled with a voluntary indicative scale for contributions or even a negotiated burden-sharing scheme that could put the UN agencies on a much more secure footing.

This objective also lies at the heart of proposals to further diversify the funding base, not only in terms of governmental and non-governmental resources but also to stop the strong dependence on a small number of donor countries and tap the funding potential of the private sector. In light of the decreasing multilateral support by many Western countries, involving non-traditional donors is an important strategic move. This could lead to both an increase in financial resources and stronger ownership and leadership by developing countries. Ultimately, it could also help pave the way for overcoming the provider–recipient thinking that reinforces not only the North–South divide in UN circles but also dominates governments and societies in the advanced industrialized world and in the global South.

UN organizations should also reach out to private actors. The secretary-general's Sustainable Energy for All initiative is an example of a large-scale, public–private partnership that promises a significant push for transforming energy systems worldwide to tackle both climate change and poverty.[38] Yet suspicions remain about nurturing too close a relationship between the UN and the corporate world.

Although some of the most recent reform attempts seem promising, none of the above will in the short or medium term be enough to change the nature of how the UN is funded. In the end, given little consensus among developing and advanced industrialized countries about what the greatest development challenges are and how the UNDS should be strategically positioned, any viable solution will need to start on a small scale and eventually prepare the ground for more fundamental and larger-scale changes. Nonetheless, it is important to think about what a more fundamental reform would entail. The most comprehensive reform and forward-looking proposal in recent times has been put forward by Bruce Jenks and Bruce Jones, who distinguish between different core functions of the UNDS (norms/standards, global public goods, assistance for crisis countries, assistance for poverty eradication) and suggest an alternative funding mechanism for each of these functions, namely assessed contributions, negotiated pledges, trust funds, core voluntary pledges and non-core contributions.[39] Pio Wennubst and Timo Mahn in turn argue for broadening the UN's operational work and establishing a system-wide funding mechanism that would be replenished from non-aid resources.[40]

The idea to have a specific tax that would benefit the United Nations and make it independent of state contributions has been formulated throughout the world organization's life—ranging from a financial transaction tax to a currency transaction tax, the taxation of aviation fuel, a maritime fuel emission tax, taxing the use of global commons, taxation of the arms trade, and a billionaire's tax.[41] Still other proposals aim more directly at citizens. A global lottery could provide the UNDS with funds, although not as reliably as taxes. New technologies surely open up more possibilities to directly reach citizens via social media and mobile phones.

Naïve as it may sound today, the time might come that the world discovers the value of an independently funded world organization that provides invaluable services to humankind. However, before such a reform can be undertaken there needs to be a broad and strong consensus about the core functions of the UNDS. Only then can an adequate level of funding be determined. The FUNDS survey found that the most important long-term structural priority for respondents from governments, the UN, and academia is increased funding for UN organizations.[42] In addition to a more secure and predictable funding base, it would be important to have a clearer understanding of what the UNDS should and should not do.

Notes

1 The UN publishes aggregated information on contributions and expenditures for operational activities on an annual basis, but with a delay of about two years. See the most recent report, *Implementation of General Assembly Resolution 67/226 on the Quadriennal Comprehensive Policy Review of Operational Activities for Development of the United Nations System (QCPR)*, Report of the Secretary-General, UN document A/69/63-E/2014/10, 6 February 2014. Additional information comes in the form of the annual statistical annexes available on DESA's homepage: https://www.un.org/en/development/desa/oesc/funding.shtml

2 *Multilateral Aid Report* (OECD, report number DCD/DAC(2012)33/Final), Figure 1.3, 17.

3 The scale of assessment is based on each member state's relative ability to pay, which is calculated based on the gross domestic product and other factors such as foreign debt and per capita income. For political reasons, the share that the United States pays is artificially limited to 22 percent of the UN's overall budget. The minimum contribution is 0.001 percent, see Klaus Hüfner, "Financing the United Nations: The Role of the United States," in *Rethinking International Organizations: Pathology and Promise*, ed. Dennis Dijkzeul and Yves Beigbeder (New York: Berghahn Books), 27–53.

4 See also *Multilateral Aid Report* (OECD, report number DCD/DAC(2011) 21/Final), 28–30.

5 OECD, "Aid to Poor Countries Slips Further as Governments Tighten Budgets," www.oecd.org/newsroom/aidtopoorcountriesslipsfurtherasgovern mentstightenbudgets.htm

6 See *Statistical Annex to the Analysis of Funding of Operational Activities for Development of the United Nations System for 2012*, Table A-1.

7 For a more extensive historical perspective, see Stephen Browne, *The UN Development Programme and System* (London: Routledge, 2011); Craig Murphy, *The UN Development Programme: A Better Way?* (Cambridge: Cambridge University Press, 2006); and Olav Stokke, *The UN and Development: From Aid to Cooperation* (Bloomington: Indiana University Press, 2009).

8 Browne, *The UN Development Programme and System*, 32.

9 See also the three phases in the UNDS's evolution as identified by Bruce Jenks and Bruce Jones, *United Nations Development at a Crossroads* (New York: New York University, Center on International Cooperation, 2013).

10 *Multilateral Aid Report* (OECD, report number DCD/DAC(2012)33/Final), Figure 1.3, 17.

11 The International Fund for Agricultural Development (IFAD), UNAIDS, UN Women, and UNRWA are the only agencies with sizable operational activities that have a core share amounting to or exceeding 50 percent. One possible explanation is that these agencies have a clearer mandate that is limited in scope/geographic focus. See *Statistical Annex to Funding Report 2012*, Table A-2.

12 *Comprehensive Statistical Analysis of the Financing of Operational Activities for Development of the United Nations System for 2007: Report of the Secretary General*, UN document A/64/75-E/2009/59, 30 April 2009.

13 Author's own calculation based on *Statistical Annex to the Analysis of Funding of Operational Activities for Development of the United Nations System for 2012*, Table A-2.

14 UNICEF Annual Report 2012, www.unicef.org/publications/files/UNICEF-AnnualReport2012_8July2013.pdf

15 Asmita Naik, "Can the UN Adjust to the Changing Funding Landscape?" *Future United Nations Development System*, FUNDS Briefing no. 2, March 2013, 3. www.futureun.org/en/Publications-Surveys/Article?newsid=8

16 *Implementation of General Assembly Resolution 67/226 on the Quadriennial Comprehensive Policy Review of Operational Activities for Development of the United Nations System (QCPR)*, 19–20.

17 The United Kingdom, the Netherlands, Sweden, and Germany alone contributed nearly 19 percent of UNDS resources in 2011. See *Statistical Annex to the Analysis of Funding of Operational Activities for Development for 2011*, Table A-5.

18 For more details on the funding profiles of donor countries, see Silke Weinlich, *Reforming the UN Development System: An Analysis of Policy Positions and Actions of Key States on Reform Options* (Bonn, Germany: German Development Institute/Deutsches Institut für Entwicklungspolitik, 2011).

19 Norway, the Netherlands, Sweden, Denmark, Finland, Belgium, Luxembourg, and Ireland together contributed more than one third of UNDS core resources in 2011. See *Statistical Annex to the Analysis of Funding of Operational Activities for Development for 2011*, Table A-5.

20 Sachin Chaturvedi, Thomas Fues, and Elizabeth Sidiropoulos, eds., *Development Cooperation and Emerging Powers: New Partners or Old Patterns?* (London: Zed Books, 2012).

21 Author's calculations on the basis of United Nations, *Statistical Annex to Funding Report 2009; 10; 11;12*, Tables A-3, A-5, B-3, www.un.org/esa/coordination/

dcpb_stat.htm and http://www.un.org/en/development/desa/oesc/qcpr.shtml;
see also Weinlich, *Reforming the UN Development System*, 61.

22 In the mid-1980s, Brasilia began to channel funds (often loans from the World
Bank or regional development banks) through the UN. It was thereby able
to work around its own administrative structures, which were slow to
reform. See Browne, *The UN Development Programme and System*, 45–46.

23 Silke Weinlich and Thomas Fues, "Aufstrebende Schwellenmächte bei den
Vereinten Nationen," in *Die großen Schwellenländer. Ursachen und Folgen
ihres Aufstiegs in der Weltwirtschaft*, ed. Andreas Nölke, Christian May,
and Simone Claar (Wiesbaden, Germany: Springer VS, 2013), 299–316.

24 In order to be eligible for ODA, many agencies identify as much of their core
budgets as possible as related to operational activities. The five largest specialized
agencies allocate between 51 and 76 percent of their assessed budget to
operational activities. See *Implementation of General Assembly Resolution
67/226 on the Quadriennial Comprehensive Policy Review of Operational
Activities for Development of the United Nations System (QCPR)*, 57.

25 Ibid., 21–22.

26 While the true costs for the management of non-core resource are estimated
to be around 15 percent of contributions, specialized agencies only charge
13 percent and funds and programs an even lower fee of roughly 7 percent. As
a partial remedy, in 2012 the General Assembly approved further increases;
the funds and programs now apply a harmonized cost-recovery rate of 8
percent, to be reviewed in 2014. See ibid., 30–2.

27 Ibid., 21.

28 Despite some successes in the Delivering as One pilot countries and elsewhere, for instance by joint programs that involved two or more UN agencies
and national partners, the fragmented and precarious funding situation is a
significant obstacle to inter-agency cooperation. See United Nations, *Independent Evaluation of Delivering as One* (New York: UN, 2012).

29 Timo Mahn, *The Financing of Development Cooperation at the United
Nations: Why More Means Less* (Bonn, Germany: German Development
Institute/Deutsches Institut für Entwicklungspolitik, 2012).

30 Naik, "Can the UN Adjust?" 4.

31 Ibid., 3.

32 See Flavia Galvani and Stephen Morse, "Institutional Sustainability: At
What Price? UNDP and the New Cost-Sharing Model in Brazil," *Development in Practice* 14, no. 3 (2004): 311–27. UNDP's strategic plan 2008–13
stipulated that the agency should reduce this form of cooperation. While in
2007, local resources accounted for about one third of total contributions,
in 2011, they are down to 18 percent. See *Implementation of General
Assembly 67/226 resolution on the QCPR*, 57.

33 Melissa Leach, Kate Raworth, and Johan Rockström, "Between Social and
Planetary Boundaries: Navigating Pathways in the Safe and Just Space for
Humanity," in *World Social Science Report 2013: Changing Global Envir-
onments*, ed. International Social Science Council (Paris: OECD and
UNESCO, 2013).

34 See Weinlich, *Reforming the UN Development System*, 81–90.

35 "Quadrennial Comprehensive Policy Review of Operational Activities for
Development of the United Nations System," UN General Assembly resolution A/67/226, 21 January 2013; see also Pio Wennubst and Timo Mahn,

A Resolution for a Quiet Resolution: Taking the United Nations to Sustainable Development beyond Aid, Discussion Paper (Bonn, Germany: Deutsches Institut für Entwicklungspolitik/German Development Institute, 2013).

36 For more information, see the website of UNDP's MDTF Partner Office: http://mptf.undp.org/.

37 See Silke Weinlich and Urs Zollinger, "Lessons from Delivering as One: Options for UN Member States," Briefing Paper (Bonn, Germany: German Development Institute/Deutsches Institut für Entwicklungspolitik, 2012).

38 Jenks and Jones, *United Nations Development at a Crossroads*, 55–58.

39 Ibid., 117–19.

40 Pio Wennubst and Timo Mahn, *Post 2015: What It Means for the United Nations Development System* (Bonn, Germany: German Development Institute/Deutsches Institut für Entwicklungspolitik, 2013).

41 Nancy Birdsall and Benjamin Lee, "Find Me the Money: Financing Climate and Other Global Public Goods," Centre for Global Development, Working Paper 248 (2011); UN Department of Economic and Social Affairs, *World Economic and Social Survey 2012: In Search of New Development Finance* (New York: UN, 2012).

42 Stephen Browne and Thomas G. Weiss, *Making Change Happen: Enhancing the UN's Contribution to Development* (New York: World Federation of UN Associations, 2012), 31.

5 Evaluating the UN development system

Robert Picciotto

Does the United Nations development system work? How can we tell? What should be done? To address these questions, this chapter probes the origins and evolution of the organization's mandate, assesses its record in aid delivery, and makes the case for a thorough reform of its evaluation arrangements.

Security, the UN's core mission

Development assistance has never been the core business of the United Nations. Article 1 of the UN Charter lists the maintenance of international peace and security as the overarching purpose of the organization. The second secretary-general, Dag Hammarskjöld, is widely reported to have argued that "the UN was not created to take humanity to heaven but to save it from hell."

Accordingly, throughout the Cold War the organization focused on defusing regional tensions, a worthy objective since the East–West ideological divide could have triggered a disastrous nuclear war. Following the implosion of the Soviet Union in December 1991, the threats to international stability posed by intra-state tensions supplanted the risks posed by interstate conflicts. Suddenly liberated from the strictures of Cold War confrontation, the United Nations was empowered to engage in far-flung peacebuilding operations in the zones of turmoil of the developing world.

Since then globalization has transformed the international system. Emerging markets have become the engine of the international economy. Trade, migration, and foreign direct investment flows have become major vehicles of resource transfer. Aid no longer holds sway except in fragile states. In parallel, security threats have evolved and multiplied due to the marginalization of least developed countries, the ascent of regional powers, the advent of transnational terrorism, and the proliferation of arms and weapons.

With the advent of non-state actors specialized in the use of violence and skilled at exploiting the borderless opportunities offered by information and communications technologies, the boundaries between interstate and intra-state security issues have become blurred. Illegal activities operating with impunity across borders constitute one of many obstacles to international stability at the intersection of security and development.

These threats to human well-being are interconnected. They include malnutrition, disease, pollution, climate change, and financial instability as well as arms trafficking, international crime, and terrorism. They cannot be solved solely through the use of defense and diplomacy instruments. They need to be tackled through international development cooperation and the production of global and regional public goods. Just as in the postwar era, security and development are two sides of the same coin but the nature of the peace and prosperity challenge has changed and the United Nations will need to adapt.[1]

Development, a second-order goal

Short of a cataclysmic world crisis, the United Nations will only change gradually. But even if reform materializes, security will always come first. To be sure, *freedom from want* will continue to be visualized as complementary to *freedom from fear*. This is in line with the intent of the postwar planners present at the creation of a new world order. Drawing on the hard-won lessons of the Great Depression, they proceeded on the assumption that a lasting peace would not be possible without institutions mandated to oversee the world economic system.[2]

To this end they chose to rely on the Bretton Woods institutions rather than the United Nations. Charter Article 55 specified that the UN should promote higher standards of living, full employment, and conditions of economic and social progress and development. But the "form follows function" principle was not heeded. Instead, the UN system was conceived as a loose assemblage of communities of practice specialized in the transfer of knowledge and skills and the identification of good practice norms within particular policy domains.[3]

The world organization remains wedded to this functional, disaggregated organizational model. Fragmentation has further increased as donor countries opted to assert control over their favored thematic initiatives through non-core funding of vertical programs. By contrast, most development assistance agencies adopted country-focused organizational structures. For example, a far-reaching country-oriented reorganization was implemented by the World Bank in 1987 in order to enhance its policy influence. Although maintaining a substantial country presence, no such reform took place in the UN and it is not in the cards.

The security and development record

With respect to its core business of maintaining international peace and security, the United Nations has performed creditably. Except where the vital interests of major powers were at stake, the UN system made major contributions to interstate security throughout the Cold War. The context changed radically following the fall of the Berlin Wall. After an initial spurt, the number of intra-state conflicts dropped by almost 50 percent between 1992 and 2003. From 2003 to 2008, the number of civil conflicts increased again but high-intensity civil conflicts remained at a low level, resulting in a 77 percent net decrease since 1988.

The UN has played a major role in peacekeeping and peacebuilding. The number of international mediation efforts rose fivefold from the 1980s to the 1990s. The number of contact groups and other political arrangements increased tenfold from 1991 to 2007. The number of peace operations went up threefold from 1988 to 2008. Sanction regimes, post-conflict peacebuilding coalitions, and war crime prosecutions also multiplied.[4]

On the development front, the United Nations was instrumental in forging a development consensus culminating in a global poverty reduction compact—the Millennium Declaration in General Assembly resolution 55/2. Remarkably, the world has already achieved the first Millennium Development Goal (MDG) target of halving the 1990 poverty rate by 2015.[5] In fact, we are now midway through a century of high and accelerating growth in the developing world, which translates into sustained economic convergence with the advanced countries.[6]

But the UN development system (UNDS) cannot take much of the credit. The acceleration of economic growth in emerging markets largely springs from these countries' own efforts. To be sure, official development assistance (ODA) played a significant supportive role in some countries and in some sectors, but the United Nations has never been a major actor on the international aid scene.[7] ODA from all members of the UNDS was only $6 billion in 2006–8, less than 5 percent of the total, and its effectiveness has long been hampered by fragmentation, high transaction costs, and poor coordination.

Implications for the United Nations

Nonetheless, the UN's indirect contribution to overall economic development has not been negligible: development cooperation is not only about aid, and war is development in reverse. From this perspective the world organization has arguably enhanced global prosperity in a major, albeit roundabout way—through its peace-building work and its humanitarian activities. Equally, aid channeled through the United Nations through non-core funding has increasingly been used for high-leverage, multi-country collaborative programs focused on the delivery of global and regional public goods. Such a role has become increasingly critical in an interconnected world.

Threats to security, including natural disasters, contagious diseases, food crises, and environmental degradation as well as terrorism, international crime, and illegal trafficking interact. Only the United Nations has the global reach and the legitimacy to help development partners tackle them in concert through diplomacy, advocacy, and knowledge-sharing. The core message of Kofi Annan's far-reaching *In Larger Freedom* report was exactly this one.[8]

Escalating security concerns help explain the rising profile of development assistance to fragile states. Development cooperation is now deliberately focused on good governance, youth employment, economic diversification, and improved natural resource management.[9] Given the existential risks associated with climate change, sustainable development considerations have also moved to the center-stage of development aid policy.

Aid today is highly fragmented while the international economy is increasingly integrated and environmental threats transcend borders. Non-aid links have become major mechanisms of resource transfer. They are dwarfing the financial impact of aid and creating new and powerful connections between industrialized and developing countries, as well as among developing countries.

Developing countries' exports are about 45 times the level of 2010 official aid flows. Foreign direct investment is more than four times as large, and remittances from migrants more than twice as large.[10] In the reverse direction, royalty and licensing fees paid by developing countries to developed countries are also substantial, and the damage to developing countries caused by climate change as a result of industrialized countries' unsustainable environmental practices is huge.[11]

Unless the UN equips itself to address explicitly the global policy issues associated with all major transmission belts of globalization, the legitimacy of the organization will be eroded. Hence, a deliberate focus on policy coherence for development combined with the provision of global and regional public goods has become the comparative advantage of the United Nations.

Pragmatic multilateralism

Global problems require global solutions. This is where the policy advocacy, knowledge-sharing, norm-setting, and global public goods delivery roles of the United Nations come together. More than ever before, leaders and institutions from around the world are discovering that broad-based sustainable development necessitates cross-border action. Thus, the UN is best conceived as a collaborative platform that transcends national borders and makes use of its legitimacy, global reach, and convening power. It has been and remains the indispensable forum that convenes sovereign states for negotiation of principled agreements on policy norms and rules of the game designed to enhance international peace and prosperity. Needless to say, political obstacles have almost always stood in the way of this mission, and it would not be practical to assess the UN's performance as if they did not exist.

Pragmatic multilateralism means exercising the art of the possible and accepting that multilateralism takes different forms. State-centric international conventions set precise principles of conduct, regulate governments' behavior, and coordinate their actions. But they are open to challenge by powerful governments as well as by a wide range of influential private interests and voluntary associations. When binding comprehensive global agreements come into conflict with national priorities or special interests, they often fail to materialize.

From this perspective, traditional multilateralism embodied by the UNDS imposes constraints that governments frequently refuse to tolerate. It follows that transaction costs and information asymmetries are minimized when the management and funding of development cooperation is left to the lowest level of executing authority at which it can be handled efficiently in line with the principle of subsidiarity. Out of necessity, partial multilateralism must be accepted as a second-best.

Thus, the collective action dilemmas embedded in classical multilateralism have given rise to a pragmatic approach to global diplomacy that entails assembling the smallest number of parties needed to have a positive impact on a given problem: minilateralism.[12] Reliance on this approach explains the rise in trust fund arrangements managed through the United Nations by tailor-made coalitions of states, private interests, and voluntary organizations.

The United Nations, a system?

Given the shift in policy priorities imposed by the rapidly evolving operating context described above, one ought to consider the overall organization as a suitable unit of account when conceiving of an evaluation function for the United Nations. Yet this is not how the current evaluation system is set up. Except with respect to inspection, all corporate oversight mechanisms mirror the stark reality of a fluid organizational network made up of diverse international agencies, treaties, and conventions, each of which has its own goals.

Specifically the unwieldy UN development system consists of 16 specialized agencies (including the World Bank and IMF, which are *de facto* not part of the system), eight functional commissions, five regional commissions, and more than a dozen other organizations and programs. It is wracked by duplication and undermined by archaic business processes. Given their separate mandates and distinctive governance arrangements, individual agencies have no incentive to comply with secretariat injunctions or to cooperate with one another.

A fair assessment of UN performance should take explicit account of the constraints built into current governance structures dictated by member states. They can be traced to the exigencies of power politics and the inevitable trade-offs between international legitimacy, responsiveness to stakeholders, and corporate effectiveness.

In particular the UN secretary-general enjoys prestige but little else. The formal authority of the post is severely limited. Yet given the interconnectedness of threats to international peace, stability, and prosperity, coherence among the initiatives taken at the program or agency level within the entire UN system is critical to performance.

Tapping synergies and improving coordination are more than ever imperatives of corporate effectiveness. Successive reforms at the United Nations have focused on delivering development aid *as one* at the country level instead of focusing on coherence and coordination in knowledge generation, norm-setting, and the promotion of principled partnerships at the global and regional levels. A major constraint has been the limited recourse to horizontal programs that cut across organizational jurisdictions in order to achieve effective results.

Even in terms of aid effectiveness at the country level, progress in all five reform dimensions of the high-profile report *Delivering as One* has been modest and partial at best, and consists of: better coordination and programing mechanisms; harmonization and simplification of operational practices; a reinforced role for resident coordinators; enhanced core and regular funding; and improved relations with specialized agencies (including the international financial institutions—IFIs).

The independent evaluation of *Delivering as One* gives an overview of the record in eight countries that volunteered to pilot the approach: Albania, Cape Verde, Mozambique, Pakistan, Rwanda, the United

Republic of Tanzania, Uruguay, and Viet Nam.[13] Despite major efforts by country teams and some achievements, the observed weaknesses were substantial.

Relying on process reforms instead of reshaping organizational structures, the UNDS has been clearly unable to *act as one* in delivering aid or influencing overall country development strategies. It is unlikely, moreover, that major donors would welcome displacement of the World Bank in this particular role. Given these strictures, the UN's comparative advantage should be sought at a higher plane.

The United Nations has lost the aid effectiveness race

In terms of aid delivery at the country level, the United Nations has proven far too fragmented and short of financial resources to compete effectively. The evidence from available aid effectiveness tables is sobering. For example, the *2008 Survey on Monitoring the Paris Declaration* confirmed that the multilateral development banks and the European Commission enjoy a significant edge over UN agencies, especially with respect to the alignment and predictability dimensions of aid effectiveness (see Table 5.1).

Similarly, a World Bank research paper synthesizes the findings of major aid-quality studies and puts forward an overall index for 11

Table 5.1 Paris Declaration indicators of donor performance

Aid agency	Harmonization	Alignment	Predictability	Aid untying	Total
AfDB	94	76	86	133	97
AsDB	97	102	134	133	117
IDB	126	90	118	133	117
WB	137	132	123	133	131
MDBs	114	100	115	133	116
EC	142	74	120	133	117
IFAD	163	144	64	133	126
UN	129	54	59	133	94
All multilaterals	127	96	101	133	114
All donors	100	100	100	100	100

Source: Better Aid, *2008 Survey on Monitoring the Paris Declaration, Making Aid More Effective by 2010* (Paris: OECD, 2008), Appendix B: Donor Data.
Note: The ratios are based on aggregate indicators for the most recent year available (2007) as follows: harmonization (indicators 9, 10a, and 10b); alignment (indicators 4, 5a, and 5b); predictability (indicator 7); aid untying (indicator 8).

multilateral institutions and 27 bilateral institutions. Once again, the United Nations was found to trail behind other donors.[14] Table 5.2 does not show the members of the UNDS in a favorable light either. The data are drawn from a comprehensive and transparent multilateral aid review carried out by the UK Department for International Development (DFID).

The vertical funds and multi-country collaborative programs deliver good or very good "value for money." The multilateral development banks also do relatively well. Much less impressive are the ratings awarded to UN organizations. Out of 21 rated by DFID, only UNICEF is rated as very good while seven are rated as good, six as adequate, and nine as poor. The same dismal message is found in a well-documented Brookings Center for Global Development (CGD) report (see Table 5.3). It shows that the United Nations ranks last for most criteria of aid quality. Fragmentation is high and efficiency low. The administrative burden imposed on partner countries is heavy.

Unless the organization engages in a strategic repositioning exercise regarding its development cooperation role and does so with the fulsome support of its member states, the share of resources flowing through the UNDS may continue to decline. Yet significant funding will be needed to achieve organizational synergy through horizontal programs connecting the security and development functions, as well as the global and country roles of the organization, more intimately. In time, lack of resources may jeopardize the world body's role as a platform for global and regional goods delivery and as a norm-setter.

The evaluation challenge

Credible evaluation systems would help the United Nations realign its corporate assets to achieve verifiable results. Here too, it has been lagging behind the multilateral development banks. The United Nations Development Programme (UNDP) and the International Fund for Agricultural Development (IFAD)—a UN organization that has adopted international financial institution characteristics—are exceptions to this rule.

While good practice standards and peer review processes focused on the independence and quality of internal evaluation systems were designed under the strong leadership of the UNDP's Evaluation Office, they have not been implemented with comparable diligence across the system.[15] The United Nations Evaluation Group (UNEG) is a loose professional network that brings together evaluation units of the UN system, including the specialized agencies, funds, programs, and affiliated organizations. The UNEG currently has 45 such members. However, there is no

Table 5.2 Value for money (VFM) ratings of selected multilateral aid organizations

Agency	Development objectives	Results orientation	Managerial strength	Partnership	Transparency	VFM
AfDB	2.8	2.0	3.0	3.0	4.0	Good
AsDB	2.8	3.0	3.3	3.0	3.0	Very good
IDB	2.3	2.7	3.0	3.0	3.0	Adequate
WB (IDA)	3.2	2.0	3.0	2.0	3.0	Very good
IFAD	3.0	3.0	2.3	3.0	3.0	Good
EC budget	2.7	2.0	2.3	3.0	3.0	Adequate
UNDP	3.0	2.0	2.3	3.0	3.0	Good
WHO	2.8	2.0	2.0	3.0	2.0	Adequate
FAO	2.7	2.0	2.0	3.0	1.0	Poor
UNESCO	2.3	1.0	1.7	2.0	2.0	Poor
UNICEF	3.3	3.0	2.7	3.0	2.0	Very good
ILO	2.2	2.0	1.7	3.0	2.0	Poor
UNIDO	1.8	2.0	1.7	3.0	2.0	Poor
WFP	3.2	3.0	2.7	3.0	2.0	Good
UNHCR	3.2	4.0	3.0	2.0	2.0	Good

Source: UK Department for International Development, *Multilateral Aid Review* (London: DFID, 2011).
Note: "Development objectives" averages ratings for role in meeting international and UK aid objectives, fragile contexts, gender, climate, poverty focus. 'Managerial strength" averages performance management, financial management, and cost consciousness. Also rated is the "likelihood of positive change."

Table 5.3 Quality of development assistance rankings

Aid agency	Efficiency	Institutions	Admin. burden	Transparency	Average
AfDB (AfDF)	2	4	12	25	10.8
AsDB (AsDF)	3	3	10	29	11.3
IDB (SF)	5	8	3	31	11.8
World Bank (IDA)	9	2	2	5	4.5
EC	11	12	9	2	8.5
IFAD	4	20	1	23	12.0
UN	15	28	24	16	20.8

Source: Nancy Birdsall and Homi Kharas, *Quality of Official Development Assistance Assessment* (Washington, DC: Brookings Institution/Centre for Global Development, 2010).
Note: See page 25 of the Brookings/CGD report. Thirty-one agencies were ranked by Brookings/CGD. The UN was represented by five agencies (UNAIDS, UNICEF, UNDP, UNFPA, and WFP).

requirement that evaluation functions report to governing bodies (instead of the head of the agency), and the lack of genuine independence constitutes a weakness of evaluation mechanisms within UN organizations.

An authoritative assessment confirms the usefulness of peer reviews in the UN evaluation system, but notes that they are not mandatory so that they tend to be undertaken mostly where the evaluation function is relatively strong.[16] Only nine peer reviews have been carried out over eight years.[17]

While the quality of evaluation systems and processes varies across the system, recurring themes nonetheless are striking: a lack of structural independence; failure to adopt explicit evaluation policies; inadequate budgets; spotty quality assurance; and limited use of evaluation findings. Another pervasive weakness has been the lack of reliable self-evaluation information at the level of individual interventions. Two solutions impose themselves: external assessment and tracking; and independent system-wide evaluations. While both are under consideration and have been so for some time, little progress is visible.

External assessment and tracking systems

Voluntary international tracking mechanisms have not filled the evaluation gap, and they have not come to terms with the reality that the United Nations should not be judged primarily as an aid organization. Through a battery of indicators, the Multilateral Organization Performance Assessment Network (MOPAN) is designed to help reach judgments about the quality of strategic management, operational management, relationship management, and knowledge management.[18] It does not address development effectiveness, and it surveys only a few multilateral organizations every year.[19]

A guidance note about the assessment of multilateral organizations' development effectiveness issued by the Development Assistance Committee Network on Development Evaluation was based on pilot tests.[20] Unfortunately this approach is heavily reliant on the prior availability of evaluative information generated by internal evaluation units. The credibility of such a "light touch" initiative is bound to be limited.

Independent system-wide evaluation

Recommendations to carry out system-wide evaluations on a regular basis have been repeatedly put forward. For example, they were called for by the High-level Panel of the Secretary-General on UN System-wide Coherence. Its November 2006 report recommended that a UN system-wide independent evaluation mechanism be established by 2008 to monitor how system-wide goals are being delivered.[21]

Specifically the high-level panel recommended that peer reviews across all UN organizations should be systematically carried out based on a common evaluation methodology. Such a system should have been in place by 2010 to permit benchmarking, inter-agency comparisons, and exchanges of best practices. But no concrete action was taken, replicating a long-standing record of foot-dragging.

The panel also argued that standardized information about UN activities, program delivery, budgets, staffing, and cost-effectiveness should be publicly available. The panelists stressed that harmonizing systems and methodologies would provide member states with a transparent overview of results from the UN development system and financial figures by area of interest and type of activity. Once again, little has been done.

The 2010 General Assembly resolution 289 requested the secretary-general—in consultation with the UNEG and the Joint Inspection Unit (JIU)—to commission a comprehensive review of the existing institutional framework for the system-wide evaluation of operational activities for development of the UN system, and to submit a report with specific recommendations to the General Assembly at its 66th session.

In June 2011, the Office of the Deputy Secretary-General (ODSG) contracted two independent consultants to conduct a comprehensive review of the institutional framework for system-wide evaluation of operational activities for development at the United Nations. This review stressed that the issue of independent system-wide evaluation has become politicized.[22] Nevertheless it proposed that the president of the General Assembly should set up a working group to explore the specific function of independent system-wide evaluations, and in this context to identify a specific role for the JIU.

The review also recommended that the secretary-general establish a process for strengthening coordination of existing ad hoc system-wide evaluation activities in the UN system, through an interim coordination mechanism in the form of a steering group. The review suggested that the JIU should be independently reviewed with a view to improving its effectiveness.

Finally, the review suggested that the evaluative role of the Department of Economic and Social Affairs (DESA) should be revisited through another independent evaluation. In parallel the UNEG should prepare guidelines for independent system-wide evaluations. Whether these recommendations will be implemented and get the issue out of the politicization rut in which it has been mired for years remains to be seen. At the end of 2013, member states decided to launch two pilot independent system-wide evaluations (GA resolution 68/229).

Reorienting the evaluation function

In terms of its global prosperity mandate and well beyond its traditional technical assistance and aid delivery functions, the United Nations could and should play a far more influential role once it recognizes that its true remit lies in knowledge creation, norm-setting, and partnership support roles.[23] The key lies in making full use of its convening power and its legitimacy at the intersection of governments, private sector institutions, and civil society organizations.

While the UN has lost the aid effectiveness race, prevailing aid quality standards are only partially relevant for its roles of catalyst, mediator, and connector that lie at the core of its distinctive comparative advantage. Current evaluations are largely focused on the aid operations of individual UN organizations. They fail to illuminate the multiple dimensions of the UN's work, especially those found at the interface of security, humanitarian action, and development cooperation, as well as those that are geared to improved coherence of public, private, and voluntary actions across borders through norm-setting and collaboration.

Recent global trends have raised the benefits of coherent multilateral action. Intensified efforts to ensure that the United Nations acts *as one* are therefore required, but they should not be directed primarily toward improved aid delivery. They should instead be designed to track

and enhance the development benefits of international conflict prevention, peacebuilding actions, and global/regional public goods creation.

It follows that the Delivering as One initiative should transcend the
country-based aid dimension. Creating incentives for bridging the
security and development divide and for creating multi-agency epistemic
communities would vastly enhance the effectiveness of the organization, since its distinctive comparative advantage lies in the coordination of conflict prevention and peacebuilding activities within fragile
states and at the higher plane of transnational challenges that cut
across security, humanitarian, and development concerns.

New evaluation policy directions

Efforts to improve evaluation in the United Nations system have been
woefully inadequate. This shortcoming is a lost opportunity, since the
evaluation function could act as a transmission belt between knowledge and policy; enhance accountability for results; help link citizens to
the organization; and improve the workings of the partnerships on
which the United Nations depends.

Emphasizing peacebuilding, norm-setting, and knowledge services
would have fundamental implications for evaluation approaches,
methods, and processes. Using a broader evaluation canvas is likely to
confirm that the UN's comparative advantage does not lie in aid
delivery. It would also provide a more accurate picture of its overall
effectiveness and comparative advantage. The full contribution of the
UN system to economic stability and social cohesion has not been
captured by evaluation processes that have neglected secondary,
indirect, and collective action benefits.

Beyond the assessment of its diverse humanitarian and development
operations, the benefits of UN activities at this higher plane should be
captured by a well-conceived evaluation function. This implies systemic
thinking and use of mixed evaluation methods adapted to the assessment
of complex interventions.

Using this broader lens, the world organization would be judged for its
distinctive contribution and its distinctive character: joint action in conflict-
prone and conflict-affected societies; the creation and use of international
norms and standards; the amplification of the voices of the poor and
underprivileged; a vigorous advocacy role for greater equality and
social inclusion; an invigorated role as a catalyst for collaborative programs involving all sectors of society; and a strengthened capacity to
coordinate international initiatives and to mobilize energies currently
scattered throughout the public, private, and voluntary sectors.

Evaluation governance

The evaluation policy directions sketched above imply organizational solutions that combine self-evaluation with independent evaluation both at the individual organization as well as at the overall system level. The foundations for an overarching approach to comprehensive and independent evaluations of the UN system would best be grounded in the good -practice standards of the Evaluation Cooperation Group (ECG) of the multilateral development banks and informed by upgraded UNEG standards. The ECG was established by the heads of evaluation of the multilateral development banks in 1996 to: strengthen the use of evaluation for greater development effectiveness and accountability; share lessons from evaluations and contribute to their dissemination; harmonize performance indicators and evaluation methodologies and approaches; enhance evaluation professionalism within the multilateral development banks; collaborate with the heads of evaluation units of bilateral and multilateral development organizations; and facilitate the involvement of borrowing member countries in evaluation and build their evaluation capacity.

A credible evaluation function for the UN development system implies a genuine effort to involve developing countries in the process. In turn, such an effort would require a major commitment to evaluation capacity development. As well, it would call for joint-evaluation governance arrangements that give greater substantive control over the evaluation process to developing country governments, organizations, and citizens.

The world organization's problems are well known: fragmentation; the specialized nature of its various agencies, funds, and programs; the sprawling multi-tier governance structure with which it is saddled, as well as the imperative of acting coherently to facilitate the alignment of global goals with local needs and capabilities. Thus, the evaluation system should be shared between strong independent internal evaluation units focused on corporate accountability and organizational learning and a system-wide independent evaluation function that addresses thematic, cross-border, system-wide United Nations activities. Regular independent assessment of internal evaluation, as well as of transparency and oversight of evaluation processes, would be the hallmarks of a sound, system-wide evaluation function.

Moreover, putting evaluation at the center of its own activities would provide the United Nations with the credentials needed to guarantee independent, high-quality evaluation work as well as fulsome stakeholders' and citizens' engagement in the global policy process. Finally, adequate evaluation structures and capabilities would allow the world organization to offer independent evaluation services to intergovernmental bodies, civil society coalitions, public–private alliances, or private philanthropies. Such services would be useful complements to the UN's norm-setting and good practice dissemination roles.

Conclusion

Reform of the United Nations is imperative. More effective multilateral action is needed to overcome policy incoherence and fill the global public goods deficit associated with a complex, interconnected, and volatile international world. Past reform efforts have yielded disappointing outcomes because they have relied on exhortation and process adjustments without tackling systemic issues.

The United Nations is the undisputed leader of peacebuilding activities in conflict-prone, fragile states. Furthermore, within an authorizing environment that favors the international financial institutions for mainstream development programs, the comparative advantage of the UN lies in norm-setting, multi-country programs, multi-sector alliances, and partnership building. Strategic repositioning of the organization toward such goals will require shifts in incentives and reorientation of donor funding toward horizontal programs cutting across organizational boundaries. Accordingly, the Delivering as One initiative should be raised to a higher plane.

The time has come to change the approach and metrics used to assess UN activities. As long as it is judged as an aid deliverer, the United Nations system will continue to be viewed as a poorer performer than it actually is. The absence of credible evaluation functions focused not only on individual organizational aid performance but also on their combined impact in terms of opinion-making, advocacy, norm-setting, knowledge dissemination, consensus-building, and peacebuilding has sold the organization short and has deprived it of the learning benefits yielded by formative evaluations.

New policy directions, greater independence, and more emphasis on organizational learning and participatory methods hold the key to an improved evaluation function at the United Nations. Adapted evaluation governance structures designed to guarantee objectivity and value added are as important as methodological rigor to ensure credibility of evaluation within the world body. The recommendations offered by the High-level Panel on UN System-wide Coherence to set up system-wide evaluation systems should be implemented.

Notes

1 Anne-Marie Slaughter, *A New World Order* (Princeton, N.J.: Princeton University Press, 2004).

2 Benn Steil, *The Battle of Bretton Woods: John Maynard Keynes, Harry Dexter White and the Making of a New World Order* (Princeton, N.J.: Princeton University Press, 2013).

3 Bruce Jenks and Bruce Jones, *United Nations at a Crossroads* (New York: New York University, Centre on International Cooperation, 2013).

4 Human Security Report Project, *Human Security Report 2009/2010: The Causes of Peace and the Shrinking Costs of War* (Oxford: Oxford University Press, 2010).

5 United Nations, Millennium Goals, www.un.org/millenniumgoals

6 Pedro Olinto and Jaime Saavedra, "An Overview of Global Inequality Trends," *Inequality in Focus* 1, no. 1 (2012): 1–4.

7 Finn Tarp, "Aid effectiveness," UNESCO, www.un.org/en/ecosoc/newfunct/pdf/aid_effectiveness-finn_tarp.pdf

8 Kofi A. Annan, *In Larger Freedom: Towards Development, Security and Human Rights for All, Report of the Secretary-General* (New York: UN, 2005).

9 Robert Picciotto, Funmi Olonisakin, and Michael Clarke, *Global Development and Human Security* (New Brunswick, N.J.: Transaction Publishers, 2007).

10 It has been estimated that 12 poor countries in East and West Africa could gain as much as \$3 trillion from new sources of oil and gas over the next 30–50 years. Larry Diamond and Jack Mosbacher, "Africa's Coming Resource Curse and How to Avoid It," *Foreign Affairs* 92, no. 5 (2013): 86–98.

11 Robert Picciotto, "Multilateral Cooperation and the Paris Process: The Road to Busan," in *Canadian Development Report 2011, Global Challenges: Multilateral Solutions* (Ottawa: The North South Institute, 2011), 59–60.

12 Moisés Naím, "Minilateralism," *Foreign Policy*, no. 173 (2009): 135–36.

13 United Nations, *Independent Evaluation of Delivering as One* (New York: UN, 2012), www.un.org/en/ga/deliveringasone/pdf/summaryreportweb.pdf

14 Stephen Knack, F. Halsey Rogers, and Nicholas Eubank, *Aid Quality and Donor Rankings*, Policy Research Working Paper 5290 (Washington, DC: World Bank, Development Research Group, 2010).

15 The Evaluation Cooperation Group has issued standards on the Independence of International Financial Institutions' Central Evaluation Departments, and the UN Evaluation Group has issued norms and standards for evaluation in the UN system. See UNEG, "Norms, Standards and Guidance," www.uneval.org/normsandstandards/index.jsp?doc_cat_source_id=4

16 Ian C. Davies and Julia Brummer, "Lessons-Learned Study of Peer Reviews of UNEG Evaluation Functions," United Nations Evaluation Group, May 2013, www.uneval.org/documentdownload?doc_id=1379&file_id=1804

17 These include evaluations of the FAO, UN Habitat, UNEP, UNIDO, WFP, OIOS, UNICEF, and UNDP. A peer review of the GEF evaluation function has also been undertaken.

18 MOPAN is managed by a network of 17 donor countries with a common interest in assessing the organizational effectiveness of the major multilateral organizations that they fund based on online surveys and interviews of MOPAN members' staff and agency clients.

19 In 2012 it reported on the African Development Bank (AfDB), the Global Alliance for Vaccines and Immunisation (GAVI), the Joint United Nations Programme on HIV/AIDS (UNAIDS), the UNDP, UNICEF, and the World Bank (IBRD/IDA).

20 "Assessing the Development Effectiveness of Multilateral Organizations: Guidance on the Methodological Approach," OECD DAC Network on Development Evaluation, June 2012, www.oecd.org/dac/evaluation/dcdndep/50540172.pdf

21 "Follow Up to the Outcome of the Millennium Summit: High-level Panel of the Secretary-General on UN System-wide Coherence," UN document A/61/583, 20 November 2006.

22 Angela Bester and Charles Lusthaus, "Independent System-Wide Evaluation Mechanisms: Comprehensive Review of the Existing Institutional Framework for System-Wide Evaluation of Operational Activities for Development of the United Nations System" (New York: UN, March 2012).

23 See Richard Jolly, Louis Emmerij, and Thomas G. Weiss, *UN Ideas That Changed the World* (Bloomington: Indiana University Press, 2009).

6   Making the UN more transparent and accountable

Richard Golding

"What is required is a Secretariat that is more empowered and flexible," former UN secretary-general Kofi Annan recommended while addressing representatives of another intergovernmental body, "and at the same time more transparent and accountable."[1] Transparency and accountability need each other and can be mutually reinforcing. Together they enable stakeholders, citizens, investors, donors, beneficiaries, and employees to hold to account those making decisions that affect them whilst potentially influencing those decisions. This chapter begins with some important generic principles surrounding the fundamentals of transparency and accountability and then analyzes some examples of how the UN system has been addressing both of these essential issues.

However, in providing such analysis and examples, it is important to keep in mind the current strategic, political, and economic conditions surrounding the UN system. In 2015 the Millennium Development Goals (MDGs) will "expire," and the global process for establishing their succession, probably for the next 15 years to 2030 and most likely through a new series of global sustainable development goals (SDGs), is already well under way but not yet concluded. This provides a potentially pivotal global opportunity to take on board renewed or even fresh commitments on how the UN system is structured and how it should realign itself to any new agreed-upon SDGs.

Setting goals is fundamental to the achievement of any activity—but it is not enough. Aligning or realigning all the available and potential resources associated with delivering on those goals is also fundamental—whether in the public or private sector. This is basic strategic thinking, but will the seven-decades-old UN system restructure or realign itself to new contemporary goals? Some old UN mandates may no longer be relevant or as relevant to the twenty-first century as when they were formulated, and some goals will pose new responsibilities for the UN.

Against this background of "opportunity for substantial reform," this chapter examines the principles of transparency and accountability in the UN system and takes a more optimistic and even provocative view of what fundamental changes could or should still be made within such a context. Without such a context, the UN system would likely continue with what amounts to mere tinkering with existing practices—or to put it in perhaps more familiar terms, change at a "glacial pace."

Transparency and accountability: what do they mean?

So what is transparency? Simply making more information available is not sufficient to achieve transparency. Flooding the arena with a continuous stream of raw, voluminous data can lead to greater opaqueness and diminish or even obliterate stakeholders' understanding of what is actually going on, with the risk that "you cannot see the wood for the trees." According to the International Transparency and Accountability Initiative (ITAI), transparency can be defined as having two pairs of key characteristics: relevance and accessibility; and timeliness and accuracy.[2] Accessibility, timeliness, and accuracy should be largely matters of fact. Relevance tends to be more a matter of opinion, which means that information can be withheld or manipulated.

A recent glaring example of the importance of transparency is the recent banking crisis and the Eurozone debt crisis, both of which resulted in enormous bailout packages for hitherto triple A-rated banks and certain governments. However, it demonstrated that there was a huge shortfall in relevant, accessible, timely, and accurate information on certain banking activities and the real financial position of certain national and local government entities. Following the Eurozone debt crisis, a recent International Monetary Fund (IMF) report defines fiscal transparency as "the clarity, reliability, frequency, timeliness, and relevance of public fiscal reporting and the openness to the public of the government's fiscal policy-making process—a critical element of effective fiscal management."[3] It is not only investors, taxpayers, and donors who may suffer from a lack of transparency but also the policymakers and decision makers themselves.

The ITAI's definition of accountability means "ensuring that officials in public, private and voluntary sector organizations are answerable for their actions and that there is redress when duties and commitments are not met."[4] They go on to refer to a UK Department for International Development (DFID) paper that describes the accountability relationship between the "accounters" and the "accountees" as being comprised of four elements: standard-setting, investigation, answerability, and sanction.

In debating the concept of accountability, there can be little argument that the above negative-sounding elements are all essential components of any accountability framework or process. While it may entail "holding someone's feet to the fire" and threatening punitive sanctions if they fail to deliver, do not the donors or "accounters" also want to see the achievement of objectives, positive outcomes, and even goals exceeded beyond expectations? Perhaps too often we focus too heavily on the necessary and important threatening aspects of accountability while ignoring or failing to give similar (or even greater?) weight to the positive and motivational aspects of management and individual empowerment in order to avoid or minimize the need to turn the threats into punitive action.

Transparency and accountability: how is the UN system doing?

This section provides a concise assessment of how the past and present UN system is doing with regard to transparency and accountability. It comprises four components: funding, accounting for dollars and results, oversight, and staff management.

Funding

The UN system is funded by a combination of assessed or core biennial contributions from member states plus voluntary or "extra-budgetary" or non-core contributions from member states, either directly, or through other multilateral organizations (such as the World Bank and EU). In some UN entities, there are also contributions from other parties although, with the exception of UNICEF, this component remains relatively small.

In Figure 6.1, analysis of the funding for the UN system's operational activities for development in the 15 years leading up to 2011 shows that contribution levels from all funding sources combined demonstrated significant, uninterrupted overall growth. It is clear that this growth is almost entirely the result of increasing voluntary contributions while the levels of assessed contributions have remained largely static. However, voluntary contributions are much less predictable, usually come with significant preconditions or earmarking, often require additional layers of reporting, audit, and oversight procedures, and result in an increasingly fragmented budgeting and accounting landscape across the whole system, with literally thousands of internal voluntary funds on top of regular or core activities. This in turn generates more administration and reporting that may increase the "accounting,"

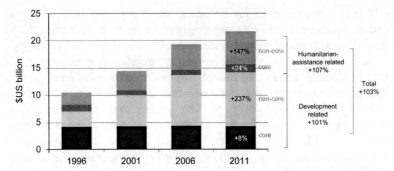

Figure 6.1 Real change over time of funding for UN operational activities for development, 1996–2011 (percentage change relative to 1996)
Source: United Nations, "Analysis of Funding of Operational Activities for Development of the United Nations System for the Year 2011," UN Department of Economic and Social Affairs, May 2013.

but such volumes and fragmentation can seriously dilute "accountability," often resulting in more opaqueness and thereby less transparency.

Given that the UN system is the frequent target of public criticism by its member states and others for being bureaucratic, wasteful, inefficient, and lacking in transparency and accountability, this sustained and steadily increasing overall funding trend is surprising and even alarming. Where else would you find such a level of constant criticism coupled with the contradiction of ever-increasing levels of investment? This reality has a lot to do with this issue of multiple sources of demands for individual donor transparency resulting in opaqueness and being unable (or even unwilling) to "see the wood for the trees."

This perhaps simplistic conclusion nonetheless provides a perspective to keep in mind when assessing and evaluating the debate about transparency and accountability within the UN system. Are there other, more structural factors that will lead to more effective results and outcomes besides persistent demands and attempts to improve transparency and accountability?

This problem will probably never completely go away until such time as there is a step-change in funding methods so that they become more long-term, generic, and most importantly better aligned to the overall development goals of the UN system, which are long-term or at least far longer-reaching than the current and persistent annual and biennial cash budgeting and funding cycles. For example, does it really make sense for an extremely important and growing agency like that of the

UN High Commissioner for Refugees, which regularly takes decisions and commits resources that are inherently long-term in nature, to be funded by voluntary, annual contributions?

Very recently, a potentially interesting development in one major UN specialized agency, the World Health Organization (WHO), seeks at least to reduce the potentially negative impact of a fragmented mix of core and extra-budgetary (or XB) funding and the fragmentation impact of growing XB funding on the organization's agreed strategic priorities. In May 2012, the WHO Assembly, for the first time, adopted a strategy and an "integrated budget" for the forthcoming biennium of 2014/2015[5] together with a commitment by member states and other third-party funding sources (e.g., the Gates Foundation) to participate in two financing dialogue sessions during which the core and XB funding requirements and commitments to support the strategy will be negotiated and agreed. The expectation is that the director-general and the senior management team will now have more certainty and support on the strategic priorities and programs to be implemented over the forthcoming biennium—and even beyond. It is hoped that this empowerment of management should contribute to better resource planning, allocation, mobilization, and coordination, leading in turn to greater and yet more simplified accountability. It is too early to assess whether or not this approach will be sustainable or a success, but other UN entities are already adopting similar approaches.

With regard to transparency of aid funding in a wider context, the International Aid Transparency Initiative (IATI),[6] not to be confused with the aforementioned ITAI, was established only in 2008 and is administered by a secretariat within the UNDP. Since its inception, it has negotiated and established an IATI standard for aid data (including annual budget and results information) and a IATI registry for participants to send and store their data, which is then publicly available through the IATI website. In addition, an associated organization known as Publish What You Fund[7] has taken the IATI standard and registry data in order to publish an Aid Transparency Index of donors. In their 2013 report, DFID was ranked first out of 67 donors in the index listing and China last. What is not yet fully clear is the extent to which a low ranking in such an index is due to the donor's lack of compliance with the published data standards or a genuine lack of transparency or withholding of data regardless of its format.

Such initiatives may be very well intentioned and provide the potential for much greater sharing of standardized data and thereby potentially more transparency—notably on funding and budgets. While still in its early stages, it is nonetheless encouraging to see such international initiatives contributing to strengthen a culture of transparency among all donors and aid providers, and that leading UN organizations are taking a positive role in its development.

Accounting for dollars, and results

When it comes to accounting for all the funds received, in one very basic sense the UN system should be one of the most transparent organizations in the world in terms of accounting for the ownership and sources of its funding. The same cannot be said for many other organizations, political parties, and private sector companies. Virtually all UN funding comes in the form of publicly reported cash contributions from national governments. All funds are declared and reported and, unlike many areas of the political and private sector, it is virtually impossible for the UN to "hide" entities or sources of funding. However, this does not mean that decisions about when and where such funds should be spent, by whom, and for what purposes are always fully transparent.

When it comes to the somewhat mundane but nevertheless critical task of accounting for and reporting on all financial revenues and expenditures across all UN entities (i.e., accounting for dollars), this has for many years been done according to a set of accounting standards developed by the UN system itself, known as the United Nations System Accounting Standards (UNSAS). However, the UN system did not formally adopt these annual or biennial cash-based accounting standards until the early 1990s. Until then, each UN organization had recorded and accounted for its receipts and expenditures according to its own cash-based accounting practices and interpretations.

It is probably being harsh to look back and criticize the UN system for such accounting practices given that almost all of its member state governments had, at least until very recently in some cases, also conducted their own domestic government accounting practices and financial reporting on essentially an annual cash basis. With the benefit of hindsight, many commentators now believe that such simplistic accounting and reporting practices within governments were a significant factor in the failure to prevent the recent sovereign debt crises.

By contrast, publicly listed and many other private sector entities abandoned cash-based accounting practices decades ago (even centuries ago in many cases). Instead they use national and international accrual-based accounting standards with full accrual accounting and valuation practices designed to provide a complete ongoing picture of all assets and liabilities, whether short- or long-term in nature.

Cash-based accounting practices, such as UNSAS, simply require all expenditures to be recorded in the accounts at the point when cash moves and regardless of whether it is being used to pay for a small but necessary expense (such as paying the monthly electricity bill), or for a much larger valuable and reuseable asset (such as a new building or a new vehicle) that may continue to deliver value and benefit to the organization for the next 10 years or more. With cash-based accounting, the full amounts are charged in the accounts at the time of purchase and, in the case of the vehicle, never appear in any future annual or biennial accounts even though the vehicle continues to be used for many years—or at least should continue to be used. Should it "disappear" for any reason, there is not necessarily any accounting or reporting impact. A key example on the liabilities side is to record and report on all future commitments to pay after-service health insurance premiums and pension benefits. The amounts involved are usually very large and very material.

In 2006, the General Assembly approved the recommendation for the UN to convert from the cash-based UNSAS to the accrual-based International Public Sector Accounting Standards (IPSAS). Soon after, various UN specialized agencies and other bodies also agreed to convert their accounting practices to IPSAS. Currently 21 UN organizations have converted to IPSAS so the adoption is almost complete across the UN system—although the core UN Secretariat and peacekeeping operations are among the last to get there. This conversion represents a very significant change not only to the way transactions are captured and recorded within the UN system, but also to judgments and assessments on future funding decisions by both management and member states.

Adoption of such accounting practices should ensure more comprehensive and prudent financial management of the organization and should also greatly reduce, if not eliminate, funding "surprises" or unplanned events and commitments such as the headquarters renovation and the increasing challenge of funding after-service health insurance commitments. There can be little doubt that such practices also promote a far greater sense of accountability among all UN stakeholders, and even enhanced transparency. It also will be further reinforced by the much-debated introduction of accrual-based budgeting across the entire UN system.

However, one critical aspect of the new IPSAS-based financial reporting system that is much harder to address is to ensure that all, or at least the majority of member state representatives who sit in UN governing body meetings, have sufficient knowledge and understanding of what they are looking at with such reporting. After all, many if not all of the governments have for many years produced their own government accounts back home also on a cash basis or something similar, and certainly not to IPSAS accrual-based standards. There is, not surprisingly, an annual cash-in/cash-out mindset among most member state representatives. Changing and broadening this mindset is one of the key challenges to improving not only transparency and accountability but also the overall quality of financial management and decision making by management and member states.

Oversight

A critical and essential aspect of the quality and reliability of any system of accountability as well as the promotion and maintenance of sustainable transparency is a comprehensive and effective system of oversight. The various principal organs of oversight within the core United Nations and the wider UN system have evolved over a considerable period of time and their establishment can be broadly summarized as follows: UN Board of Auditors (BOA), 1946; UN Panel of External Auditors (PEA), 1959; Joint Inspection Unit (JIU), 1966; UN Office of Internal Oversight Services (OIOS), 1994; and UN Independent Audit and Advisory Committee (IAAC), 2007.

The BOA represents those government audit institutions who provide the external audit service for the core UN and its various funds and programs. As the various specialized agencies joined the UN system in the years that followed, the wider PEA was established to broaden the external auditors' "forum" beyond the core BOA. Both bodies still function.

The JIU comprises 11 inspectors. The initial enabling General Assembly resolution was in 1966, and it started operations in 1968. The number of inspectors has remained unchanged since then. The JIU mandate enables inspections, evaluations, and investigations to be carried out by the 11 inspectors across the UN system, including the specialized agencies and the International Atomic Energy Agency.

It was not until 1994, almost fifty years after its birth, that the United Nations established the Office of Internal Oversight Services (OIOS). It provides three key oversight functions: internal audit, evaluations, and investigations, which fall under the overall responsibility of the OIOS under-secretary-general, who is appointed by the secretary-general.

Similar but smaller internal oversight divisions or departments have also been established in the various specialized agencies. While the OIOS has grown steadily over the years, reaching a total headcount of

327 staff in 2012, the oversight divisions in most other UN entities are far less numerous; and some of the smaller agencies have just one or two internal auditors as permanent staff.

Looking back, it is somewhat surprising that the various UN organizations took so long to institutionalize these critical internal oversight organs. It can be argued that the JIU exclusively fulfilled such an internal oversight role for some 30 years with its broad, system-wide mandate, albeit with fixed, very limited resources. However, as was illustrated in Figure 6.1, the 1990s witnessed a dramatic acceleration in the overall funding and activity levels of the UN system, especially in development activities; and, in parallel, member state concerns about accountability, inefficiency, waste, and fraud intensified.

In addition, a more recent initiative has been the establishment of independent oversight or advisory committees, with the UN General Assembly setting up its own committee—the IAAC—in 2007. Other such committees with similar names and responsibilities have also been established by almost all other UN organizations. Such committees provide supposedly independent advice to UN governing bodies on the adequacy and effectiveness of each of the various oversight functions. These groups reflect a growing trend, which had its roots in the private sector, with publicly listed companies across many jurisdictions being required to set up such "audit committees" as independent advisory bodies to boards. Many national government institutions in member states have followed this trend. The levels of independence of members of these now important UN system committees from the governing bodies that they advise has become or is becoming very strong, whereas this was less so in the initial stages.

Of all the internal oversight functions, the largest tends to be the internal audit function, where there has been another important recent trend with regard to internal audit reports in that OIOS now makes all its final internal audit reports publicly available. Some other UN organizations are also following this trend. There are inevitably some security, privacy, and confidentiality safeguards that form part of this procedure, but it is nonetheless a positive step toward greater transparency. Such a move is also undoubtedly having some impact on the style and quality of internal audit reports. Many governments and almost all of the private sector do not make such reports publicly available, and so the United Nations is quite exceptional in this regard.

Turning to the evaluation function, the under-secretary-general for OIOS told the UN Evaluation Group during its "evaluation week" in April 2013 that "evaluation has yet to become a fully robust and comprehensive function and integral to how a programme works."[8]

Also, the last Quadrennial Comprehensive Policy Review report in 2012 included the following statement: "The lack of adequate results-based management capacity, including evaluation capacity at country level, undermines the quality of results-based management at the agency and inter-agency level."[9]

Most would agree that evaluation is a critical oversight function, but evaluations can also be seen as exercises in both self-congratulation and ineffectual intellectual posturing as results and outcomes are debated within evaluation reports. Other challenges can include the failure at the outset of any program to clearly define and agree expected results and outcomes, and that in turn undermines any future evaluation efforts. Also many programs—whether for development projects, technical assistance, or even implementation of norms and standards—can take many years before results, outcomes, and impacts can be accurately assessed. Because of such delays, evaluations are not always carried out and, even if they are, the results may no longer be pertinent or useful.

The function of investigations also remains a critical component of the UN system's oversight practices. It has, sadly, been a "growth industry" within the UN system and especially within the OIOS, and most notably since the embarrassing investigation of the Iraq Oil-for-Food Programme that used a combination of both internal OIOS investigators and external investigators over several years. Investigation staff numbers are also slowly rising among the funds, programs, and specialized agencies. It is difficult, if not impossible, to assess whether this is because the levels of fraud and misconduct are increasing, or whether there has always been an inherent level of fraud and misconduct and the various investigations are backlogged so that officials are basically playing catch-up in working through both reported and not-yet-reported cases.

There has been a long debate within the UN system about the relationships between these three critical oversight functions and how they should be organized. As already described, the core OIOS has all three functions under one under-secretary-general; and this practice is followed by some, but not all, other UN organizations where sometimes evaluations come from a separate division. Practitioners of each function will rightly argue that they are different professions, skill sets, and career paths—and there is solid evidence to support this view. There is a case for saying that a strong, professional internal audit team, together with a responsive management team, will gradually build stronger and more effective internal controls. This approach should, in the long term, result in less fraud and malpractice, and so fewer investigations will be needed. Would internal audit be more effective being in its own separately managed division from investigations? In the private sector, these two disciplines or professions are almost always separated. Why not within the UN system?

Such arguments are linked as well to the critical question of the level of independence and objectivity for each of these functions. It is normal practice in business as well as in many government sectors for internal audit to be an in-house function but with direct reporting access to the governing body or audit committee as well as the chief executive officer. This dual-reporting line is the case now in most UN organizations, although there is still some concern that the CEO, director-general, or executive director still has too much direct influence and even final say on the internal audit and internal oversight budget and resources. Independence would be strengthened if the internal audit budget were reviewed and approved directly by the governing body based on advice from the oversight committee. This in turn would increase the function's ability to hold the entity head and the management team accountable. The same point can be made for the evaluation and investigations functions.

A further, more controversial proposal to strengthen independence for any or all of these three oversight functions is to consolidate the resources into three distinct, UN system-wide functions with a core team of professional staff for each one serving the entire UN system. Such a practice would require shared funding from all UN organizations, and it would be accountable to the governing bodies and management of each of them—similar to the JIU's mandate but with far greater resources and implementation capabilities.

There are two principal arguments in favor of such a robust effort. The first is the necessity of independence; three distinct entities would avoid the criticism that auditors, evaluators, and investigators should not be auditing, evaluating, or investigating staff who are on the same payroll and thereby less likely to dilute or avoid reporting any bad news. The second argument is that, especially for the UN organizations with small oversight teams, the new entities would provide a strong career path for the oversight staff themselves, which, in turn, would improve staff retention and promotion, which, in turn, should improve the overall quality of the group's work and service to its clients. A 2011 JIU report of the investigations function in the UN system recommended that this function be centralized for the entire UN system, based mainly on the necessity for independence.[10]

However, there is considerable resistance to such a consolidation of oversight functions among most, if not all UN entities, with the strong, almost ingrained belief and culture that each UN entity needs its own staff to work on its own business. The arguments will continue until a management culture evolves that welcomes scrutiny, especially from "the outside."

Staff management, individual accountability

Underneath all these activities, systems, and functions associated with promoting transparency and accountability across the UN system, there lies what could be termed "the bottom line" when it comes to the two key pillars of transparency and accountability: individual accountability. If all UN staff members—whether as one member of a large team in a large office, or a program supervisor, or an HQ department head, or the chief executive—are not transparent in their activities and, most importantly, not held fully accountable for their actions and results, all the wider organizational processes, reports, and functions with respect to accountability are diluted or rendered ineffective.

Holding organizations accountable means, in practice, holding the individuals who work in them accountable—or at least enough of them. Truly effective staff performance appraisal is arguably the most difficult and challenging task that needs to be carried out by any manager or supervisor at any level in any public or private organization. The UN system is no exception, and this fundamental accountability test remains its biggest challenge for making significant and even dramatic improvements to accountability.

Staff performance appraisal can be viewed as mundane and even not strategic, but it lies at the heart of any accountability system and, if done effectively, stimulates and sustains overall performance improvement. If done poorly or not at all, it promotes incrementalism, inertia, and stagnation. Most UN organizations, like other large twenty-first-century organizations, have a staff performance appraisal process that typically requires an annual or biennial formal objective-setting exercise for all staff members with their immediate supervisors followed by an appraisal and performance rating at the end of the performance period, which is typically documented and gets filed. Over the years, there have been long periods where such a process was either never followed or, if it was, led to performance ratings that were often consistently overstated due to supervisors opting out of their responsibility.

There is now stronger evidence that staff performance appraisals are at least being documented and some evidence of more realistic performance ratings being recorded. However, this is still only the start of the long road to truly effective performance measurement and accountability.

Holding someone accountable against a set of previously agreed objectives is only worthwhile and meaningful for the organization and its stakeholders if exceptional performance can be somehow recognized and rewarded in a tangible way and that under-performance can be the subject of real remedial action and, if necessary, sanctions. If the persons being held accountable, regardless of their grades and seniority, see no tangible impact, positive or negative, it is bound to influence individual and collective performance—and profoundly if it persists over years and becomes ingrained in the organizational culture.

Many businesses and some governments apply "forced distributions" or bell-curves to overall performance ratings allocated to staff each year.[11] Merit systems for the highest performers and some form of personal development, improvement, or sanction system for the lower performers is fundamental to ensuring meaningful accountability. The topic of merit awards is sensitive, especially within the publicly funded UN system, but some form of accelerated progression within a salary grade could form the basis of a distinctive but modest merit award; and some are already using such a process. The sanction element for lower performers is always the most challenging task, but member states and UN management finally need to tackle this critical shortfall in UN management practices. They should start what may be a sensitive and lengthy process through the gradual introduction of employment contract conditions for new staff that make a clear and definitive link between contract termination rights and performance appraisal results. Clearly a reasonable appeals process would remain to obviate any abuse on either side.

A further key element of individual transparency and accountability concerns the relatively recent introduction of ethics officers and personal financial disclosure (FD) policies to many UN entities. With the UN Secretariat and its funds and programs, this requirement for senior staff and staff from other designated functions (such as procurement officers) has been in place for some time, with officials being required to file annual returns on the financial and other interests of themselves and their immediate family members. This information is then independently spot-checked and verified with advisory services to deal with any potential conflicts of interest. Regular obligatory training and awareness programs on ethics and conflicts of interest are also delivered. Some of the UN specialized agencies have also introduced the requirement for such filings but have yet to provide any independent verification or spot-checks. Such verification is essential to provide credible transparency and accountability. Without it, such FD filings can be justifiably criticized as being "just paper."

Conclusion

The first UN secretary-general, Dag Hammarskjöld, provides a final insight: "You are merely the lens in the beam. You can only receive, give, and possess the light as the lens does."[12]

He provides a straightforward reminder that transparency and accountability illuminate otherwise hidden or shady realities; yet this illumination serves to change behavior and thus reality.

In order to further improve transparency and accountability in an increasingly globalizing, technology-driven world, it can be said that the UN system is making some deliberate and positive changes as the consolidation of strategy, budget, and funding coupled with greater management empowerment. Moving to accrual-based accounting and IPSAS-based reporting practices is a little-understood yet crucial change that should promote more informed and responsible funding decisions and financial management; the hoped-for introduction of system-wide accrual-based budgeting would complement this process well.

Oversight resources and processes have continued to evolve in recent years and the advent of new oversight advisory committees has begun to add genuine weight and credibility to governing body deliberations on oversight. However, the issue of independence of internal oversight is an argument that will not die. Given the growing clamor for greater consolidation and even the merging or realigning of UN organizational mandates, the time is approaching when system-wide oversight functions will make such overwhelming sense as to be irresistible. These developments are hardly guaranteed, but would enhance independence and objectivity while simultaneously creating the basis for modern, professional resources with a real critical mass that can serve the whole UN system rather than individual organizational interests.

It will become increasingly hard for those UN organizations yet to set up strong and verifiable financial disclosure processes supervised by a competent ethics office to avoid doing so. The rest of the world is moving in this direction, and again the UN system cannot continue as an outlier.

Finally, can the UN system progress toward an environment and culture in which high-performing individuals are recognized and rewarded at the same time that under-performance is documented and actioned? Strong, meaningful, and effective staff appraisal and performance management are the essential seeds of a more transparent and accountable UN system.

As indicated at the outset, 2015 represents a potentially pivotal opportunity for the UN system to establish medium-term targets to transition and realign itself behind a new set of globally agreed twenty-first-century

SDGs. Such a moment has probably not arisen since 1946. Some of the more profound proposals for change in this chapter may be given new impetus if they are being pursued in the context of the first major structural reforms since the world organization's initial year of operations. It surely is possible. Otherwise, do we really want to reach 2046 with the same 100-year-old UN organizations with the same mandates, the same culture, and the same lack of transparency and accountability?

Notes

1 Kofi A. Annan, "Message to the Conference of Heads of Government of the Caribbean Community," St. Lucia, 3 July 2005, www.un.org/News/Press/docs/2005/sgsm9980.doc.htm
2 Transparency and Accountability Initiative, *Definitions*, www.transparency-initiative.org/about/definitions
3 "Fiscal Transparency, Accountability, and Risk," International Monetary Fund, August 2012. https://www.imf.org/external/np/pp/eng/2012/080712.pdf
4 Transparency and Accountability Initiative, *Definitions*, www.transparency-initiative.org/about/definitions
5 "Proposed programme Budget 2014/2015," World Health Organization document A66/53, 20 May 2013. Geneva: WHO.
6 International Aid Transparency Initiative, www.aidtransparency.net
7 Publish What You Fund (www.publishwhatyoufund.org) is funded in part by the Hewlett and Open Society Foundations.
8 UN Office of Internal Oversight Services, *Homepage*, www.un.org/Depts/oios/index.htm
9 Angela Bester, "Results-Based Management in the United Nations Development System: Progress and Challenges," New York: United Nations Department of Economic and Social Affairs, July 2012.
10 M. Deborah Wynes and Mohamed Mounir Zahran, *The Investigation Function in the United Nations*, JIU Report JIU/REP/2011/7 (Geneva: UN, 2011).
11 There will always be in any one year or biennium around 15 percent at the highest rating level and around 5 percent at the lowest level, with other ratings at 2 or 3 levels in between, or a similar distribution pattern.
12 Dag Hammarskjöld, *Markings* (New York: Knopf, 1964).

Part III

The requirements of war-torn states

Part II

7   Aligning UN development efforts and peacebuilding

W. Andy Knight

In a 2008 address to the Group of 77 (G77) developing countries, UN Secretary-General Ban Ki-moon reiterated that the UN development agenda should be as important as the organization's work in the areas of peace and security and human rights. He went on to suggest that these three areas are "interlinked and mutually reinforcing"; and for that reason, the UN needs to ensure that the attempts to strengthen the organization should be accompanied by an effort to develop "a stronger development pillar."[1] This chapter argues that strengthening the UN's development pillar requires an alignment of the organization's work in this area with its peacebuilding (including its humanitarian, peacekeeping, and human rights) activities. In other words, strengthening the development pillar cannot be accomplished in a vacuum. Complex interdependence in our globalizing world has resulted in the intertwining of development and peacebuilding agendas, so much so that these areas are now considered to be "indissolubly interconnected."[2] This reality is especially clear in the countries in which the United Nations is concentrating its activities and is generally viewed as having a comparative advantage.

Aligning the development and other pillars that support UN efforts to maintain international peace and security is not a new idea. In fact, one can argue that the founding fathers had this in mind when the UN Charter was drafted. Indeed, the Preamble underscores the determination of member states to "save succeeding generations from the scourge of war," "reaffirm faith in fundamental human rights," and "promote social progress and better standards of life in larger freedom." Here, there is an implicit recognition of the need for the UN to pursue security, development, and human rights simultaneously if the world organization was to achieve its primary goal of maintaining international peace and security. Charter Article 1 is more explicit in designating the UN system as "a centre for harmonizing the actions of nations in the attainment of these common ends." Yet, during the first 60 years of its existence, the UN system operated in an uncoordinated fashion, as its main organs, agencies, and sub-units developed more or less autonomous governance mandates and arrangements and exhibited fiefdom characteristics. Despite a series of efforts at institutional reform, attempts at coordinating the work of the organization at headquarters and in the field in pursuit of the UN's primary mandate, were futile until around the year 2000.[3]

Development is really a process of societal change geared to improving the lives of people. This implies more than simply increasing the quantity of resources available to a society or expanding its wealth. In fact, development is about improving all the indicators that lead to better quality of life: access to education and healthcare, better employment opportunities, access to clean air and safe drinking water, reducing the threat of crime and violence, providing an environment in which people have the political freedom to choose. Economic growth is a means to an end when it comes to development.

Peacebuilding, too, is a process of societal change—the purpose of which is to identify and support those structures within a society that will strengthen and solidify peace. The goals of peacebuilding are: to prevent and resolve violent conflicts; to consolidate peace once violence is reduced; to reconstruct societies that have been torn apart by violent conflict; and to avoid a relapse into violent conflict. Furthermore, peacebuilding "seeks to address the proximate and root causes of contemporary conflicts including structural, political, socio-cultural, economic and environmental factors."[4] Thus, peacebuilding is particularly important for post-conflict societies in that it becomes a means of ensuring that those societies build peace that is sustainable. Building sustainable peace in countries emerging from armed conflict is a complex and multidimensional undertaking.[5] It involves planning, programming, prioritizing, and resource allocation; and it is a long-term process that involves addressing root causes of conflict and dealing with a variety of stakeholders, beginning with the citizens of the target country. Peacebuilding is not limited to security processes; it must also embrace developmental processes—hence the link to development.

The UN development system encompasses a range of different functions—from technical assistance to intergovernmental policy-making, norm-setting, advocacy, research, and information. But it has become increasingly difficult and artificial to define. The world organization is called upon to address essential development-related concerns of security, emergency humanitarian response, and human rights. To what extent can and should its development efforts be considered separately from its other roles, particularly in low-income and fragile states? What might be the organizational implications of closer alignment between the UN's human development and human security roles? In the complex interdependent world of the twenty-first century, it would be foolhardy to treat UN development activities as separate and distinct from the other roles that it plays. This chapter focuses specifically on the ways in which UN system-wide reforms have attempted to facilitate the alignment of the UN development and peacebuilding pillars.

The UN development pillar

On 14 October 2013, Ambassador Le Hoai Trung, the Vietnamese permanent representative at the United Nations, spoke on behalf of the Association of Southeast Asian Nations (ASEAN) during a debate in the UN on "Operational Activities for Development." In his statement, he reiterated the importance of the UN system's development pillar.[6] ASEAN countries, like several other countries in the global South, understand the importance of the UN development system because they have benefited from its operational activities.

Certainly, ASEAN member states recognize the importance of the comparative advantage of various UN funds, programs, and specialized agencies that are part of the UN development pillar. But Trung expressed serious concern about the decline in major donors' aid to developing countries over the past two years. This decline is linked to the global economic crisis and the particularly tight budgets of the members of the Organisation for Economic Co-operation and Development (OECD) as a result of the global financial crisis. The drop in official development assistance (ODA) comes when developing countries have been "hit by the knock-on effects of the crisis."[7] It is notable that the UN development system has seen an increase in contributions from developing countries (about 16 percent in nominal terms since 2006), half of which came in the form of core contributions. But these contributions amount to less than 2 percent of the overall funding for UN development initiatives and are often spent within the country contributing.[8] While increased contributions from developing countries to the UN development system are noteworthy, the Vietnamese ambassador called for the strengthening and intensification of development cooperation between the global North and the global South.

UN development activities are considered important by developed countries as well. This explains the global deliberations in the form of UN summits since the 1990s—including the Millennium Summit (2000) and the World Summit (2005)—and the subsequent UN meetings that have created strong commitments by the global North and the global South to strengthen and broaden the UN development agenda. The UN system has in fact become a central player in the establishment of what is now known as the "development pillar." The primary reason for this is that the UN system is the only multilateral body with a universal mandate that can align development activity with other important intersecting goals such as maintaining peace and security, protecting human rights, and providing humanitarian assistance to those faced with complex emergencies.

Yet some critics argue that the UN development pillar is weak and that the world body's work in development is lagging behind other areas of its work—peace and security, humanitarian affairs, and human rights. For such critics, development appears to be the lowest of the UN's priorities. To improve the situation, the UN development system would have to strengthen its analytical capacities and engage in cutting-edge analyses of major emerging issues, improve its strategic planning and integration capacity, strengthen the regional dimension of its work, gain a better understanding of new trends in cooperation (e.g., South–South cooperation and triangular cooperation), provide greater support to the UN Economic and Social Council (ECOSOC), and provide greater support for the implementation of client-oriented service delivery of projects at the country level.[9]

As mentioned, development is about more than just improving the economic well-being of people. It also is about providing people with the capacity for sustained multidimensional well-being, which requires addressing issues beyond mere growth and income. One also has to take into consideration factors that could threaten sustained well-being, such as violent conflict and insecurity, human rights abuse, humanitarian crises, and natural and human-made catastrophes. Therefore, aligning the UN's development pillar with security, peace-keeping, human rights, and humanitarian action would seem to be logical in our complex interdependent world.[10]

Inching closer to aligning development and peacebuilding

Boutros Boutros-Ghali made passing reference in his *An Agenda for Peace* to the interconnectedness of preventive diplomacy, peace-making, peacekeeping, and peacebuilding. While he recognized "the obvious connection between democratic practices—such as the rule of law and transparency in decision-making—and the achievement of true peace and security in any new stable political order," the former UN secretary-general still treated development, security, and human rights as quite separate and distinct. Perhaps this dichotomy explains why Boutros-Ghali produced *An Agenda for Development* and *An Agenda for Peace* as two separate reports. Although the latter was a response to a request from the Security Council to analyze and recommend ways of strengthening the UN system's capacity for preventive diplomacy, peacemaking, and peacekeeping, it stopped short of proposing an explicit alignment of development, security, and human rights activity.

Yet, there was an opportunity for him to recommend such an alignment when he put forward his concept of the peacebuilding toolkit.[11] An analysis of that toolkit demonstrates that Boutros-Ghali was very close to envisioning this alignment. His conception of peacebuilding was about addressing the deepest causes of conflict (e.g., economic despair, social injustice, and political oppression) so that countries coming out of conflict would not relapse into violence. The peacebuilding toolkit was therefore an attempt "to help states move from a merely negative peace—the absence of violence—to a positive peace marked by the deeper social, political, and economic features that help make society work."[12]

Boutros-Ghali's conceptualization of peacebuilding contains the early outlines of what later became known as the disarmament, demobilization, and reintegration (DDR) process. The former secretary-general envisioned that some of the elements involved in peacebuilding would be linked directly to preventing the recurrence of violent conflict. These elements include: disarming warring factions, restoring law and order, decommissioning and destroying weapons, repatriating refugees, reintegrating internally displaced persons into their communities, providing advisory and training support for security personnel, improving police and judicial systems, monitoring elections, de-mining and other forms of demilitarization, providing technical assistance to fledgling states coming out of conflict, advancing efforts to protect human rights, reforming and strengthening institutions of governance, promoting formal and informal participation in the political process, and facilitating social and economic development.

Because Boutros-Ghali's conception of peacebuilding was premised on the construction of lasting peace, he was acutely aware that it had to involve more than just the cessation of violence; it also necessitated strategies for economic development, the protection and promotion of human rights, the solidification of the rule of law, the establishment of democratic and accountable structures and processes, social equity, environmental sustainability, and the meting out of justice balanced with the encouragement of reconciliation between ex-combatants and other members of the target society. This signals recognition of the need to align the development pillar with UN's peacebuilding activities.

From the mid-1990s, the United Nations embraced the DDR process as an essential element of its multidimensional, post-conflict peacebuilding and reconstruction efforts. Indeed, DDR programs have become quite commonplace in UN peace operations,[13] and their intent has been to build security, reconstruct the social fabric of, and develop human capacity in countries coming out of conflict so that a sustained, long-term peacebuilding capacity can be established once UN missions are terminated. But the involvement of a multiplicity of actors in DDR programs explains recent concerns with consolidating, coordinating, and integrating the DDR activities of these actors.[14]

For instance in Liberia, the UN adopted the lead role in the DDR program. But UNICEF assumed responsibility for disarming and demobilizing young combatants who were aged 17 years or younger, while at least six other agencies were involved in the DDR processing of adult ex-combatants on the ground, including the World Food Programme (WFP), the World Health Organization (WHO), ActionAid, and the United Nations Development Programme (UNDP). One of the largest DDR programs in Africa—the Multi-Country Demobilization and Reintegration Programme (MDRP) is headed by the World Bank, and it involves 40 other Western and African governments, nongovernmental organizations (NGOs), and regional organizations. While the multidimensional nature of DDR programs requires multiple players in their execution and management, in many cases coordination is difficult and confusion is the norm.[15]

The objective of the DDR process, according to the UN's DDR Resource Centre, is "to contribute to security and stability in post-conflict environments so that recovery and development can begin." This entire process, linked to broader national recovery, is a complex one, "with political, military, security, humanitarian and socio-economic dimensions." One of the other major aims of DDR is to address the post-conflict security problems that arise when ex-combatants are left without livelihoods or support networks (other than their former comrades) during the transition from conflict to peace. By relieving combatants of weapons and by taking these individuals out of their military structures and routines, the DDR process can then facilitate their integration into society and help them become active participants in the peace process.[16]

Disarmament refers to the collection, documentation, control, and disposal of small arms, ammunition, explosives, and light and heavy weapons of combatants and often of civilians in a conflict zone. It also involves the establishment of arms management initiatives (e.g., programs for safe storage and/or destruction) as well as de-mining programs. When conflict ends through a negotiated settlement, ex-combatants are generally induced to give up their weapons voluntarily. When conflict ends via a clear military victory, the victor will more often than not coerce the vanquished to surrender their weapons. Where UN peacekeepers are involved in the disarmament phase of DDR, they are generally charged with the collection, safe storage, and sometimes destruction of weapons. In theory, by taking weapons out of circulation, a more secure environment is created in which the peace process can coalesce and development can begin. But there can be major problems during this phase. For instance, some combatants may try to disarm multiple times in order to reap financial benefits when money is being offered in exchange for weapons. There have also been instances in which ex-combatants withhold the best weapons in their arsenal.

Demobilization is a process by which conflicting armed groups are induced to disband their military organization and shift from combatant to civilian status. It involves registering and processing individual ex-combatants in temporary centers. It also requires the massing of troops or rebel forces in cantonment sites, encampments, barracks, or other assembly areas; the provision of transitional support/assistance packages to help ex-combatants and their families meet their immediate basic needs, such as food, clothes, shelter, medical services; short-term remedial education, training, employment, and tools (this is usually called reinsertion); psychological counseling and trauma healing support; and transportation to get to their home community. In most cases, the dividing line between reinsertion and reintegration is not clear. Given DDR political and security objectives, it is perhaps useful to view the reinsertion phase as a bridge between demobilization and reintegration.[17] Problems can also occur at this phase of the process, especially as is often the case when there are inadequate funds to support demobilization and reinsertion.

Reintegration is a longer-term social and economic process with an open time-frame designed to facilitate the assimilation of ex-combatants in a way that allows them, and their families, to adapt to civilian life in communities that may not necessarily be ready to accept them. In most cases, this process involves: provision of cash or some form of compensation package in exchange for the commitment of ex-combatants not to return to conflict; providing them with longer-term job or career training; initiating sustainable income-generation projects; repatriating refugees and displaced persons; and establishing a forum and process for truth and reconciliation. This stage of the DDR process is probably the most arduous and is usually accompanied by efforts to rehabilitate war-affected individuals and reconstruct damaged national infrastructure. It is clear how these efforts can nourish the environment for development.

In some cases, surplus militia and other ex-combatants may be encouraged to merge with a new national military force as part of security sector reform during this phase of DDR. This process is a critical factor in successful post-conflict peacebuilding agendas because no peace can be assured unless order is maintained—and, often, the best method of ensuring order may be through a unified national army. In any event, reintegration is sustained when indigenous capacity is enhanced, ex-combatants and other war-affected individuals become productive members of their communities, and post-conflict societies learn how to address conflicts in nonviolent ways.

There is some debate as to whether or not the "R" stage of DDR should entail a focus on (or an enhancement of) longer-term reintegration. Some scholars argue that longer-term reintegration is not part of the DDR process. The rationale is that a conceptual line needs to be drawn between "an individual's status as ex-combatant and his/her status as civilian."[18] However, this "line" seems particularly artificial. If in fact the main purpose of DDR is to contribute toward building sustainable peace, longer-term reintegration should be included. As noted, the UN has recognized this need, and has placed greater emphasis on long-term reintegration and uses the term "reinsertion" to refer to the short-term process of reintegration.[19]

Clearly the DDR process is multidimensional and complex because of the political, military, security, humanitarian, and socioeconomic dimensions. Its primary goal is to address the post-conflict security challenge that stems from ex-combatants being left without livelihoods or support networks once wars come to an end and during the critical transition period from conflict to peace. DDR programs seek to support ex-combatants' economic and social reintegration so they can become stakeholders in peace and productive members of their communities. There are serious concerns among some observers that some ex-combatants receive disproportionate benefits during the post-conflict phase. However, one can argue that such disproportionate benefits may be a small price to pay for the establishment of security in war-torn societies, particularly if obstacles and blockages to broader recovery efforts can be eliminated and a return to violence forestalled.[20]

As Neclâ Tschirgi put it, "post-conflict peacebuilding has become an international growth industry."[21] This development is reflected to a large extent in the exponential growth in the peacebuilding literature. But it may also be a result of responses to a UN blue ribbon panel report that called on the world body to expand its global peace support role by aligning security and economic development goals and activities.

The Brahimi report: making the security-development nexus more explicit

The report of the Panel on United Nations Peace Operations (known as the Brahimi report because of its chair) was released in August 2000 and fully acknowledged the link between peacekeeping, peacebuilding, and socioeconomic development. The panel recommended a number of peacebuilding tools and strategies to be part of any peace support operation. These included: the adoption of quick impact projects (QIPs), the establishment of a DDR fund, the adoption of a "doctrinal shift" away from civilian policing to "rule of law" teams, the creation of a pilot peacebuilding unit, and regularized funding of the Electoral Affairs Division at UN headquarters in New York.[22]

The Brahimi report recognized that force alone cannot create peace but only a space within which peace can be constructed. The report made the connection between security, socioeconomic development, and the rule of law. But its focus was more on coordinating the various elements of peacebuilding—as its recommendation for a new peace-building unit within the Department of Political Affairs at the UN demonstrates—than on aligning the development pillar with the UN system's humanitarian, peacekeeping, and human rights activities. But we know that "strong, legitimate security institutions that are inte-grated within wider national governance frameworks and development plans can be powerful champions of national development."[23] The explicit focus on aligning those pillars came shortly after the release of the Brahimi report, with the Millennium Declaration.

The Millennium Declaration and new focus on pillar alignment

On 8 September 2000, at the end of a three-day Millennium Summit in New York, UN member states adopted the Millennium Declaration in the General Assembly.[24] That declaration explicitly linked the three pillars of security, development, and human rights in the organization's search for a "peaceful, prosperous and just world." But the Millennium Declaration was not explicit in demonstrating how these pillars could be aligned to achieve the Millennium Development Goals (MDGs). It was UN Secretary-General Kofi Annan who first urged the international community of states and civil society to consider aligning these pillars.

In the Millennium Declaration, a bold and inclusive new vision for humanity was laid out with the intent of channeling the positive elements of globalization for the benefit of all. There was thus a distinct emphasis on the development pillar (development and poverty eradication) in that document when it declared that "no individual and no nation must be denied the opportunity to benefit from development." But one can also see in that document a suggestion that development must be aligned with security (freedom from the fear of violence) and human rights ("The equal rights and opportunities of women and men must be assured").[25]

In his 2005 report *In Larger Freedom*, Annan conceptualized world peace as being established on three pillars: security, development, and human rights. He recognized, particularly after the attacks of 11 September 2001, that the safety, prosperity, and freedom of people around the globe must be viewed as "indivisible." He came to the realization that in our world of rapid technological advances, increasing economic interdependence, globalization, and dramatic geopolitical change, we can no longer operate as though peace, development, and human rights can be achieved independently of each other. According to Annan, we cannot enjoy development without security; we cannot enjoy security without development; and we cannot enjoy either without respect for human rights.[26]

In Larger Freedom was interpreted to mean an alignment of UN goals to ensure "freedom from want," "freedom from fear," and "freedom to live in dignity." These things could not be achieved separately, in the former secretary-general's view. And Annan worked hard to ensure that this conceptual nexus between the three pillars would spur UN member states to align the efforts and resources of various parts of the UN system to maximize the impact of the world body on delivery of its primary goal. Supplementing the *In Larger Freedom* report are the reports on the World Social Situation (2005); the Millennium Development Goals (MDGs); the World Economic and Social Survey (2006); the 2006 ECOSOC ten-year action plan to generate employment and decent work for all; the Millennium Debt Relief Initiative; the pledge by DAC members to meet the minimum target of 0.51 percent of gross national product (GNP) by 2010 and 0.7 percent of GNP by 2015; the G8 members' pledge to grant $50 billion in official development assistance (ODA) mostly to African countries; the Millennium Villages; establishing a permanent forum on indigenous issues; the promotion of the rights and dignity of people with disabilities; the

Global Fund to Fight HIV/AIDS, TB and Malaria; the implementation of New Partnership for Africa's Development (NEPAD); and the integrated DDR unit at the UN. Many parts of the UN system are responsible for addressing a range of human rights issues. For instance, the core intergovernmental mechanisms—the General Assembly, the Security Council, ECOSOC—and subsidiary organs make policy decisions with human rights implications on a regular basis. But within the development system, the Office of the High Commissioner for Human Rights (OHCHR) provides advice and gives support on human rights issues to those intergovernmental bodies. That office has also undertaken to mainstream human rights in system-wide UN work. Mainstreaming human rights has been instrumental in linking the UN development pillar to peace and security and humanitarian affairs.

This mainstreaming effort began in 2009 when the UN secretary-general called for the establishment of an inter-agency group—the UN Development Group's Human Rights Mainstreaming Mechanism (UNDG-HRM). The primary purpose of this mechanism was to strengthen the UN's responses to requests from member governments who wanted support to help them fulfill their human rights obligations. The OHCHR chairs this inter-agency body and guides the HRM toward meeting the strategic priorities of the UN Development Group, namely to promote policy and operational coherence; to provide direct support to resident coordinators and UN country teams as they drive mainstreaming efforts at the local or country level; to provide support to member states as they attempt to fulfill their human rights commitments; to support the strengthening of national human rights protection systems when governments expressly request such support; and to assist with the integration of human rights issues in the overall UN Development Group's advocacy with respect to development issues.

Over the past decade or so, the UN's humanitarian relief system has responded to over 1,000 natural disasters and complex emergencies across the globe. But as early as 1971, General Assembly resolution 2816 created the disaster relief coordinator position and established the Office of the UN Disaster Relief Coordinator in Geneva. The Department of Humanitarian Affairs (DHA) was established in 1991 by General Assembly resolution 46/182 within the UN Secretariat precisely for the purpose of supporting mobilization, funding, and co-ordination of humanitarian action in response to complex emergencies and natural disasters. As part of UN reform efforts in 1997, the DHA became the Office for the Coordination of Humanitarian Affairs (OCHA). It focuses on trying to understand the needs of its clients and works closely with partners to strengthen coordination mechanisms and improve the evidence base for humanitarian decision making and the allocation of resources. In 2010 OCHA introduced an "Associate Surge Pool" (ASP) solution and a Stand-By Partnerships Programme (SBPP) to ensure that humanitarian experts can be dispatched on short notice to target countries affected by the world's worst disasters. They involve the coordination of close to 2,000 men and women from over 30 offices across the globe to ensure that effective assistance reaches those in need.[27]

OCHA manages a Central Emergency Response Fund (CERF)—a pooling mechanism (with a $450 million grant facility) for humanitarian agencies to draw on during cases of complex humanitarian emergencies. This office is headed by the emergency relief coordinator who acts as a focal point for governmental, intergovernmental, and nongovernmental relief activities and is staffed by OCHA. In 2012 its financial tracking tools managed humanitarian donations (approximately $8.8 billion) from some 130 countries to assist about 54 million people affected by humanitarian crises.[28] The Inter-Agency Standing Committee (IASC) has brought the UNHCR and OCHA into closer coordination at both the country and global levels. The IASC engages in needs assessment, information management, early warning and preparedness, gender and humanitarian action, and common advocacy efforts.[29]

Human rights, humanitarian action for the most vulnerable, and the rule of law were not only reaffirmed at the Millennium Summit, they were actively supported by a number of specific actions within the world organization, including: the establishment of international tribunals for the former Yugoslavia and Rwanda (1993 and 1994, respectively); the establishment of the Special Crimes Court for Sierra Leone; the establishment of Extraordinary Chambers in the Courts of Cambodia; the calls for a tribunal to be set up in Lebanon after the assassination of the Lebanese prime minister Rafik Hariri; the creation of the truth and reconciliation tribunal for Burundi; the establishment of the International Criminal Court (ICC) in Rome; the establishment of the Human Rights Council; the emergence of the "responsibility to protect" norm; and the creation of "cluster leadership" within the UN to provide more systematic predictability to humanitarian assistance to vulnerable populations during complex emergencies.

Conclusion

The establishment of recent humanitarian, human rights, and justice mechanisms and initiatives represents an attempt to align the UN's different pillars. If development infers the social, economic, and political processes that unlock human capacities while reducing vulnerabilities in a society, then development is intrinsically linked to peacebuilding activities. This chapter presents evidence that member states and the Secretariat have made attempts to align the UN's development pillar with the quest to achieve its primary mandate of maintaining international peace and security and preventing war. However, Secretary-General Ban Ki-moon clearly recognizes the difficulty in achieving such alignment.[30]

Efforts also have been made to align the UN development pillar with human rights, humanitarian, and justice activities. However, if the UN system is to properly align its peacebuilding and development functions, considerable additional structural and institutional reforms are required to "deliver as one" at the country, regional, and global levels. Among other things, we would list reforming the Security Council, disciplining the General Assembly, revitalizing the role of ECOSOC to better coordinate post-2015 MDGs, making continued changes to the UN Secretariat to improve its efficiency and effectiveness, and carefully reviewing the mandates of all UN bodies to eliminate overlap and redundancy. But aligning development and peacebuilding pillars would also involve better coordination and cooperation between the UN and regional organizations in a subsidiarity arrangement. System-wide coherence and country-level coordination will have to include both state and non-state actors, including NGOs and business communities, and assist national societies in developing cultures of peace.

Drawing on the advice of UNDP administrator Helen Clark, the UN development system "must leverage from the UN's founding Charter and its convening power to inspire, lead, and co-ordinate the efforts of others, building alliances and networks for the MDGs and sustainable development, and for peace and human rights." The UN development system "should, in 21st Century parlance, become the ultimate social network."[31] It is a social network that must reach beyond the confines of the UN system to embrace a multiplicity of actors—global, regional, national, local—and multidimensional tasks.

Notes

1 Secretary-General's Remarks at the Group of 77 Chairmanship Handover Ceremony, 11 January 2008, www.un.org/sg/statements/?nid=2950
2 "Report of the Secretary-General on the Work of the Organization," UN General Assembly document A/61/1, 16 August 2006. Note that the European Union also considers "development and peacebuilding to be intrinsically linked." See "Linking Peacebuilding and Development," European Peacebuilding Liaison Office, February 2011. www.eplo.org/assets/files/2.%

20Activities/Working%20Groups/PeDS/EPLO_Statement_Linking_Peace building_and_Development.pdf

3 W. Andy Knight, *A Changing United Nations: Multilateral Evolution and the Quest for Global Governance* (New York: Palgrave, 2000).

4 Neclâ Tschirgi, "Peacebuilding as the Link between Security and Development: Is the Window of Opportunity Closing?" International Peace Academy, December 2003. www.un.org/esa/peacebuilding/Library/Peace building_as_link_IPA.pdf

5 Tom Keating and W. Andy Knight, eds, *Building Sustainable Peace* (Tokyo: United Nations University Press, 2004).

6 "ASEAN Reiterates Importance of Development Pillar in UN Work," *Vietnam Plus*, 17 October 2013.

7 "Development Aid to Developing Countries Falls Because of Global Recession," Press Release, Organisation for Economic Co-operation and Development, 4 April 2012.

8 "ASEAN Reiterates Importance of Development Pillar in UN Work," *Vietnam Plus*, 17 October 2013.

9 "Brief Background Note on 'Strengthening the Development Pillar of the UN,'" UN Executive Committee on Economic and Social Affairs, October 2007. www.un.org/en/development/other/ecesa/private/meetings/documents/2007%20ECESA%20Minutes/Strengthening%20dev%20pillar%20-one%20p ager%20final.pdf

10 On complex interdependence, see Robert O. Keohane and Joseph S. Nye, "Interdependence in World Politics," in George T. Crane and Abla Amawi, eds, *The Theoretical Evolution of International Political Economy: A Reader*, 2nd edn (New York: Oxford University Press, 1997), 122–40; and Robert Keohane and Joseph Nye, *Power and Interdependence* (Boston, Mass. and London: Little, Brown, 1979).

11 Boutros Boutros-Ghali, *An Agenda for Peace: Preventive Diplomacy, Peacemaking and Peace-keeping* (New York: UN, 1992).

12 Elisabeth King and Robert O. Matthews, "A New Agenda for Peace," *International Journal* 67, no. 2 (2012): 277; see also Keating and Knight, eds, *Building Sustainable Peace*.

13 UN Department of Peacekeeping Operations, *Second Generation Disarmament, Demobilization and Reintegration (DDR) Practices in Peace Operations* (New York: UN, 18 January 2010).

14 See www.unddr.org/iddrs/ (accessed 24 February 2013).

15 Stephanie Hanson, "Backgrounder: Disarmament, Demobilization, and Reintegration (DDR) in Africa," Council on Foreign Relations, 16 February 2007. New York: UN.

16 UN DDR Resource Center, "What is DDR?" www.unddr.org/what-is-ddr/introduction_1.aspx

17 Nicole Ball and Luc van de Goor, *Disarmament, Demobilization and Reintegration: Mapping Issues, Dilemmas and Guiding Principles* (The Hague: Netherlands Institute of International Relations, 2006).

18 Ibid., 3.

19 See, for example, www.unddr.org

20 See www.un.org.np/ddr/role.php (accessed 17 May 2013).

21 Neclâ Tschirgi, "Post-Conflict Peacebuilding Revisited: Achievements, Limitations, Challenges," International Peace Academy, 7 October 2004, 1.

https://www.un.org/esa/peacebuilding /Library/Post_Conflict_Peacebuilding_IP A.pdf
22 See William J. Durch, Victoria K. Holt, Caroline R. Earle, and Moira K. Shanahan, *The Brahimi Report and the Future of UN Peace Operations* (Washington, DC: The Henry L. Stimson Centre, 2003).
23 Alan Bryden, "Pushing Pieces Around the Chessboard or Changing the Game? DDR, SSR and the Security-Development Nexus," in Albrecht Schnabel and Vanessa Farr, eds, *Back to the Roots: Security Sector Reform and Development* (Zurich, Switzerland: Lit Verlag, 2011), 201–24.
24 "United Nations Millennium Declaration," UN General Assembly resolution 55/2 (A/55/L.2), 8 September 2000.
25 Ibid.
26 "In Larger Freedom: Towards Security, Development and Human Rights for All," UN General Assembly resolution A/59/2005, 21 March 2005.
27 Nina Gillman, *Interagency Coordination During Disaster: Strategic Choices for the UN, NGOs and other Humanitarian Actors in the Field* (Baden-Baden, Germany: Nomos Publishers, 2010), 21.
28 See UN Office for the Coordination of Humanitarian Affairs, "OCHA Annual Report 2012," http://unocha.org/annualreport/2012/year-in-review
29 See www.humanitarianinfo.org/iasc/pageloader.aspx
30 "Report of the Peacebuilding Commission on its Fifth Session," UN Security Council (S/PV.6805), 12 July 2012.
31 "Helen Clark: 'Conference on Future of the UN Development System,'" UN Development Programme, 18 November 2010, www.undp.org/content/undp/en/home/presscenter/speeches/2010/11/18/helen-clark-wilton-park-conference-on-future-of-the-un-development-system

8   The economics of peace

Is the UN system up to the challenge?

Graciana del Castillo

Several countries in the Middle East and North Africa are emerging from war and violence, and the Syrian civil war will not go on forever. With risks not only for the region but for the world as a whole, the time is past due for the UN system to engage in a broad-based debate on how to improve its record in dealing with countries embarking on the complex transition to peace and stability. This chapter analyzes the different dimensions of such transitions and focuses on the economics of peace, on the UN system's operational capacity, and on the premises, lessons, and practices of previous cases that should be debated in order to improve the world body's record in assisting war-torn countries. It also provides a cautionary note on how to measure success in such situations.

The multidimensional transition to peace and stability

Despite the peculiarities of each case, countries need to address the root causes of conflict to make the complex transition to peace and stability irreversible. It is in this context that countries embark on a multi-dimensional transition to establish security (the security transition); create participatory political systems, and respect for the rule of law and human rights (the political transition); foster social cohesion and national reconciliation (the social transition); and engage in the econom-ics of peace so as to create stable, dynamic, and inclusive economies that would enable ordinary men and women—including the youth and uneducated—to have jobs and earn a decent living (the economic transition).

Since countries came out of Cold War–related confrontations in the early 1990s, this transition has proved incredibly difficult, not only for the countries involved, but also for the international community of states that has been ill-prepared to support them effectively. Failure in any one of the four dimensions of the transition would—as indeed it often happens—put the others at risk. It is understandable, and to be expected, that such an overwhelming process would necessarily take a long time and would entail formidable challenges (see Table 8.1). This is why effective support from the UN system is so important for countries undergoing transition.

Humanitarian relief to provide food, shelter, potable water, and medical care helps to save lives and provides minimum levels of consumption for subsistence in the short run. Delivering such aid through UN agencies and nongovernmental organizations (NGOs) has proved rather effective and financing has been generally available—even if less than the amounts requested by governments.

However, economic reconstruction that stimulates investment, production, food security, and job opportunities has proven largely unattainable in states emerging from war or other violent chaos. Such

Table 8.1 Complex and multidimensional transition to peace and stability

Transition:	From:	To:
Security	Violence and insecurity	Improving public security; Creating national security forces; Disarming and demobilizing former insurgent groups; and De-mining of roads and fields.
Political	Lawlessness and political exclusion	Developing a participatory government at the national and local levels; Promoting respect for the rule of law; and Promoting human, gender, and property rights.
Social	Sectarian/ethnic, religious, ideological or class confrontation	Promoting national reconciliation and social cohesion; Developing framework to address grievances through peaceful means; and Reintegrating demobilized combatants into society and productive activities.
Economic	War-torn and corrupt war economies, state-controlled policies and large macroeconomic imbalances	Rehabilitating infrastructure and services; Eradicating illicit activities; Establishing a simple and flexible macro/microeconomic framework; and Creating dynamic, inclusive, and sustainable economies.

countries cannot move into sustainable long-term development unless they engage first in an intermediate and distinct phase—"the economics of peace"—which must aim at reactivating the economy while minimizing, at the same time, the high risk that these countries have of relapsing into conflict.[1] Indeed, over the last decade every new civil conflict took place in countries where conflict was endemic.

Reactivation of the economy in war-torn countries requires that they move along the following path (with terms used interchangeably in brackets):

ECONOMICS OF WAR
(or UNDERGROUND WAR ECONOMY)
↓

ECONOMICS OF PEACE
(or ECONOMIC RECONSTRUCTION)
(or ECONOMIC TRANSITION)
↓

ECONOMICS OF DEVELOPMENT
(or LONG-TERM DEVELOPMENT)
(or DEVELOPMENT AS USUAL)

Figure 8.1 The economics of war, peace, and development

To avoid a relapse into conflict, the reactivation of the economy requires conflict-sensitive economic policies—unlike many of those advocated by the Bretton Woods institutions—to create the kind of growth that benefits the large majority and is sustainable, meaning that it is not going to disappear as soon as foreign forces and civilians leave the country and aid withers. The reactivation of the economy is also essential so that the other dimensions of the transition—security, political, and social—can be carried out and financed without the country falling into an aid dependency trap.

UN operational capacity

While different aspects of humanitarian relief are covered by different UN agencies, economic reconstruction per se has proved to be, to paraphrase Jeffrey Sachs, an "institutional orphan" in the UN system: no one organization has a specific mandate to address it.[2] Some multilateral organizations and donor governments have created or expanded specialized departments to deal with issues of reconstruction but there is no organization within the UN system with a specific mandate. For example, the UN Development Programme (UNDP) has the Bureau for Crisis Prevention and Recovery (BCPR) and the World Bank has a new Center on Conflict, Security and Development (CCSD). Operationally, however, the process of economic reconstruction has proved to be mostly fragmented, chaotic, and wasteful and has often incurred large costs in terms of peacekeeping operations or military forces to keep the peace.

In 2000 the Brahimi report (named after its chair) noted that effective "peacebuilding" is, in effect, a hybrid of political and development activities targeted at the sources of conflict. For this reason, it concluded that the UNDP was best placed to lead peacebuilding operational activities, in cooperation with other UN agencies and the World Bank.[3]

Given that such development organizations as the UNDP and the World Bank have a clear mandate to collaborate with governments, former insurgents and those who should give up arms cannot generally see them as impartial players. As argued in my book *Rebuilding War-Torn States*, only the UN Secretariat can be an impartial arbiter in the negotiations between governments and armed groups that need to be reintegrated into society and into productive activities. This impartiality is the key to establishing programs and in allocating funds during reconstruction, where different groups or different parts of the country cannot necessarily count on the government's goodwill at a given point in time, but should nevertheless be beneficiaries of government services and aid money.

The UN Secretariat, however, has several operational shortcomings that prevent it from playing a leading political role in economic reconstruction. Although peacekeeping missions now have a deputy special representative for "humanitarian relief and reconstruction," it is normally the UNDP's executive director who is appointed to that position and makes all decisions regarding the economics of peace. The UN, therefore, loses its comparative advantage as an impartial arbiter. Having one person in charge of two very distinct activities—requiring not only different policies but also different expertise to implement them—conflates the basic distinction between "humanitarian aid" and "reconstruction aid" that Allen Dulles made in his book, *The Marshall Plan*.[4] This distinction was the key to the effective reconstruction of Europe after World War II. In the post–Cold War period, the same distinction can clearly be associated with failure in reconstruction leading to aid dependency.[5]

In 2005 UN member states made the decision to create the intergovernmental Peacebuilding Commission (PBC) as well as a Peacebuilding Support Office (PSO) within the UN Secretariat to make lasting the transition from war to peace. But the PSO lacks any operational capacity, which is indeed a problem since that is where the UN has largely failed in assisting countries in the transition. The UN Secretariat needs such capacity since economic reconstruction and national reconciliation, including through reintegration of former combatants, have proved critical in supporting the transition to peace and stability—but also in derailing it. Their neglect has led to a dismal record: the UN itself reckons that roughly half of the countries that embarked on a multifaceted transition to peace since the end of the Cold War—either through negotiated agreements or military intervention—have reverted to conflict within a few years.[6]

Of the half that managed to keep the peace, the large majority ended up largely dependent on foreign aid.[7] A few countries such as Afghanistan have the infamous record of having both relapsed into conflict and becoming one of the most aid-dependent countries in the world, along with Liberia. Moreover, aid dependency has not necessarily led to improvements in the well-being of the population. Mozambique, for example, often hailed as a success story by the UN and the World Bank for keeping the peace and growing fast, remains at the bottom of the UNDP's Human Development Index (HDI).

There are only a few exceptions to this dismal record; El Salvador, for example, stands out on both grounds. Compliance with the UN-brokered peace agreement led to a perfectly observed ceasefire, in stark contrast to so many others—Angola, Rwanda, Timor-Leste, Iraq, and Afghanistan relapsed into even bloodier conflicts. El Salvador also managed to keep the peace and more than triple income per capita with unusually low levels of aid for a war-torn country.[8]

The dismal past record requires soul-searching on the part of the UN, its programs and agencies—including the Bretton Woods institutions—on how to improve their assistance to countries in the difficult transition to peace and stability.[9] At the same time, the UN lacks an institutional memory[10] in this area that could facilitate learning from relative success stories such as that of El Salvador, and particularly from positive and negative lessons experienced in the country.[11]

Both soul-searching and the creation of an institutional memory are particularly necessary as aid becomes scarcer in the aftermath of the global financial crisis, which has brought unimpressive growth, higher unemployment, crumbling infrastructure, fiscal imbalances, and larger taxpayer scrutiny in donor countries. Aid to war-torn countries competes with funding to address issues of long-term development, pandemics, natural disasters, and environmental problems worldwide.

What follows are some ideas for reflection and debate on how the record could be improved, particularly as the UN system embarks on future operations. Funding such operations is going to be particularly difficult as taxpayers—ranging from those in the United States to those in China, and all in between—become more skeptical about providing aid to distant countries through the UN system as reports on waste, incompetency, and corruption increasingly make the headlines.[12]

Premises, lessons, and best practices for debate

Ignoring the peculiarities and special needs of war-affected countries— strikingly different from those of other fragile states—as well as carrying out economic reconstruction under the misguided policies and misplaced priorities of development as usual, has been a major factor in the dismal record of economic reconstruction. Although each country is different and requires its own strategy, the experience of the last two decades has allowed us to identify a number of premises, lessons, and best practices that national policymakers and the UN system, as well as other bilateral and multilateral stakeholders and non-state actors, should keep in mind to improve the provision of aid and technical assistance to war-affected countries.

The economics of peace phase has proved particularly challenging, since the country must reactivate the economy while moving away from the economics of war—that is, the underground economy of illicit and rent-seeking activities that thrive in situations of armed conflict or chaos and that will make the establishment of governance and the rule of law difficult, if not impossible. This key move requires overcoming the interests of spoilers that have an economic stake in drug production and trafficking, smuggling, arms dealing, extortion, and the many other illicit and profitable activities that thrive during wars. As Thomas G. Weiss and Peter Hoffman note, unusual predatory economic opportunities abound during reconstruction. In addition to those already listed, aid manipulation is an important factor to deal with.[13]

Because countries emerging from domestic armed conflict, as those at war, do indeed share a number of characteristics with weak countries in the normal process of development, they are often lumped together as "fragile states."[14] The similarities, however, should not lead to the conflation of their needs. In fact, during the economics of peace phase, countries coming out of conflict have special needs and face a double challenge— that is, a "development-plus" challenge. Moreover, policymaking in war-torn states, as in other crisis-affected countries, must be quite distinct from those unaffected by war or other kinds of chaos.[15]

Policymakers should start addressing the normal socioeconomic challenges of the country very early on in the process. This was particularly needed in the case of poor countries such as Mozambique,

Liberia, Sierra Leone, East Timor, or Afghanistan, which exhibited some of the worst social and economic indicators in the world and which perennially were at the bottom of the Human Development Index. At the same time, however, these countries had to accommodate the extra burden of peace-related commitments.

Indeed, a number of activities—which are not necessary in weak countries not affected by conflict—are critical to address the grievances and special needs of groups involved in civil conflicts and to ensure their support of the peace process. These activities include the rehabilitation of services and infrastructure throughout the conflict-ravaged country; the creation of a simple and flexible macroeconomic framework for effective policymaking and for the accountable utilization of large volumes of aid that are typically given to post-crisis countries; the return of refugees and internally displaced persons; and the clearance of mines in villages and in the fields as a precondition for resettlement and production.[16] They also include the reform of the armed forces and the creation of a civilian police force to maintain public security, as well as the demobilization of militia groups and their reintegration into society through their inclusion into the security forces or productive activities. All of these peace-related activities targeted at conflict-affected groups have serious financial implications, but are indispensable for the effective reconstruction of the country and the reconciliation of its people. Without them, security would easily deteriorate, as in fact it has in many countries in transition.

Because the economics of peace takes place amid the complex and multidimensional transition to peace and stability—not independently from it—and because of the extra financial burden of carrying out peace-related projects, economic reconstruction is fundamentally different from development as usual. The most important challenge is to prevent the recurrence of hostilities—that is, to make peace irreversible. This entails the complex political task of addressing the root causes of the conflict, and it is for this reason that the UN is best placed to take the lead in establishing the economics of peace.[17]

Because there cannot be development without peace, it should be accepted by all parties involved that the objective of peace and reconciliation should always prevail over that of development—if the two ever clash as they often do, particularly with regard to budgetary allocations. Moreover, hard-learned lessons from the past indicate that policy in war-torn countries, just as in other crisis situations, should be tailored to take into account five basic differences from development as usual (see Table 8.2). These differences arise from: the horizon over which economic policies can be planned (i.e., short versus medium and long term); the treatment of different groups (i.e., preferences versus equal treatment for all); the amount of aid (i.e., sharp spikes versus low and stable flows); the establishment of the rule of law (i.e., national government versus foreign forces); and the involvement of the international community in national affairs (i.e., intense and intrusive versus nonexistent).[18]

Because the overriding objective in war-torn countries is to avoid reverting to war or generating new social conflicts, emergency policies should be adopted without delay, even if they are not optimal in the long run. This means that policymakers lack the luxury, typical of development as usual, of planning with a medium- and long-term framework in mind. At the same time, aid to groups most affected by the conflict, that is, the "reconstruction principle," should have priority over the "normal development or equity principle" of treating equally all groups with the same needs.

Because aid spikes follow crises, national ownership of reconstruction policies must be assured even amid the large interference from the international community of states, which is inevitable in the presence of such a large amount of aid and often of foreign troops. Also, corruption needs to be checked since large volumes of aid facilitate it.

Because of these five basic differences, it should come as no surprise to anyone that optimal economic policies are not always possible or even desirable during this phase. This was not accepted (in fact, it was almost heresy) when the author first raised it at the Office of the UN Secretary-General in the early 1990s as well as at the IMF in the late 1990s.[19]

Paul Collier, a former director of the Development Research Group at the World Bank, acknowledged as much in 2008 when he wrote:

> Indeed, until recently, the organizations dedicated to economic development did not systematically distinguish post-conflict settings

Table 8.2 Policymaking under normal development vs conflict situations

Normal Development	Conflict Situations
Medium- and long-term framework	Requires (distortionary) emergency programs
Application of the "development principle"	Application of the "reconstruction principle"
Low and stable foreign assistance	Sharp spikes in foreign assistance
Government establishes rule of law	Foreign troops and police support rule of law
Political involvement of international community considered as interference	Intensive and often intrusive political involvement

as requiring a distinctive approach. Yet policy in the post-conflict phase needs to be distinctive, both that of the government and that of the donor agencies. It should not be simply development as usual.[20]

In the same year, in a major speech on countries in reconstruction, World Bank president Robert Zoellick finally recognized that "development projects may need to be suboptimal economically—good enough rather than first-best."[21]

But organizations are slow to change, even if their leaders acknowledge the need; development organizations and experts may resist a choice that seems obvious. In fact, they often insist that the country adopt optimal economic policies from the very beginning, even if such policies threaten the consolidation of peace, as has occurred in different ways in countries as far apart in time and distance as El Salvador, Haiti, Timor-Leste, and Afghanistan. Rather than making peace, stability, reconciliation, the elimination of the illicit economy, and food security the focus of the intermediate phase, these organizations focused on establishing highly productive policies and programs, and world-class institutions, and on achieving poverty alleviation and the UN Millennium Development Goals (MDGs). Experience shows that countries need to move through the economics of peace and away from the economics of war before they can fully engage in the economics of development.[22]

By proposing that development organizations lead peacebuilding operations, the Brahimi report promoted a continuation of the failed development-as-usual approach to economic reconstruction, which has proved so ineffective in consolidating peace.[23] Such policies, which ignore political and security realities, have normally benefited a small elite over the large majority. By neglecting to reactivate the subsistence rural sector on which the large majority often depends for food and livelihoods, policies have often led to food and aid dependence and large trade deficits that these countries can ill afford. Such policies have been a major factor in the dismal record in establishing lasting peace and stability in war-torn countries across the world.

Development-as-usual policies have also been a factor in the high costs that the international community has incurred to keep the peace in countries such as Liberia, Afghanistan, and the Democratic Republic of the Congo (DRC). In Liberia, for example, the UN peacekeeping operation (UNMIL) cost the equivalent of two-thirds of the country's GDP in 2009–11. As UNMIL departs, the government must make a major effort to maintain security, which will require a painful reallocation of budgetary resources. Similarly, as foreign troops withdraw from Afghanistan, the government will need to assume operational and maintenance costs for security that will be difficult to sustain. More effective and inclusive economic reconstruction policies adopted from the very beginning, in which a large part of the population receives a peace dividend in terms of better living conditions and improved livelihoods, would have made such excessive security expenses unnecessary.[24]

How to measure success?

An important issue for debate in the UN system is how to measure success in war-torn countries. Different organizations often compliment themselves on the high growth rates of countries that they support in the transition to peace and stability. They call attention to growth in Liberia and Afghanistan, for example, to validate their strategy and to conclude that they are on the right track to building peace in those countries. With substantial aid flows and a large international presence (both civilian and military), such high rates of growth are hardly surprising when starting from a low base. Reactivating growth under such conditions is rather easy to achieve but very hard to sustain. Moreover, it often creates a number of economic and social distortions such as inflation in non-tradable goods, difficulties for the most vulnerable groups in accessing services and meeting basic needs, and a poor quality civil service, since the few people who are qualified for such positions are naturally drawn to higher paying jobs with international organizations. These distortions may affect the country for years to come.

Similarly, the degree of aid dependency should be factored into measures of success. Many complain that countries in Africa get much smaller levels of aid per capita than those in the Balkans. But this measure is grossly misleading because it does not show how the aid affects peoples' lives. What matters is not the nominal amount, but what aid represents in terms of peoples' income and in terms of the purchasing power in the respective countries.

Table 8.3 shows that in the 10-year period following the Dayton Peace Agreement, Bosnians received $221 per person on average for this period (t_0–t_9). This is significantly more than the $72 that Mozambicans received during a similar period. However, in the case of Bosnia, the amount received per capita represented less than 20 percent of the average per capita income of the population. In the case of Mozambique, aid added 40 percent to per capita income, more than twice as much. Furthermore, the same dollar amount could buy a significantly larger amount of food and other basic necessities in Mozambique than in Bosnia, a much more expensive country. Thus the relative impact of aid was larger in Mozambique than in Bosnia.

Table 8.3 Aid comparison across war-torn countries

ODA	t_0	t_1	t_2	t_3	t_4	t_5	t_6	t_7	t_8	t_9	$t_0–t_2$	$t_0–t_4$	$t_0–t_9$
Per capita (US$)													
Afghanistan[1]	57	67	93	110	111	181	172	213	213	216	73	88	143
Bosnia[2]	293	251	246	250	345	195	169	145	140	176	263	277	221
Liberia[3]	37	72	73	82	212	360	141	376	197		61	95	172
Rwanda[4]	140	139	75	36	53	53	40	36	42	38	118	89	73
Mozambique[5]	99	78	78	67	55	57	61	47	51	53	85	75	72
El Salvador[6]	72	70	53	51	52	48	31	31	30	40	65	60	53
As % of GDP													
Afghanistan[1]	32	35	44	45	42	57	47	50	40	37	37	39	43
Bosnia[2]	45	26	19	17	22	13	11	8	6	7	30	26	18
Liberia[3]	21	37	33	35	74	112	44	110	50		30	40	57
Rwanda[4]	60	56	35	13	18	21	19	18	22	18	50	36	31
Mozambique[5]	76	60	54	46	27	25	24	18	22	24	63	53	42
El Salvador[6]	7	6	4	3	3	3	2	1	1	2	5	4	3

Source: Calculated by author using data from the World Economic Outlook Database (April 2013); OECD total ODA (accessed 12 May 2013).
Notes: The table reports aid during the first decade of the transition to peace in the reported countries; it also reports the average aid flows during the first 3 years (t0–t2), 5 years (t0–t4), and 10 years (t0–t9).
[1] Afghanistan: 2002–2010.
[2] Bosnia and Herzegovina: 1995–2004.
[3] Liberia: 2003–2011 (hence last column averages aid over 9 years instead of 10). As of November 2013, data for ODA in 2012 was not available.
[4] Rwanda: 1994–2003.
[5] Mozambique: 1992–2001.
[6] El Salvador: 1992–2001.

Table 8.3 also shows that in some countries (Bosnia, Rwanda, Mozambique, and El Salvador) aid fell over time and the average for the first 10-year period is lower than in the first 3-year period (t_0–t_2). In others (Afghanistan and Liberia), however, aid flows increased during the first decade—a clear indication that dependence was not falling, as it should have been. What the table does not show is that Mozambique continued to receive aid amounting to 24 percent of its GDP on average during the second decade. After two decades of such large aid flows, the 2013 HDI placed Mozambique 185th among 186 countries.[25] This is indeed striking, and clearly calls into question not only the definition of success—since the World Bank and UN organizations often refer to Mozambique as a fast-growing and successful post-conflict country—but also the nature of the support that the UN system is providing for economic reconstruction in the country.[26]

Donor policies are often focused on improving infrastructure and services that mainly benefit domestic elites and foreign investors. Success should be measured by whether the lives and livelihoods of the large majority of men and women have improved and by whether the country can stand on its feet and move into a normal development path.

Conclusion

How can the UN system provide more effective assistance? There is indeed a desperate need for more efficient use of available aid and for better-directed technical assistance to war-torn countries in their transition to peace and stability. The United Nations, together with its programs and agencies, is best placed to support countries in such a transition. The UN system should focus on how to achieve these goals, particularly in light of the fact that new donors such as the Gulf countries, which will be key in financing policies in the Middle East, and China, which is playing an increasing role in Africa, are reluctant to channel aid through the UN system because of its high cost, ineffectiveness, and waste.

Among the things to be debated is how the UN system uses its resources. Should it continue to spend money on repetitive reports and conferences, unnecessary translations, and first-class travel,[27] or should those resources be channeled toward supporting war-torn countries to create local capacity and improve local livelihoods, which constitutes the only way to achieve lasting peace and stability? Clearly, cutting resource waste should be a priority concern.

The UN system needs also to debate specific ways to make itself more relevant in supporting war-torn countries through the economics of peace phase. Such debate should involve practitioners throughout the

UN system, policymakers and parliamentarians in donor countries, other multilateral and bilateral donors, academics, and nongovernmental actors, including NGOs and private companies that are increasingly operating in war-torn countries. Just as importantly, it should involve policymakers and other experts from these countries, who are not normally participants in discussions about their own future.

Several proposals have been made to improve the effectiveness and accountability of aid and to create a level playing field for the majority, including through the creation of "reconstruction zones." By putting foreign investors and local communities in a position to work together, such zones could help countries achieve food security, provide viable employment for the large majority including the youth, and become less aid dependent. Given the poor record of the past, debating this and other such proposals that contribute to thinking outside the box could be productive.[28]

The UN system should also explore ways that aid can be channeled increasingly through the government so that it can subsidize micro, small, and medium-sized enterprises in the agricultural, manufacturing, and services sectors to hire workers—including former combatants and other conflict-affected groups. With labor costs thus reduced, and with strong support from the UN system, existing and potential local entrepreneurs could decide to invest both for the domestic and foreign markets, even under the conditions of uncertainty and high risk that characterize those countries.[29]

These and other policies focused on employment creation, the utilization of local ingenuity and local inputs, and foreign capital could help war-torn and other conflict-affected countries to move toward peace and stability. The UN system needs to debate ways to improve its support of governments in rebuilding their own countries and to reduce its own operational and overhead costs. Otherwise, direct cash payments to the poor will become increasingly used as an alternative to channeling aid through the UN system, particularly since it seems to be working well in different settings.[30]

Only by helping governments to establish their legitimacy in the provision of security and services, and in the creation of a level playing field for the large majority in the rural sector and in the establishment of a favorable business climate for other sectors, will the UN, its programs and agencies, succeed in reducing young people's motivations to embrace insurgencies and uprisings.

Notes

1 See in particular, Graciana del Castillo, *Rebuilding War-Torn States: The Challenge of Post-Conflict Economic Reconstruction* (Oxford: Oxford

University Press, 2008), 31–33, 40–47; "The Economics of Peace: Five Rules for Effective Reconstruction," *Special Report #286* (Washington, DC: United States Institute of Peace, September 2011); and "Building Peace and Stability Through Economic Reconstruction," *UNIDIR Resources*, www. unidir.org/files/publications/pdfs/building-peace-and-stability-through-economic-reconstruction-en-417.pdf

2 See Jeffrey Sachs's introductory remarks at the Columbia University "Conference on Peace through Reconstruction," 23 October 2009, available at http://capitalism.columbia.edu/view/events/conference

3 See "United Nations Report of the Panel on United Nations Peace Operations," UN document A/55/305, August 2000, 8.

4 Allen W. Dulles, *The Marshall Plan*, ed. Michael Wala (Providence, R.I.: Berg Publishers, 1993).

5 For a discussion of the relevance of the Marshall Plan to transitions to peace since the end of the Cold War, see Graciana del Castillo, *Rebuilding War-Torn States*; and *Guilty Party: The International Community in Afghanistan* (Bloomington, Ind.: Xlibris, 2014).

6 Secretary-General Kofi Annan mentioned this figure in his report *In Larger Freedom* (New York: UN, 2004), 70. The UN does not seem to have updated this figure, and we have seen many countries reverting to war since. Analysts using a wider sample, which includes countries that are not going through the complex multidimensional transition discussed above, have estimated probabilities of relapsing into conflict ranging from 40 to 50 percent. What matters more than an exact figure is that war-torn countries have a much larger probability of going back to war than others, and that is why policies should be conflict-sensitive.

7 OECD Official Development Assistance (ODA) data used in this chapter include only economic and humanitarian aid at concessional terms, and exclude military and counter-narcotics assistance. They also exclude private sources of aid (NGOs, foundations, and private individuals). Thus, they are an underestimate of total aid.

8 For a comparison between the El Salvador and Mozambique situations 20 years after the signature of their respective peace agreements, see Graciana del Castillo, "The Political Economy of Peace," *Project Syndicate*, 12 January 2012. www.project-syndicate.org.

9 The Bretton Woods institutions have improved the way that they support these countries, although much remains to be done. For a detailed analysis of how those institutions have assisted these countries over time, see Graciana del Castillo, "The Bretton Woods Institutions, Reconstruction and Peacebuilding," in *Ending Wars, Consolidating Peace: Economic Perspectives*, ed. Mats Berdal and Achim Wennmann (London: Routledge for The International Institute for Strategic Studies, 2010), Chapter 4; *Rebuilding War-Torn States*, 66–77; "Economic Reconstruction of War-Torn Countries: The Role of the International Financial Institutions," *Seton Hall Law Review* 38, no. 4 (2008): 1265–95; and "Post-conflict Economic Reconstruction and the Challenge to the International Financial Organizations: The Case of El Salvador," *World Development* 29 (December 2001): 1967–85.

10 Three of the most important initiatives that Secretary-General Boutros-Ghali supported to deal with reconstruction in war-torn countries are largely

unknown, including *An Inventory of Post-Conflict Peace-Building Activities* (New York: UN, 1997); the *International Colloquium on Post-Conflict Reconstruction Strategies* (Vienna: UN, 1995); and the Minimalist Monetary and Fiscal Frameworks prepared for the IMF at the request of the secretary-general for these countries. See del Castillo, *Rebuilding War-Torn States*, 31–33, 55–56, 72–74, and 280–81.

11 See Alvaro de Soto and Graciana del Castillo, "Obstacles to Peace-building," *Foreign Policy* 94 (Spring 1994): 69–83 for some of the early problems that the UN faced in El Salvador; Marrack Goulding, *Peacemonger* (London: John Murray, 2002), 241–43 for problems with the renegotiation of the land program that he claims saved the peace process; del Castillo, "Arms-for-Land Deal: Lessons from El Salvador," in *Multidimensional Peacekeeping: Lessons from Cambodia and El Salvador*, ed. Michael Doyle and Ian Johnstone (Cambridge: Cambridge University Press, 1997) for an analysis of the problems with implementation of the program; and del Castillo, *Rebuilding War-Torn States*, Chapters 7–8, for a detailed analysis of the experiences of El Salvador and Kosovo with economic reconstruction, the role of the UN in them, and the problems the organization faced in assuming the leading role.

12 See, for example, Jack Healy, "In Afghanistan, A Village Is a Model of Dashed Hopes," *New York Times*, 8 August 2011, for the waste with the UNDP's Alice-Ghan housing project for returnees in Afghanistan.

13 Thomas G. Weiss and Peter J. Hoffman, "Making Humanitarianism Work," in *Making States Work: State Failure and the Crisis of Governance*, ed. Simon Chesterman, Michael Ignatieff, and Ramesh Thakur (Tokyo: UN University Press, 2005), 299–300. See also James Cockayne, "Crime, Corruption and Violent Economies," in Berdal and Wennmann, *Ending Wars, Consolidating Peace: Economic Perspectives*, chapter 10.

14 See Rachel Gisselquist's presentation at the UNU-WIDER Conference on Fragility and Aid—What Works? New York, 25 October 2013.

15 See del Castillo, "Auferstehen aus Ruinen: Die Besonderen Bedingungen des Wirtschaftlichen Wiederaufbaus nach Konflikten" ("Post-Conflict Reconstruction: A Development-Plus Challenge") *der Überblick* (*Foreign Affairs*) 4 (December 2006), www.der-ueberblick.de/ueberblick.archiv/one.ueberblick.article/ueberblick0596.html?entry=page.200604.042. See also del Castillo, "Post-conflict Peace Building: A Challenge for the United Nations," *CEPAL Review*, no. 55 (April 1995): 27–38, at 30, for a discussion of the "double challenge" of normal socioeconomic development and the need to settle for "less than optimal policies" in their economic reform efforts so as to accommodate the additional financial burden of reconstruction and peace consolidation.

16 In some countries the need for de-mining was urgent and expensive. After more than two decades of war, Afghanistan, for example, had become one of the most mined countries in the world. De-mining was imperative not only for the safety of the population but also for the reactivation of agricultural production.

17 Both the UNDP and the World Bank rejected requests by the UN Secretary-General's Office to support the land program on the grounds that they supported "all farmers." See del Castillo, *Rebuilding War-Torn States*, Chapter 7.

18 Ibid., Chapter 4.

19 See Graciana del Castillo, "Post-Conflict Peacebuilding: The Challenge to the UN," 29–30. See also del Castillo; "Post-conflict Reconstruction and the Challenge to the International Organisations," 1970 and 1978.
20 Paul Collier, "Postconflict Economic Policy," in *Building States to Build Peace*, ed. Charles T. Call with Vanessa Wyeth (Boulder, Col.: Lynne Rienner, 2008), 103.
21 Robert Zoellick, "Securing Development," speech to the International Institute for Strategic Studies, London, 12 September 2008.
22 For empirical evidence on how these issues were addressed in these countries and other countries, see de Soto and del Castillo, "Obstacles to Peacebuilding"; and del Castillo, *Rebuilding War-Torn States*.
23 Despite his well-known diplomatic skills, Lakhdar Brahimi has never shown any special interest on the economic issues that could have provided support to his political policies in Afghanistan and elsewhere. See del Castillo, *Guilty Party*.
24 IMF balance of payments data show that the cost of UNMIL was $600 million a year on average in 2009–11, in a country where GDP only averaged $900 million a year. The security costs in Afghanistan have been detailed in del Castillo, *Guilty Party*, Chapter 20.
25 UNDP, *Human Development Report 2013: The Rise of the South* (New York: UNDP, 2013).
26 Mozambique is one of the UN's pilot countries for Delivering as One (DaO). However, the UN has been criticized for taking a non-strategic approach to development assistance and for having lost influence, especially because it represents a small fraction of total ODA to Mozambique. Operationally, in spite of DaO, "the UN's challenges are fragmentation, duplication, lack of focus, competition between the agencies for funding, inefficiency, inadequate coherence, inefficient operation." See UN Mozambique, *Delivering as One: Country-led Evaluation 2010*, 54, www.mz.one.un.org/por/Resources/Publications/Delivering-as-One-Evaluation-Report, 2.
27 For evidence on waste and inefficiencies, see del Castillo, "The Economics of Peace."
28 See Graciana del Castillo, "Reconstruction Zones in Afghanistan and Haiti: A Way to Enhance Aid Effectiveness and Accountability," *Special Report #292* (Washington, DC: United States Institute of Peace), October 2011; "Aid and Employment Generation in Conflict-affected Countries: Policy Recommendations for Liberia," Working Paper no. 2012/47 (UN/WIDER, Helsinki, Finland, 2012); *Guilty Party*, chapter 22; and "Leveling the Afghan Playing Field," *Project Syndicate*, 8 August 2013, www.project-syndicate.org/
29 See Graciana del Castillo and Edmund Phelps, "A Strategy to Help Afghanistan Kick Its Habit," *Financial Times*, 3 January 2008, and "The Road to Post-war Recovery," *Project Syndicate*, 9 July 2007, www.project-syndicate.org/
30 See, for example, Joseph Hanlon, Armando Barrientos, and David Hulme, *Just Give Money to the Poor: The Development Revolution from the Global South* (Sterling, Va.: Kumarian Press, 2010); Sarah Murray, "NGOs Tread Gingerly when Matchmaking," *Financial Times*, 23 June 2011; Annie Lowrey, "Ending Poverty by Giving the Poor Money," *New York Times*, 20 June 2013; and Tim Harford, "The Undercover Economist: How to Give Money Away," *Financial Times*, 12 July 2013.

9 Can peacebuilding drive the UN change agenda?

Michael von der Schulenburg

Peacebuilding constitutes a profound change in the way that the United Nations pursues its core mandate of maintaining international peace and security. Indeed, peacebuilding has replaced traditional peacekeeping and has become the UN's main operational response to contemporary threats to peace and security. This chapter describes the changes that are brought about by peacebuilding, explores the shifts in the global security environment that made peacebuilding necessary, and outlines the political developments that made peacebuilding possible. Finally, this chapter explores peacebuilding's impact on the UN development system and how it could drive a reform agenda.

Peacebuilding is understood as all activities aimed at bringing peace and development to fragile and conflict-ridden countries. All UN action undertaken within member states is different from traditional UN peace operations—that is, between member states. The former are hence called "peacebuilding missions."[1]

Changes brought about by peacebuilding

Under the general notion of peacebuilding, the UN has moved away from its original task of preventing armed conflict and ending wars between member states toward actions in weak and failing member states, and more specifically to help end intra-state wars and to assist them in regaining national sovereignty. Peacebuilding is the UN's response to a changing global security environment in which interstate wars have virtually disappeared and the main threat to peace and security originates from intra-state armed conflicts; the Security Council's involvement in civil wars and failing states results because armed non-state actors are a danger to international peace and stability. Therefore, central to peacebuilding are failing and conflict-prone states that are unable—or that are seen to be unable—to achieve internal peace and stability, and to provide basic public goods and services to citizens.

Despite the importance of peacebuilding for UN peace operations, there is still no generally accepted definition. In 2007 the UN Policy Committee agreed to a rather limited non-political description of the process.[2] Probably a better version[3] is a combination of national and international efforts designed to assist post-conflict[4] fragile countries in breaking the vicious cycle of armed conflict; returning to security, peace, and national understanding; and building a more tolerant, inclusive, and democratic society with effective and transparent national state institutions that are accountable to citizens and bound by human rights and the rule of law. To deal with the complexity of the problems in post-conflict countries, the UN would have to mobilize the technical and operational capabilities from across the UN system in order to re-establish internal security, promote national reconciliation, advocate human rights protection, and promote the rule of law, as well as provide humanitarian and development assistance.

UN peacebuilding missions that arrive, often with thousands of military and police personnel and large numbers of international experts, in a fragile post-conflict country constitute a deliberate and planned interference—though time limited—in its internal affairs. Such a presence could be light, as in most special political missions, but also could take the form of temporarily controlling key sovereign state functions, including police, border security, elections, or even actual government functions. Furthermore, UN peacebuilding missions often arrive not only with a set of fixed values but also with a state model that is based on liberal democracy, the rule of law, and a market economy. Such a model leaves little room for local politicians to develop any deviating views over their country's future political and economic systems.

Because peacebuilding constitutes interference into the internal affairs of a member state, it is potentially a risky and dangerous tool. To distinguish peacebuilding missions from other (military) outside actions, they should be strictly limited to fragile and conflict-ridden countries that are no longer able to solve their internal conflicts without external assistance and with conflicts that constitute a threat to international peace and security. They should be authorized by the Security Council with mandates that specify their purposes and time-frames. And their ultimate aim should be to restore state sovereignty by helping create the necessary political, institutional, social, and economic conditions for the exercise of such responsibilities.

When it was introduced in 1948 and 1956, peacekeeping was an addition to the UN's operational toolbox. Although not mentioned in the UN Charter, it would become one of the most important UN instruments for maintaining international peace and security. However, at its inception and throughout the Cold War, UN peacekeeping was usually used to end wars between states—not within states.

When peacebuilding emerged after the end of the Cold War, it was an even greater novelty because, in strict legal terms, it could be seen as an abrogation of the UN Charter's noninterference principle in Article 2 (7). However, it can be argued that peacebuilding is evidence of the extraordinary flexibility of the United Nations and its members in reinterpreting and adapting the UN Charter. Peacebuilding may ultimately be of greater significance for the UN than traditional peacekeeping. The additional task of maintaining the internal peace of member states amounts to a considerable expansion of the world organization's responsibilities, with consequences for the UN's operational system.

Changes that made peacebuilding necessary

During its first 45 years, the UN sent its peacekeepers exclusively to monitor ceasefires between member states, separate their belligerents, and supervise the withdrawal of foreign troops from the territory of another country.[5] When the concept of peacebuilding was officially introduced by former UN secretary-general Boutros-Ghali in his *An Agenda for Peace* in 1992,[6] the United Nations found itself in the middle of an upsurge of intra-state wars, largely a consequence of the Cold War's end that brought into the open many internal conflicts that had been suppressed or shrouded by East–West politics. Responding to successive waves of civil wars has since marked the UN's involvement in conflict management.

In 1989, Namibia, Mozambique, and East Timor were still fighting for their independence, and in Liberia the first of two civil wars broke out. In 1991, Somalia collapsed and the brutal civil war in Sierra Leone began, while the violent break-up of the former Yugoslavia led to a series of separate internal wars. In 1992, Bosnia's civil war made the headlines, as did the second phase of Angola's civil war. In 1990, Rwanda descended into civil war that, despite a peace agreement, led to the 1994 genocide. In addition, there was Burundi's civil war (1993–2005) and the war between royalist and Maoist forces in Nepal (1996–2006). Largely abandoned by their former Eastern and Western patrons, the civil wars in El Salvador, Guatemala, Angola, and Afghanistan continued to fester.

A second wave of intra-state wars began in 1999 when anti-independence forces took control of East Timor, and armed conflict broke out in the

Central African Republic in 2001. Sudan became a matter of great concern with the intensification of its war with its southern provinces over independence that had started already in 1983, and the civil war in its Darfur province that began in 2003. In 1996, the Congo, once again, fell back into chaotic violence that triggered a serie of internal wars, some with the military involvement of its immediate neighbors. Even the formerly prosperous Côte d'Ivoire descended into civil war in 1994 that lasted until 2011. The US-led interventions to remove the Taliban regime in Afghanistan in 2001 and Saddam Hussein in Iraq in 2003 resulted in further internal violence that continues to date.

Conflicts resulting from the Arab Spring could be considered a third wave of intra-state conflicts. A different type of violence often results in civil war, which includes armed uprisings and military backlash in Tunisia, Libya, Bahrain, Yemen, Egypt, and Syria.

Relatively new are so-called internationalized intra-state wars in which one or several foreign armed forces are directly engaged in a local civil war. The best examples are Sierra Leone, where initially the Economic Community of West African States (ECOWAS) and later UK armed forces fought the Revolutionary United Front; Afghanistan, where the North Atlantic Treaty Organization (NATO) forces are confronting the Taliban opposition; and Mali in 2013, where French troops prevented Islamic fundamentalists from taking control of the country, and later in the Central African Republic.

By contrast, interstate wars, once the raison d'être of the UN, have almost disappeared. The war against Saddam Hussein's regime following his annexation of Kuwait in 1991 was the last major international war in which regular armies of various countries fought each other. The Ethiopia/Eritrea and the Sudan/South Sudan conflicts are best considered as extensions of previous civil wars, and their impact has remained largely local.

According to the latest published numbers by the Peace Research Institute Oslo and the Uppsala Conflict Data Program[7] in 2012, a total of 32 armed conflicts were ongoing worldwide.[8] Only the conflict between Sudan and the recently independent South Sudan is classified as an interstate war. Of the estimated 38,000 civilian and military battle-related deaths in 2012, about 99 percent were the result of intra-state wars.

Since World War II the number of battle-related deaths has dropped considerably, which is even more significant if we consider that the world's population has tripled since then.[9] Whereas the average annual battle-related deaths[10] were estimated at 417,000 from 1946 to 1949, they declined to 230,000 annually from 1980 to 1984. From 1995 to 1999, battle-related deaths fell to 83,000 annually; and as already mentioned, this number dropped in 2012 to 38,000—even including those killed in the Syrian civil war.[11]

This decline in the human cost of armed intra-state wars around the world would hardly justify high-level international attention were it not for the deeper concern over threats emanating from conflict-prone fragile states. Especially after the 9/11 attacks in 2001, Western countries increasingly feared that failed states could become safe havens for international terrorism and transnational crime. Fragile states also trigger humanitarian disasters and lead to flows of refugees and illegal migration. All this can have a ripple effect on neighboring countries, the region, and ultimately, developed countries.[12]

The latest Failed State Index by the Fund for Peace[13] rated 35 countries under "alert," meaning that they could implode at any time. A further 73 countries are under "warning," indicating that there are reasons to be concerned about their future internal stability. Of the total 178 countries in the survey, 108 are considered to have shaky political systems—a staggering 61 percent of surveyed countries have different degrees of weakness on the failing states list.

The large number of fragile states and, even more importantly, states with active internal armed conflicts, are a threat to international peace and security. For this reason, the UN Security Council has increasingly authorized peace operations in fragile states. The tool to do this is peacebuilding.

From peacekeeping to peacebuilding

Throughout the Cold War, peacekeeping was essentially a military matter: UN peacekeepers would, often in accordance with a ceasefire agreement, monitor the pulling back of the armed forces of the warring states behind a ceasefire line or act as a buffer between them along a ceasefire line. In other cases, UN peacekeepers monitored the withdrawal of foreign troops or prevented their infiltration into a member state.

These operations implemented ceasefire agreements and had few other political ambitions. None of them was instrumental in concluding a peace agreement—indeed, an oft-cited criticism is that they protect the status quo and keep unsavory regimes from collapse. This situation changed dramatically with the end of the Cold War in 1989 when the Security Council sent, in quick succession, multidimensional UN peacebuilding missions[14] to help end armed intra-state conflicts: Namibia (1989–90), Angola (1991–95), Cambodia (1991–93),

Mozambique (1992–94), Somalia (1992–93), Liberia (1993–97), Rwanda (1993–94), and Bosnia (1995–2002). After some initial failures of these new types of peace missions, it took the Security Council a few years before approving a new series: in Haiti (1997), the Central African Republic (1998), Kosovo (1999), Sierra Leone (1999), the Congo (1999), East Timor (1999), Afghanistan (2002), Liberia (2003), Burundi (2004), Côte d'Ivoire (2004), and Sudan/Darfur (2007).

Despite the fact that UN peacekeepers were now sent to solve conflicts within countries, their mandates remained largely military. But separating warring national armies who had agreed on a ceasefire and acting within a country that had just emerged from an armed conflict were very different tasks. UN peacekeepers were increasingly involved in something far more complex; they had now also to disarm regular and irregular combatants, regain control over contested territories, take over internal security, protect civilians, and reform national security forces.

In addition, these missions were now faced with humanitarian and development tasks, and peacekeepers increasingly turned to civilian experts, including burgeoning numbers of police, which altered the structure of UN peace operations. Military peacekeepers became part of a wider UN effort that included police units as well as civilian experts able to deal with issues from reconciliation to writing a constitution, from elections to dealing with civil society, from human rights and the rule of law to fighting transnational crime, from institution-building to development.[15] The UN soon realized that its interventions in intrastate conflicts were far more complex, risky, and costly,[16] and that this needed a new approach.

Initial adjustments were ad hoc rather than based on any visionary strategy. The failure to recognize the complexity and very different requirements of the new type of UN in-country operation may have contributed to a number of the first-generation post–Cold War peacekeeping operations going wrong—usually the following four are listed as such: Angola, Somalia, Rwanda, and Bosnia. The three principles that governed traditional peacekeeping operations—consent, impartiality, and minimum use of force in self-defense—no longer had the same traction in intra-state conflicts. For example, the UN's failure to authorize NATO airstrikes against pro-Serbian forces attacking UN-declared safe zones in 1993–95 can be found in the principle that the UN could only operate with the consent of all parties, including the pro-Serbian forces. In Rwanda, the reluctance of the UN to agree to General Roméo Dallaire's pleas to authorize a surprise attack on illegal pro-government weapons depots was the result of fears that this could undermine the UN's supposed neutrality. New York was caught in the mindset of traditional peacekeeping. However, by then the political contexts had changed, and UN peacekeeping operations had become *de facto* multidimensional peacebuilding missions.

It was not until September 2005 that the General Assembly and Security Council—following the recommendations of the High-level Panel on Threats, Challenges and Change and the World Summit—recognized peacebuilding as a core UN activity and established the UN Peacebuilding Commission (PBC), the UN Peacebuilding Support Office (PBSO), and the Peacebuilding Fund (PBF). What had started mostly as ad hoc responses to a rise in intra-state conflicts over the previous 15 years found a home in new institutional structures.[17]

Changes that made peacebuilding possible

After the Cold War, civil wars were already common, but Moscow and Washington no longer protected their client states or regimes from interference by the UN or any other international body. Even more important, a global consensus gradually emerged about the "right" form of a political and economic state system.

From the General Assembly back to the Security Council

Since 1989 the Security Council had assumed the function spelled out in the UN Charter, the power to decide on collective action for maintaining international peace and security. Prior to the fall of the Berlin Wall, the work of the Security Council had been largely obstructed by East–West antagonisms and the use or threatened use of the veto. Initially, the Soviet Union was mainly responsible for a gridlocked Security Council, but from the 1970s onward it was increasingly the United States and to a much lesser extent also France and Britain that used their veto powers to block decisions. In 1971 when the People's Republic of China took over the seat of the Republic of China (Taiwan) in the Security Council, a legitimate member of the Group of 77 was also among the permanent five (P-5) members; and Beijing used its veto power to block decisions that infringed on the national sovereignty of newly independent states, irrespective of the circumstances.[18] Given the general atmosphere of mistrust, many important international security concerns never even reached the Security Council.

Recourse to the General Assembly was seen by many countries as a way to sidestep the paralysis in the Security Council.[19] The General Assembly made decisions about the Korean War (1950–55), the division of Palestine (1947), the independence of Libya (1952),[20] and even the creation of the first UN Emergency Force (UNEF I) that became the model for most subsequent UN peacekeeping missions. However, in the late 1960s, recently decolonized states began to dominate the General Assembly. By 1980, 120 of the 154 member states (or 78 percent) represented in the General Assembly were organized in the Group of 77 or Non-Aligned Movement (NAM). The main themes now became decolonization, anti-apartheid, the plight of the Palestinian people, the price of raw materials, and even a new international economic order. Not surprisingly, newly independent countries rejected any form of interference in their internal affairs. The General Assembly was unable to deal with the issue of fragile states or approve UN operations when the Security Council could not.

A new dawn for the Security Council came with the end of the Cold War, including renewed calls for reform. The new-found cooperation among the P-5 led to a proliferation of new UN peace missions. While the Security Council had only approved 16 peacekeeping missions in 15 conflict areas during the Cold War, by 2012 it had approved a total of 68 new peace missions in 41 different conflict areas.[21] In other words, in the 23 years since the end of the Cold War (1989–2012), the UN initiated and fielded over three times as many UN peace missions as during its first 44 years (1945–89).[22]

But far more significant than the increase in UN peace missions was the change in their mandates. Of the 41 conflict areas in which the UN intervened, 24 UN operations (about 60 percent) were in intra-country conflicts and had to various degrees peacebuilding agendas.[23] With these missions, the Security Council had introduced the principle of intervening in a member state—but if, and only if, this was considered necessary for maintaining international peace and security.[24]

From peoples' democracies to liberal democracies

Any UN mission in a post-conflict country with the mandate of helping rebuild its society, state institutions, and economy should be based on internationally acceptable political and economic systems—on a kind of "model state." Prior to 1990, no such model existed. Aside from the East–West ideological divide, many newly independent countries experimented with different governance systems: the rural classless society of the Khmer Rouge, the dynastic autocracy in North Korea, the "empire" in Central Africa, the Jamahiriya system in Libya, as well as one-party systems and dictatorships. These variegated political, social, and economic systems could only coexist while the UN observed the principle of noninterference in the affairs of member states. It was inconceivable that the UN would assist any country in setting up peoples' democracies, empires, or authoritarian regimes.

Following the break-up of the Soviet Union and its satellites in 1991–92, there was a steady spread of electoral democracy. Today, the vast majority of UN member states have a democratic constitution and accept the principle of the rule of law. Freedom House estimated that while in 1989 about 41 percent of all countries surveyed were democracies, the proportion by 1994 had already increased to 64 percent.[25] In 2006, the Democracy Index of the Economist Intelligence Unit (EIU)[26] listed 76 percent of all countries they surveyed as either full or part democracies. And although it may be a long way from having well-functioning democracies, the principle of democratic governance was no longer contested.

In December 2007 the General Assembly took the unprecedented step in resolution 62/7 of reaffirming "that democracy is a universal value based on the freely expressed will of people to determine their own political, social and cultural systems and their full participation in all aspects of their lives." The resolution goes on to urge the UN and other international organizations to spread democratic values by sharing experiences and providing technical advice.

The economic transition from socialist (and various mixed systems) to free-market systems was even faster and more widespread than the democratic transition as countries such as China, Viet Nam, Iran, and Saudi Arabia adopted free-market economies while keeping their respective political systems.

The general acceptance of a democratic state model along with a liberal market economic system facilitated the possibility of UN intervention into member states; and UN peacebuilding missions now had a roadmap for helping rebuild societies, democratic state institutions, and economies based on private capital. It allowed assistance to non-state actors such as political parties, nongovernmental organizations, religious and traditional leaders, and the media—all activities that had previously been unthinkable.

Consequences for the UN development system

Peace and development are inseparable and mutually reinforcing components of any peacebuilding operation. Key to the success of peacebuilding is not only the extent to which peacebuilding missions are able to achieve greater internal security, but also their ability to provide a peace dividend in the form of new opportunities, jobs, justice, health, and education. Development has become an integral part of any peacebuilding mission. In the words of the so-called Brahimi report: "effective peacebuilding is, in effect, a hybrid of political and development activities targeted at the source of conflict."[27] If the recommendations of the High-level Panel of Eminent Persons on the Post-2015 Development Agenda[28] are followed, political considerations of peace and security will gain even greater impetus.

In many ways, the UN's operational capacities and management structures have lagged behind the increasingly complex requirements of peacebuilding. In particular, the challenge remains critical for the notoriously fragmented UN development system.[29] There is also a disconnect with the other pillars of the UN operational system such as the rule of law, human rights, and humanitarian relief, but above all with the political and security pillar. Although some UN agencies such as the UN Development Programme (UNDP) have made solving conflicts a central objective,[30] the overall UN development system tends to see development as a separate agenda and shies away from submitting to Security Council political mandates. UN development activities follow traditional approaches of government-centered development assistance, and isolated project-by-project approaches are often driven and inspired by donor demands rather than the local needs of post-conflict peacebuilding.

Development assistance requirements in fragile post-conflict countries are often huge and complex. Largely because of its internal problems, the UN development system does not play a leading role in major peacebuilding operations. Following the Bonn Peace Agreement for Afghanistan in 2001, for instance, member states decided to make individual countries responsible for different aspects of post-conflict reconstruction. And in Iraq following the US-led invasion, foreign troops took the lead in launching reconstruction and recovery efforts. In November 2013, the UN secretary-general and World Bank president announced a joint initiative for Mali's recovery and for the Great Lakes region. However, in the emphasis on the interconnectedness of peace and development, the UN development system appeared largely sidelined—in fact, this initiative was later "camouflaged" by developing yet another "strategic framework" for United Nations–World Bank collaboration.

Among other things, the World Bank has made considerable inroads into the UN's core business of international peace and security. For example, in Sierra Leone the World Bank was in charge of demobilization, disarmament, and reintegration. Although the recoveries of Afghanistan and Iraq were anything but successful, the decisions to sidestep the UN development system must, nonetheless, be understood as votes of no-confidence. Largely because of its fragmentation, the

UN development system is today unable to lead, plan, or implement comprehensive national reconstruction and recovery strategies in fragile conflict-ridden countries. This does not necessarily imply that its projects and programs are unsuccessful, but that UN development activities remained project-oriented and piecemeal.

However, assisting fragile, conflict-ridden countries will remain the foremost challenge for the future United Nations. The UN development system must therefore make greater efforts to adapt to the special requirements of peacebuilding operations and accept working under a Security Council political mandate. More specifically, under peacebuilding operations in post-conflict situations, the UN development system should:

- Accept and support the *single political leadership principle* for all peacebuilding missions under a special representative or executive representative of the secretary-general (SRSG or ERSG) and abandon its present insistence on a parallel development track under a deputy SRSG or resident coordinator.
- Support a *single peacebuilding strategy* in which development aspects are integrated with political, security, human rights, rule of law, and humanitarian aspects.
- Ensure that the various components of a peacebuilding mission come together behind a *single message approach* and support joint outreach programs.
- Bring development activities *in line with the political work* of the UN. Institution- and capacity-building programs should make greater contributions to forming a more democratic and inclusive society; programs directed at public services such health, education, and vocational training should incorporate aspects of national reconciliation, of greater national inclusiveness, of reducing inter-communal tensions, and of catering for war-affected populations.
- Give greater focus on *distinctive peacebuilding programs* responding to post-conflict needs and build its in-house capabilities to design and support such programs. This could include ones to turn a war economy into a peace economy; to support national truth and reconciliation commissions; to sustain civil society organizations; to support all-inclusive constitution-writing processes; to facilitate the return of internally displaced persons and refugees; to support the social and economic integration of ex-combatants, child soldiers, women and girl slaves, war orphans, invalids, and other war-affected populations; and to assist the re-creation of a national police force and justice system.

- Be *less government-centered* in its programming and learn to work closer with other national stakeholders, including political parties, opposition groups, trade unions, civic associations, traditional and religious leaders, women and youth groups, and the media.
- Develop measures to *ensure greater national ownership*, especially for post-conflict situations in which national sovereignty is limited and government institutions are not (yet) fully functioning.
- Make greater efforts to develop a *coherent and integrated programs approach* that responds to the complexity of post-conflict situations and that allows various UN agencies to work together within the same effort.

Because the UN development system has been working in post-conflict countries for several years, many of the suggested program adjustments are in one way or another being implemented. However, such efforts remain ad hoc and are not codified. There is a role for the Peacebuilding Commission in facilitating the deployment of the UN development system as an integral part of UN operations in conflict-ridden countries.

Conclusion

The world continues to be beset by internal violence, civil wars, and failing states. Member states undoubtedly will make renewed demands on the United Nations to mount effective peacebuilding missions. And if Syria is an indication of the future, peacebuilding missions may become even more complex and difficult. The UN system faces the stark challenge that its fragmented response mechanisms are out of sync with the multidimensional approach required for successful peace-building. Substantial reforms of the UN system to improve its operational effectiveness and efficiency through greater coherence have previously failed because of a lack of political will among member states and often strong resistance within the UN departments and organizations that saw their particular interests threatened. An illustration of how the system can be made to work is found in Box 9.1.

Box 9.1   Peacebuilding in Sierra Leone: a success that did not stick

The United Nations Integrated Peacebuilding Office in Sierra Leone (UNIPSIL) was established in October 2008 as a purely civilian, Department of Political Affairs–led successor mission to two types of UN peacekeeping missions: from 1999 to 2005, the UN Assistance Mission in Sierra Leone (UNAMSIL)—a full-fledged peacekeeping mission with up to 17,000 peacekeepers; and from 2006 to 2008, a smaller operation. UNIPSIL—a reduced peacekeeping mission with military observers—was something of a special case as it started 10 years after the signing of the Lomé Peace Agreement and six years after the end of all hostilities.

From the outset, UNIPSIL joined the entire UN country team that included the 17 resident UN organizations to form a fully integrated peacebuilding mission. This effort was facilitated because the executive representative of the secretary-general was also the UN resident coordinator, the humanitarian coordinator, the UNDP resident representative, and the designated official for security. By combining these functions in one person, the UN peacebuilding mission in Sierra Leone became one of the rare examples of a "single leadership."

This centralization helped the mission to develop a single peacebuilding strategy, the "Joint Vision for Sierra Leone" in 2008. This joint vision is probably the only example within the United Nations that brought together all of the UN's political, security, development, human rights, rule of law, and humanitarian activities in a single strategy, which allowed a concentrated focus on peacebuilding issues. The first joint vision included only 20 joint programs; the second had only 7 programs. Linked to the joint vision were joint programming and evaluation, joint resource mobilization, joint outreach activities, joint sub-offices and transport facilities, joint administrative and medical services, and shared expert staff.

This integrated peacebuilding mission became an example of how the UN's political and development activities in the field can be successfully combined in a post-conflict country. It represents an example of how the UN development system could help meet the post-2015 challenges, if the prevailing institutional and "cultural" divisions among UN agencies, funds, and programs can be overcome. Integration with the UN country team proved economical for UNIPSIL, costing only 3–4 percent of the previous UN peacekeeping mission, UNAMSIL.

The UN integrated mission in Sierra Leone was based on the following principles:

- *National ownership and inclusiveness* through down-scaling the UN presence, working with local organizations and staff to build local capacity, engaging with political institutions such as the parliament, political parties, and autonomous commissions, and supporting civil society and traditional and religious leaders, as well as the media;

- *Peace and development* as a focus instead of peace and security; peacebuilding concentrated more on improving social indicators in areas such as employment, education, and health;
- *Steady transition* by phasing out peacekeeping while building on its achievements, and phasing in development activities to establish a more standard UN country team of development organizations; and
- *International partnerships* created by coordinating activities with other bilateral and multilateral donors, including the World Bank, the International Monetary Fund, and the African Development Bank. The ERSG and World Bank representative jointly chaired regular donor coordination meetings. Informally, the United Kingdom acted as a lead country partner, having earlier intervened militarily and then strongly advocated UN peacebuilding operations in the Security Council and the Peacebuilding Commission.

To facilitate national ownership, the government needed its own peace and development strategy. In 2008 there were at least 32 separate strategic framework documents or sector development plans coexisting, with few linkages. These planning documents had been prepared by or for one or another UN organization, bilateral donor, or other multilateral donor. The government had five separate planning documents. The UN and World Bank helped the government to prepare a single strategy and by the end of the year, the *Agenda for Change* had been agreed,[31] which was submitted to the PBC in June 2009 and became the only peacebuilding framework for the country. Consequently, donors adjusted their respective development plans in support. The relationship between national and international planning frameworks made single joint annual progress reports possible.

The quick response from the UN Peacebuilding Support Office in providing financing from Peacebuilding Fund was crucial for the success of the integrated peacebuilding approach; it was the glue that helped keep the political and development mandates together. In June 2009, with the help of the Peacebuilding Support Office, the Peacebuilding Commission held a High-level

Special Session on Sierra Leone[32] in New York that was attended by the secretary-general and by most permanent representatives of countries in the PBC. The president and most of his cabinet participated through a video link with Freetown, and Sierra Leone's delegation included members of the opposition and civil society. The message from all sides was in support of a single national strategy, the *Agenda for Change* and a single integrated UN sub-strategy, the Joint Vision.

Sierra Leone provided an example of how, in a post-conflict context, such integration is possible, with benefits to the host country and considerable cost-efficiencies. However, despite the fact that, in a radio interview in 2010, the secretary-general called the UN operation in Sierra Leone "the best and most advanced UN integrated peacebuilding mission,"[33] the experience was not recognized by UN headquarters as a model for future UN peace missions. The core principle of "one UN—one leadership—one strategy—one message" was not sustained. The traditional dichotomy between political/security and development/humanitarian aspects was no longer addressed in other integrated mission planning. No subsequent missions have had a single UN leadership or single UN strategy that incorporated all aspects of UN activities. SRSGs are often political nominees with little or no experience with UN operations, happy to leave humanitarian and development work to others. In fact, new UN peace missions no longer use the term "integrated peacebuilding."

The main reason for the Sierra Leone example being quietly dropped was undoubtedly that it clashed with the separate institutional interests of the UN organizations' headquarters as well as with UN Secretariat departments. The fear may have been that such integration would ultimately raise questions about the fragmentation of decision making in headquarters and could make some parts of the central administration appear redundant. In the words of the former head of the Department of Political Affairs, the integration of the Sierra Leone mission far surpassed any integration that existed in New York, with no one acknowledging ownership of activities in the country. The Peacebuilding Commission also failed to defend the integrated approach, a denial of its mandate. In short, the UN has failed to learn an important lesson and develop a sustainable model of a more effective and integrated approach to its interventions in conflict-prone states.

The need to deploy successfully in fragile, conflict-ridden countries could provide a promising opportunity to reform the UN system, at least in a specific area where it presently matters most—peacebuilding. Instead of trying to reform the entire UN system, reforms aiming at an integrated and coherent UN approach for peacebuilding missions should in principle be easier to implement. Reforms aimed at UN operations in fragile and conflict-ridden countries would be target-oriented and time-bound. They would not require shaking up the whole UN system and would not threaten vested institutional interests within the United Nations. In fact, individual UN organizations could see such reforms as potential win–win solutions and actively support them.

It may also be easier to persuade member states to support reforms that are limited to peacebuilding operations. Failing and conflict-ridden countries are high on the agenda of member states, and it is considered important that peacebuilding missions be successful. Here the Peacebuilding Commission, with its special peacebuilding mandate and its more representational membership, could play a central role for member states in driving the reform agenda. It is an opportunity that the PBC has not yet seized.

Notes

1 This usage deviates from the present use of the term "peacebuilding mission," which the Department of Peacekeeping Operations (DPKO) or the Department of Political Affairs (DPA) calls either "peacekeeping missions" or "special political missions," respectively.
2 The UN Secretary-General's Policy Committee decision of 22 May 2007 stated:

> Peacebuilding involves a range of measures to reduce the risk of lapsing or relapsing into conflict by strengthening national capacities at all levels of conflict management, and lay foundations for sustainable peace and development. Peacebuilding strategies must be coherent and tailored to the specific needs of a country concerned, based on national ownership, and should comprise a carefully prioritized, sequenced and therefore relatively narrow set of activities aimed at achieving the above objectives.

> See the UN Peacebuilding Support Office website, www.un.org/en/peace building/pbso/pbun.shtml

3 See also different definitions collected in Alliance for Peacebuilding, *Peacebuilding 2.0: Mapping the Boundaries of an Expanding Field* (Washington, DC: Alliance for Peacebuilding, 2012).
4 The term "post-conflict" is misleading, for even when the fighting stops the armed conflict will most likely not be over; otherwise a UN peacebuilding mission would not be necessary.

5 The UN Operation in the Congo (ONUC) in the 1960s was the odd mission out; although initially tasked with supervising the withdrawal of foreign troops, it quickly got entangled in local politics and was drawn into using offensive military force. ONUC became a major East–West controversy; had it not been for the end of the Cold War, no such mission would ever have passed the Security Council again.

6 Boutros Boutros-Ghali, *An Agenda for Peace* (New York: UN, 1992).

7 Lotta Themner and Peter Wallenstein, "Armed Conflicts, 1946–2012," *Journal of Peace Research* 50, no. 4 (2013): 509–21.

8 Themner and Wallenstein define armed conflicts as "contested incompatibilities" over control of territory or a government that result in at least 25 battle-related deaths per year, a very low bar for observing armed conflicts.

9 Joshua Goldstein, *Winning the War on War: The Decline of Armed Conflict Worldwide* (New York: Penguin, 2011).

10 These numbers include deaths of fighting forces and civilians caught in an armed conflict, though not deaths resulting from war-related famine and illnesses.

11 Themner and Wallenstein, "Armed Conflicts, 1946–2012."

12 The recent tragedies in the Mediterranean that killed hundreds of illegal migrants have also drawn renewed attention to the problem of fragile states.

13 Fund for Peace, *The Failed States Index 2013*, http://ffp.statesindex.org/rankings-2013-sortable

14 The first post–Cold War peacebuilding mission was Operation Salam in Afghanistan (1989–93) following the withdrawal of Soviet troops from Afghanistan in December 1989. Although this was one of the largest UN missions, it is not reflected in any UN statistics, possibly because it did not "belong" to DPKO or DPA and was simply forgotten.

15 The UN used "traditional" peacekeeping missions in the 1991 Iraq–Kuwait war, the 1993 Ossetia war, the 1994 Chad–Libya conflict, and the 2000 Ethiopia–Eritrea dispute.

16 The UN peacekeeping mission that helped end the civil war in Sierra Leone in which about 75,000 people lost their lives required 17,500 peacekeepers, whereas UNIIMOG that helped end the Iran–Iraq war in which over half a million people lost their lives had only about 400 UN military observers; the cost of the UN missions to Sierra Leone may have been eight to nine times that of the Iran–Iraq mission.

17 Ejeviome Eloho Otobo, "A United Nations Architecture to Build Peace in Post-Conflict Situations," *Development Outreach* 11, no. 2 (2009): 46–49.

18 How important the veto rights were became apparent when in 1950 the Soviet Union's temporary withdrawal from the Security Council allowed the remaining four permanent members to approve military action against North Korea's invasion of South Korea.

19 In 1970 the General Assembly adopted a resolution giving itself the right to arbitrate in local conflicts if the Security Council proved unable to act.

20 Libya was the first country to obtain independence under a General Assembly resolution in 1952. The resolution made Libya an independent kingdom with the leader of the Islamic Sanusi order becoming its first (and last) king.

21 The difference between the numbers of conflict areas and UN peace missions results from the fact that some conflict areas had two or more successive missions.

22 See lists of peacekeeping and special political missions published on the DPKO (www.un.org/en/peacekeeping/operations/) and DPA (www.un.org/wcm/content/site/undpa/main/about/field_operations) websites.
23 One could even argue that the number of missions in intra-state conflicts is larger, as ex-Yugoslavia, Ethiopia–Eritrea, and the Prevlaka peninsular disputes had their origin in such conflicts.
24 Humanitarian reasons, including the protection of civilians, are often mentioned as further justifications for UN intervention.
25 "Freedom in the World 2013: Democratic Breakthroughs in the Balance," Freedom House, January 2013. www.freedomhouse.org/report/freedom-world/freedom-world-2013
26 "Democracy Index 2012: Democracy at a Standstill," Economist Intelligence Unit, 14 March 2013. https://www.eiu.com/public/topical_report.aspx?campaignid=democracyindex12
27 "Report of the UN Panel on United Nations Peace Operations," UN document A/55/305, 21 August 2000.
28 High-level Panel of Eminent Persons on the Post-2015 Development Agenda, *A New Global Partnership: Eradicate Poverty and Transform Economies through Sustainable Development* (New York: UN, 2013).
29 FUNDS, a project of the Ralph Bunche Institute, lists 31 UN agencies, programs, and funds with separate field development efforts in post-conflict countries, each with their own governing bodies, field offices, representatives, operational approaches, reporting lines, and management structures.
30 In 2000, the UNDP created its Bureau for Crisis Prevention and Recovery; it is therefore not surprising that the UNDP has developed into a major partner in UN peacebuilding operations.
31 The World Bank accepted the *Agenda for Change* as its standard poverty reduction strategy.
32 See "Outcome of the Peacebuilding Commission High-level Special Session on Sierra Leone," UN document PBC/3/SLE/6, 12 June 2009.
33 Kelvin Lewis, "Sierra Leone a Success Story, says Ban Ki-moon in Freetown," Radio France International, 16 June 2010, www.english.rfi.fr/africa/20100616-ban-ki-moon-salutes-sierra-leone-its-democracy

Part IV

Toward a reformed UN development system

10 The UN and the post-2015 Development Agenda

David Hulme and Rorden Wilkinson

Determining what the shape and content of the post-2015 Development Agenda (post-2015 DA) will be once the Millennium Development Goals (MDGs) have expired has generated a great deal of analytical energy. Some has been created by governmental processes; much more has been produced by an array of civil society actors keen to have their say on (and in) the shape of the post-MDG development regime. At the core of the post-2015 debate has been an official process. This involved a 28-member high-level panel (HLP) appointed by the UN secretary-general and chaired by Indonesia's President Bambang Yudhoyano, Liberia's President Ellen Sirleaf, and UK Prime Minister David Cameron. With input from government actors, UN agencies, and civil society, the HLP produced its report, including 12 "illustrative goals" for the post-2015 Development Agenda, in May 2013. Adding to the complexity of debate and the multitude of actors are two other related complications resulting from two UN processes—an open working group of 30 member states is still producing a set of sustainable development goals (SDGs), and a UN System Task Force (led by the UN Department of Economic and Social Affairs, DESA) has produced a technical report and other documents but not yet an agreed and coherent agenda or conversation.[1] The result has been a veritable storm of activity.

Yet for all the energy generated, the activities, deliberations, and final report of the UN high-level panel suggest that the post-2015 DA will not be dramatically different from its predecessor.[2] While the HLP identifies human rights and inequality as essential issues, the illustrative goals give little concrete attention to them. Goal 10, "Good governance and effective institutions," is more ambitious than the MDGs, but there is considerable doubt about what would be acceptable to the UN's membership in 2015.

This does not bode well for a thorough reform of the United Nations development system (UNDS). Perhaps we should not be surprised because that kind of *volte face* would signal a dramatic change in the UNDS and would be unprecedented, conceptually counter intuitive, and anatomically improbable. What we should take away from the post-2015 debate is that it has largely unfolded as business-as-usual for UN organizations, national governments, and civil society organizations; we are likely to see only incremental developments in both the post-2015 DA and operational activities of the UNDS.

Why? Historically, each UN development regime has been the product of incremental evolution. Changes have tended to be within—and indeed, have almost always reinforced—existing ways of operating, however inadequate, rather than offering clear departures from what preceded in order to improve understanding or goal-setting or delivery. This does not mean that there has been nothing to celebrate in the development of the UNDS. Quite the contrary. It is simply that, as Margaret Joan Anstee reminds us, both the development system and "the MDGs are not an innovation but a continuation of what has gone before."[3] There is no reason to suppose that alterations in the post-2015 regime or the supporting development apparatus will break this pattern.

There is little to suggest, in short, any fundamental departure from existing ways of operating. While we know that radical transformations in the evolution of global institutions are possible, they are rare. In the absence of a fundamental alteration in global power relations or crises out of which new institutional forms are forged, most institutions tend toward piecemeal adjustments that reinforce existing modes of behavior and produce strikingly similar outcomes.[4] As Robert Cox puts it, "institutions reflect the power relations prevailing at their point of origin and tend ... to encourage collective images [by which he means behavior consistent with] ... these power relations."[5]

The UNDS's structure, moreover, is so diffuse and atomized that its capacity to generate (as well as carry through) a transformed—and, we might add, transformative—development agenda and establish a new system is severely curtailed. As Stephen Browne and Thomas G. Weiss argue, the UNDS is characterized more by its diffusion than its coherence:

> The so-called system that engages in development activities in developing and transition-economy countries includes more than 30 organizations (variously called funds, programmes, offices, and agencies). There is also an equivalent number of supportive functional commissions and research and training organizations.[6]

Inevitably, the UNDS that will result from the post-2015 deliberations is likely to be a continuation of business-as-usual irrespective of the shifts in the interests and influence of some key players in world politics. This chapter aims to explain why this is the case. We begin with an examination of the political economy of the post-2015 DA, offering a short analytical history of the immediate run-up to the formulation and implementation of the MDGs in order to contextualize the argument that follows. We then explore what has been "achieved" by the MDGs to explain why the "progress" that has been achieved under their guise is likely to generate incremental adjustment rather than wholesale reform. We then analyze the continuities and changes in the processes shaping the "new" goals and contrast them with the MDG processes. Here we focus on the changed global context; the ideas that are competing to provide a different conceptual framework for the "new" goals; the actors and institutions leading the process; and the way the changed material capabilities of regions, and of countries, is redefining processes. The next section reviews the prospects for the post-2015 DA. We argue that any potential "deal" in 2015 might appear to be quite different from the MDGs, but the post-2015 DA will not be transformative in terms of strengthening the UN and its agencies, nor will it have much leverage over the broad array of global institutions, national governments, or social norms.

The MDGs—processes of formulation and implementation

The origins of the MDGs lie, in part, in a rolling series of UN summits and conferences from the 1990s that simultaneously sought to capture the momentum of the immediate post–Cold War era and to dilute the neoliberal orthodoxy espoused by the Bretton Woods institutions.[7] The purpose was, as Ingvar Carlsson and Shridath Ramphal put it, to move beyond "the constraints of the cold war that so cramped the potential of an evolving global system ... seized of the risk of unsustainable human impacts on nature [and] mindful of the global implications of human deprivation."[8] These summits and conferences were classic UN-type processes with member states formulating lengthy and often somewhat incoherent "declarations" through combinations of long-winded and last-minute diplomatic negotiations and compromises.[9]

The origins of the MDGs can also be found in the attempts in the mid-1990s by the Organisation for Economic Co-operation and Development's (OECD) Development Assistance Committee (DAC) to rekindle political and public interest in foreign aid. As part of this activity, DAC produced a list of six International Development Goals (IDGs),[10] which were selected from the declarations of UN summits and conferences and repackaged in a results-based management (RBM) framework.[11] The selection implicitly focused upon OECD members' priorities; and while some donors shifted to IDG frameworks for programming aid, most developing countries ignored them.

The United Nations came back to center stage in the goal-setting process in 1998, as Kofi Annan prepared for the Millennium Assembly. The world body sought to develop an agenda that would both advance its development mandate and support Annan's efforts to reform the UN system. The Millennium Declaration reaffirmed the UN's principles, rallied support for all the organization's purposes (peace, development, environmental protection, human rights, and others) and redefined "development" as "development and poverty eradication." For a time, it looked as though the world might end up with two sets of development goals—a UN set and the OECD's IDGs. However, a meeting of the UN, OECD, World Bank, and International Monetary Fund (IMF) in Washington, DC, in March 2001 managed to reach a compromise. The content and format of the IDGs was made the basis for the MDGs with the addition of Goal 7 (environmental sustainability) and Goal 8 (a global partnership for development). This final goal was pushed by developing countries, which demanded that the goals specified "what" developed countries would contribute to the development process. While the rich countries agreed under pressure to include Goal 8, they made sure that the text with the targets for their "commitments" was different from that of the other goals because the September 2001 General Assembly only approved the previous seven with specific targets for developing countries. As a result, such countries as India and the United States regularly pointed out that they had agreed to the Millennium Declaration but not the MDGs.

The confused implementation of the MDGs followed. The UN set up the Millennium Project and the Millennium Campaign to advance the MDGs, but real power remained with the World Bank and IMF. These institutions controlled the national-level process of preparing country-specific Poverty Reduction Strategy Papers (PRSPs) and negotiating Medium Term Expenditure Frameworks (MTEFs) that determine levels of public expenditure in many developing countries. Whatever the ideals behind the MDGs, development in aid-dependent countries remained focused on planning for foreign aid (rather than domestic resource mobilization), while "national ownership" of the process and content of the PRSPs grew only slowly.

So what have the MDGs achieved?

It is very difficult to assess what the MDGs have contributed to development with any precision.[12] There is no counterfactual—"what would have happened if the MDGs had not been agreed?" Indeed, most MDG goal achievement is not directly related to the MDGs as things had been getting better for much of humanity with increasing speed over the late twentieth century. And these underlying processes continued into the 2000s—to which data on economic growth and human development, growth and national governance, and reduced levels of violent conflict and physical violence testify.[13]

That said, a number of "additional" contributions can be linked to the MDGs and related processes (such as the PRSPs and debt forgiveness). There is evidence that the MDGs helped stop (or at least stall for a while) the decline in foreign aid from OECD members.[14] Within aid programs, and some national budgets in developing countries, allocations for poverty reduction and human development increased. Improvements have also been reported in the availability and quality of poverty data and in aid coordination.

At times the MDGs also appear to have provided a "hook" leading to greater media coverage of the issues of global poverty and international development—events that are normally newsworthy only when human suffering and catastrophes reach harrowing levels. This coverage may have had an impact on public awareness in some OECD countries, such as the United Kingdom, but it had minimal impact in terms of challenging or changing international social norms around poverty alleviation.[15]

That said, it is certainly the case that the MDGs have not been transformative in terms of catalyzing a global anti-poverty movement,[16] nor in terms of securing the Goal 8 commitment to a global partnership for development. Goal 8 was a grand promise, but the record of achievement is unimpressive. There was a little movement forward in the World Trade Organization's Doha round, which had been deadlocked since July 2006 (though formally only from July 2008). The provisions of the "successful" December 2013 Bali package were meager, with the "development" content with benefits for developing countries eliminated from the negotiations. Meanwhile, global climate change negotiations have been meandering for some time, and the World Bank and IMF's governance reformed marginally.[17]

More controversially, the case could be made that the MDGs are the world's biggest lie. Under pressure at the turn of the millennium, the globe's richest countries and most powerful corporations managed to explain to the world how the new millennium would be better for developing countries than the previous one. But then, "business as usual" returned. Arguably, global capitalism (and its winners) gained a wider acceptance and ultimately legitimacy for a market-based orientation at the lowest possible price. Critics argued that the MDGs were regressive when compared to the UN Declaration of Human Rights of 1948, and that the MDGs failed to identify who was responsible for target achievement—national governments or multilateral agencies or the General Assembly.

The emerging Post-2015 Development Agenda

The intergovernmental efforts to address "what comes after the MDGs" are behind schedule, at least in part because the UN Secretariat and secretary-general explicitly blocked debate about the shape of the post-2015 DA until 2011. The agenda of the MDGs+10 UN Summit in 2010 was circumscribed so that it focused only on the MDGs. The rationale was that any discussion of what followed would draw attention away from the pressing need to improve finance for, and the implementation of, the MDGs. In 2011 this UN proscription was relaxed, and in 2012 debate about the post-2015 Development Agenda was unleashed. Yet, while the post-2015 DA has become a major debate in international development and particularly foreign aid circles, it is in no sense a "big" issue outside of these limited groups.

There are numerous reasons, but two are especially noteworthy. First, the contemporary historical moment is quite different from 2000–2001. The world is no longer unipolar—though what multipolarity means for international goal-setting is unclear. The pressure that a millennium event put on world leaders to show up in New York and reach an agreement does not exist. Equally, the turn toward multilateralism by the United States after the 9/11 terrorist attacks has faded, and international social agreements have reverted to their lowly place in the pecking order of global summitry. Moreover, austerity measures put in place in the wake of the 2008 financial crisis have ensured that foreign aid budgets have been reduced while the migration of poor people to industrial countries is being presented as a domestic issue in them rather than as a way of meeting economic and social goals in developing countries. In the United States, for instance, it seems unlikely that the Obama administration would risk showing too much interest in the welfare of non-citizens who are not a threat to national security (especially when the administration is being challenged domestically for focusing on the welfare of poor/low-income US citizens).

Second, the changing material capabilities of many developing countries in the early twenty-first century have also had an impact on post-2015 DA processes. Following the Rio+20 conference, Latin American countries (and particularly Brazil) have focused on leading negotiations for a set of sustainable development goals (SDGs) that include poverty eradication—rather than a set of poverty eradication goals that include sustainability. The leaders of these countries see the SDGs as more relevant to their needs and interests, especially as recent growth means that national politics are increasingly about middle-class voters and poverty is viewed as a residual rather than a structural problem. Relatedly, African countries that have experienced growth, and often progress in important dimensions of human development,[18] are no longer so aid dependent and are adopting a more assertive stance in post-2015 DA negotiations. Indeed, African finance ministers, supported by the African Union (AU), have been pushing a growth agenda as the frame for the post-2015 DA—an about-face in policy terms from the MDG period.

Moreover, pressures from the "developing world"[19] revealed themselves in the February 2013 declaration that came out of the second HLP meeting in Monrovia that highlighted the need for the post-2015 DA to incorporate the SDGs and identified "structural transformation" as central to any future goals. However, how the new "big" powers will shape the post-2015 DA remains unclear. The Indian media have lambasted their government for not recognizing that the post-2015 DA is a relatively easy and low-cost way for India to develop a soft-power strategy. No one seems sure about how China will engage.

Changed circumstances are not the only feature of the post-2015 deliberations that are different from those of the MDGs. Notable changes have occurred in the foundational ideas that are being contested. The MDG debate resulted in the adoption of a multidimensional understanding of poverty. For many progressive think-tanks and policy advocates, the main focus of the post-2015 debate has been on how to incorporate inequality into the post-2015 DA. UN organizational heads and their secretariats, academics, and think-tanks have all argued for tackling the "causes" of poverty by seeking reduced national and international inequality.[20] However, this rhetorical argument does not have widespread actual support in wealthy countries. The case for reducing inequality is well made, but it is unlikely that the political economy of the contemporary era will permit such a move. The power of US interests (which would see economic inequality reduction as potentially "pulling down" US incomes and wealth) and the private sector (concerned that this would mean higher personal and corporate taxes and perhaps even "global taxes") seem likely to block any movement to reduce the huge gap between the global "haves" and "have-nots."

Another idea that has been advancing is that economic growth should be at the heart of the post-2015 DA. The MDGs barely touched growth.[21] Indeed, it could be argued that growth was kept off the MDG agenda so that it remained under the guidance of the World Bank and IMF and was not part of any UN General Assembly–based process. This time around African leaders have argued that growth has to be central to development goals and strategies. In the post-2015 DA growth is often conceptualized as "structural transformation,"[22] and the HLP Monrovia Declaration argued structural transformation to be essential. The HLP's final report also identified growth and employment targets in Goal 8 (create jobs, sustainable livelihoods, and equitable growth) of its "illustrative goals."

Perspectives on whether the inclusion of growth in a post-2015 DA is progressive or regressive vary. The positive case says that this would permit economic, social, and environmental policies to be integrated and would reduce the influence of aid donors on development strategies. The negative case claims that once growth is on the agenda it will crowd out social and environmental goals and might even reverse the gains made by the human development agenda in recent years.

Latin American countries have powerfully advocated a greater focus on the environment and climate change so that the idea of "sustainable development" originally fleshed out in the late 1980s seems certain to be a component of any post-2015 DA. Indeed, an indicative set of SDGs has now been published and will be the major focus of the General Assembly's 2014 69th session. While this idea has been associated with Latin American countries, it can be seen as a continuation of the Brundtland Commission's work under UN auspices decades earlier.[23]

Finally on ideas, human rights, governance, democracy, and accountability/transparency are commonly identified as crucial components of any post-2015 DA. The final HLP report included an illustrative Goal 10 to "Ensure good governance and effective institutions." Whether this goal can be defined in a way that does not pose a challenge to emerging powers (which could view it as shorthand for adopting Western political institutions) remains to be seen.[24] If the targets focus on state capacity and technical transparency, they might be acceptable. By contrast, if they focus on democracy and human rights, they are likely to become contextual "principles"—lauded in the preambles of post-2015 DA documents but not turned into specific targets or indicators. Moreover, it is worth noting in this context the naïve belief formerly peddled by rich world leaders that democratization in all contexts is essential to foster economic and social development has been undermined by events in Egypt and elsewhere after the "Arab Spring."

Certain institutions (understood as authoritative organizations) shaped the emergence of the MDGs—UNICEF, the UN secretary-general and

Secretariat, UNDP's Human Development Report Office, the OECD, the Group of 77, the Holy See, and many others. In contemporary debates, the commitment—or lack thereof—of such institutions will be an important determinant of outcomes. The UN secretary-general and Secretariat remain at the center of the official processes, but many doubt whether the present secretary-general has the same passion for "development" as Kofi Annan. The UNDP, which played an important role in the millennium processes through promoting the idea of human development and through the powerful influence of its leader (Mark Malloch-Brown), seems less influential now. DESA, which might be expected to be a leading player, is coordinating the UN System Task Force but is seen by many as remaining on the intellectual sidelines—as it did 15 years ago. The Group of 20 (G20) placed the post-2015 DA before its 2013 Summit, but it seems less committed than was the Group of 7/8 in the late 1990s.[25] The United Kingdom is seeking to continue its self-selected role as global cheerleader for the rich world to prioritize tackling global poverty. In contrast, the United States (with its economic and political power) remains quietly on the sidelines as it did in the 1990s. The OECD is active but also seems to appreciate that this time around foreign aid cannot be a core issue. Civil society activity is most obvious in the global North (such as in the Beyond 2015 Network), which has become a concern for such Southern think-tanks as the Southern Voices Initiative coordinated by the Dhaka-based Centre for Policy Dialogue.[26] This time around NGO and civil society inputs are professional and polished compared to the passionate, messy, and unscripted processes of the summits of the 1990s. However, there are also "new" actors. The AU is much more active and may be orchestrating a relatively coherent African voice into the post-2015 DA.

The UN system and the post-2015 Development Agenda

In many ways, the specifics of a post-2015 outcome matter little. Together they are unlikely to constitute a game changer in terms of the differences that they make to everyday lives or to drive a fundamental transformation of the UNDS. Rather, the point of exercises such as these is to put in place a statement of how development actors should interpret prevailing global economic orthodoxy without actually threatening its core tenets. It is nonetheless important to determine more precisely what the relationship between the UN system and the post-2015 DA will be. We do this by focusing on two aspects: first, the role of the system itself in shaping the post-2015 DA—in leading ideational and norm-setting processes; and, second, in the way the post-2015 DA may have an impact upon the UN system—that is, whether it will foster performance-enhancing reform or simply allow the UNDS to continue to drift.

Formally, the United Nations is at the center of the post-2015 DA because of its unique claim to global legitimacy. Any new deal will be agreed or not at the General Assembly in 2015, or in later years if negotiations drag on. In practice, the UN system appears to have become more of a venue for debating the post-2015 DA than a lead contributor to the debates (as it was in the 1990s). This partly reflects the style of senior management—coordinating rather than leading— and partly the failure of any part of the system to spearhead the processes or the ideational contests (as did UNICEF and later the UNDP in the 1990s). DESA, which might have been expected to have played a leading role in the 1990s and at present (as it leads UN Statistics), lacks the influence and capacity to shape international debates. It has proven unable to convert its critical stance on neoliberal growth into a coherent agenda or strategy for development—hardly surprising in light of its limited financial resources and feeble human resources.

The post-2015 DA will be a political compromise, as were the MDGs. But the underpinning processes—national elites arguing for national self-interest; semantics to get around value differences; compromises that allow all parties to show that they got their way; big players not engaging so others have to judge how to move toward the positions of the powerful—certainly will not be challenged by the UN system promoting an agenda. The leaders of the post-2015 DA will likely be the IMF and World Bank rather than core UN bodies. For example, Homi Kharras (ex-World Bank) was the lead author on the final HLP report in May 2013; and the Bank's Public Sector Management Group had a clear proposal for HLP Goal 10 (governance) targets and indicators by July 2013, while DESA and the UNDP were still at an early consultation stage.

While growth (Goal 8 of the HLP report) looks like it will be prominent in the post-2015 DA, the UN system has done relatively little to provide clear guidance on how growth can create employment and raise productivity in informal as well as formal labor markets. The leading ideas come from economists at the World Bank or economists at universities in the United States who work closely with the Bank.

So if the UN system's contributions to shaping the post-2015 DA are relatively limited, can the same be said of the impact that the post-2015 DA is likely to have on UN operations and performance? The answer depends not so much on the goals included in the post-2015 DA, but much more on the modalities for implementation. The "deal" agreed by the UN and international financial institutions (IFIs) for the MDGs was basically that the UN could have the international agenda while the IFIs could retain control of what happened at the country level through PRSPs (later PRSs) and MTEFs. Although the Millennium Project sought to challenge this division of labor—through MDG-based national development strategies—this challenge only functioned in a limited number of small, aid dependent countries such as Mongolia. As a result, the MDGs contributed little to driving forward enhanced program design or implementation by UN organizations. After 2015 the strengthening of UN activity at the national level seems much more likely to be a function of UN reform initiatives, such as Delivering as One, than of the content of any post-2015 agenda.

Conclusion

While the UN system had a significant input into the MDGs through its summits and conferences and the championing of the human development agenda and multidimensional understandings of poverty, UN contributions to the post-2015 DA are more modest. In effect, the United Nations has become the venue for debating the post-2015 DA but is much less engaged in shaping the content of any agreement. This is partly because of the prevalence of emerging powers now and partly because of UN staff's limited capacity to promote ideas or take on leadership roles.[27] The UN's major role may be getting an agreement through diplomacy, negotiation, and compromise rather than promoting any radically new way of tackling development problems. The tactic is likely to be deploying "message entrepreneurs," who can achieve a final deal at the General Assembly and with the agreement of key UN organizations, rather than norm entrepreneurs striving to dramatically change the ways in which social problems are framed.[28] The ideas about "structural transformation" that have most recently shaped the work of the HLP come from economists at the World Bank or at elite universities in New England. Whether such an approach actually aligns the goals of economic growth, human development, and sustainability, or simply gives economic liberalization a human face, is a moot point.

Although civil society groups continue to present the post-2015 DA as potentially "transformative," the actual development agenda is unlikely to mobilize support (financial, political, or technocratic) that would dramatically redefine global goals and action plans. The forces shaping the post-2015 DA look as though they may permit it to be progressive (by including the productive sector as well as social policies) but not transformative (not reformed global governance, progressive agreements on trade and climate change, or targets for reducing inequality). As with the MDGs, the focus will be on *what* the goals are, but not on *how* they can be achieved. Specifying strategy is still too contentious for UN member states with their varying views on the trade-offs between efficiency and equity and on whether economic liberalization or more heterodox policies should be pursued. The result is that there is likely to be little transformative about the post-2015 DA. Step changes will not be forthcoming, either in the way the development system operates or its constitution. Thus, we need to look elsewhere for drivers for change.

The consequences for the UN development system are that the post-2015 DA is likely to reinforce the tendencies that have become evident over the course of the MDG era. The UNDS will likely continue to be a venue for coordinating debate and not an intellectual player in itself as it was often in the past. The post-2015 DA will do nothing to address the atomization of the UNDS, nor will it generate a substantively different transformative approach to poverty and its alleviation that moves beyond what we currently have. Our knowledge of the system's history and current structure should have prepared us to expect little else. In the absence of a visionary program of action—and a concomitant implementation plan—we are likely to see the incremental evolution of poverty eradication initiatives rather than a concerted global effort to end poverty.

Notes

1 DESA, *Realising the Future We Want for All* (New York: UN, 2012).
2 HLP, *A New Global Partnership: Eradicate Poverty and Transform Economies through Sustainable Development: The Report of the High-Level Panel of Eminent Persons on the Post-2015 Development Agenda* (New York: UN, 2013).
3 Margaret Joan Anstee, "Millennium Development Goals: Milestones on a Long Road," in *The Millennium Development Goals and Beyond: Global Development after 2015*, ed. Rorden Wilkinson and David Hulme (London: Routledge, 2012), 20.
4 Rorden Wilkinson, *The WTO: Crisis and the Governance of Global Trade* (London: Routledge, 2006), 14–18.
5 Robert Cox, *Approaches to World Order* (Cambridge: Cambridge University Press, 1996), 99.
6 Stephen Browne and Thomas G. Weiss, *Making Change Happen: Enhancing the UN's Contribution to Development* (New York: World Federation of United Nations Associations, 2012), 4.
7 See David Hulme, *Global Poverty* (London: Routledge, 2010), and "Global Poverty Reduction and the Millennium Development Goals: A Short History

of the World's Biggest Promise," Brooks World Poverty Institute Working Paper 100, University of Manchester, 2008.

8 Ingvar Carlsson and Shridath Ramphal, "Co-Chairmen's Foreword," in the Commission on Global Governance, *Our Global Neighbourhood* (New York: Oxford University Press, 1995), xx.

9 Michael G. Schechter, *United Nations Global Conferences* (London: Routledge, 2005), 107–53.

10 OECD, *Shaping the 21st Century: The Contribution of Development Cooperation* (Paris: OECD, 1996).

11 In the 1990s RBM was popular in many OECD countries as a way of getting the public sector "to work." This also appealed to DAC as RBM gives the funding agency a powerful position over implementers (i.e., developing countries).

12 See Rorden Wilkinson and David Hulme, eds., *The Millennium Development Goals and Beyond: Global Development after 2015* (London: Routledge, 2012).

13 Charles Kenny, *Getting Better: Why Global Development Is Succeeding— And How We Can Improve the World Even More* (New York: Basic Books, 2011); Daron Acemoglu and James Robinson, *Why Nations Fail: The Origins of Power, Prosperity and Poverty* (London: Profile, 2012); and Steven Pinker, *The Better Angels of Our Nature: Why Violence Has Declined* (London: Penguin, 2011).

14 Hulme, *Global Poverty*.

15 Sakiko Fukuda-Parr and David Hulme, "International Norm Dynamics and the 'End of Poverty': Understanding the Millennium Development Goals," *Global Governance* 17, no. 1 (2011): 17–36.

16 The Make Poverty History Campaign was the apogee of MDG social action, but it was really only visible in the United Kingdom. The Global Call to Action Against Poverty (GCAP) has an impressive network of partners and countries but has not managed to mobilize civil society much beyond "stand up" events. See Clive Gabay, *Civil Society and Global Poverty: Hegemony, Inclusivity, Legitimacy* (London: Routledge, 2012).

17 James Scott and Rorden Wilkinson, "What Happened to Doha in Geneva? Re-engineering the WTO's Image While Missing Key Opportunities," *European Journal of Development Research* 22, no. 2 (2010): 141–53; Rorden Wilkinson, *What's Wrong with the WTO and How to Fix It* (Cambridge: Polity, 2014); Matthew J. Hoffmann, "Climate Change," in *International Organization and Global Governance*, ed. Thomas G. Weiss and Rorden Wilkinson (London: Routledge, 2014); BRICS Information Centre, "Fourth BRICS Summit: Delhi Declaration," 29 March 2012, www.brics.utoronto. ca/docs/120329-delhi-declaration.html; Robert H. Wade, "Emerging World Order? From Multipolarity to Multilateralism in the G20, the World Bank and the IMF," *Politics and Society* 39, no. 3 (2011): 347–78.

18 Most obviously in the amazing reductions in child mortality that have occurred in many countries over the last decade.

19 The rise of the emerging economies makes the separation of countries into "developed" and "developing" categories increasingly anachronistic.

20 Dolf te Lintelo, *Inequality and Social Justice Roundtable Consultation* (Brighton, UK: Institute of Development Studies, 2011); Naila Kabeer, *Can the MDGs Provide a Pathway to Social Justice? The Challenge of*

Intersecting Inequalities (Brighton, UK: Institute of Development Studies, 2011); UN Research Institute for Social Development (UNRISD), *Combating Poverty and Inequality*, Beyond 2015 Brief no.1 (Geneva: UNRISD, 2011).

21 One could argue that the dollar-a-day income target incorporates growth but that goal can also be achieved by redistribution (and especially through social protection policies).

22 Ricardo Hausmann, César A. Hidalgo, Sebastián Bustos, Michele Coscia, Sarah Chung, Juan Jimenez, Alexander Simoes, and Muhammed A. Yıldırım, *The Atlas of Economic Complexity: Mapping Pathways to Prosperity* (Cambridge, Mass.: Harvard University Center for International Development, 2011).

23 World Commission on Environment and Development, *Our Common Future* (Oxford: Oxford University Press, 1987).

24 The authors' involvement in these processes has revealed the considerable tensions between UN agencies involved in goal-setting, with DESA, the UNDP, and the World Bank having competing ideas about what the "governance" targets and indicators should be.

25 The G7/8 regularly had debt forgiveness and "Africa" high up on its agendas in the late 1990s.

26 Initiatives such as PARTICIPATE, involving 25 Southern NGOs, have Northern origins—it is financed by the UK Department for International Development and managed out of the Institute of Development Studies, Sussex (see www.participate2015.org).

27 The high-profile heads of UN organizations in the 1990s (such as Jim Grant at UNICEF, Nafis Sadik at the UN Population Fund, and Mahbubul Haq at the Human Development Report Office) took on major roles as norm entrepreneurs and effectively used their agencies as organizational platforms for international social norm promotion. The heads of these agencies in the 2010s are more focused on internal management and have more modest profiles. See the publications of the UN Intellectual History Project, especially Richard Jolly, Louis Emmerij, and Thomas G. Weiss, *UN Ideas That Changed the World* (Bloomington: Indiana University Press, 2009).

28 See Fukuda-Parr and Hulme, "International Norm Dynamics." A possible exception to this might be the adoption of Sabina Alkire's multidimensional poverty index by the UNDP's *Human Development Report*. If this were to be widely used it would reinforce the human development element of global goals and reshape the understanding of the geography of poverty.

11 "We the peoples" in the UN development system

Roberto Bissio

This chapter focuses mainly on the participation of civil society actors in UN deliberative processes concerning development issues. It summarizes the evolution of the relation between the world organization and nongovernmental actors, which is rooted in the UN Charter itself. Over seven decades, the UN has established working relations with non-profits and stimulated them to play diverse roles that contribute to the functioning of the world body and the fulfillment of its mandate. Since the turn of the century, private for-profit actors (mainly large corporations) have been encouraged to associate with the UN in a variety of ways. Those "partnerships," largely unaccountable and still not properly evaluated, risk displacing and jeopardizing the relationships with voluntary organizations at a moment when the world body seeks public support to embark on a new development agenda.

From NGOs to civil society

The opening words of the UN Charter are "We the peoples of the United Nations." They are quoted every time there is a discussion about how ordinary citizens can directly relate to the UN—not just through their member governments, which in turn derive their legitimacy from the claim of representing their peoples. Charter Article 71 encourages the Economic and Social Council (ECOSOC) to "make suitable arrangements for consulting with non-governmental organizations [NGOs]," and the Department of Public Information (DPI), created in 1946, has been inviting NGOs to annual conferences since then.

Over the past few decades, NGO participation in UN-sponsored events has increased dramatically, and more especially since the end of the Cold War. Fifty-seven NGOs were accredited to the UN Conference on Human Rights in Tehran (1968). That number grew to 114 organizations for the World Conference of the International Women's Year in Mexico City (1975), and 163 for the Third World Conference on Women in Nairobi (1985). Around 300 NGOs are said to have been accredited to the Stockholm Conference on the Human Environment in 1972. Twenty years later, there were 1,378 officially accredited NGOs for the 1992 Rio Earth Summit, at which some 18,000 people attended parallel events. At the Fourth World Conference on Women in Beijing (1995), some 2,600 NGOs were accredited and some 300,000 people took part in parallel events. It was the series of global UN conferences of the 1990s that essentially rewrote the UN agenda and attracted thousands of NGOs, "establishing the UN as an institution where citizen voices could be heard and have influence."[1]

"Is this huge industry [of NGO participation] all built on one flimsy, conditional sentence in the UN's Charter?" asked the UN Secretariat in a background document it had prepared for the Cardozo panel commissioned to study the issue in 2003. The paper concludes that "the importance of civil society within the UN system reflects more the changing nature of the world we live in and the contemporary challenges of global governance than the deliberate efforts of the UN to elevate the contributions of NGOs."[2] Thus, it was active pressure from civil society to be included and heard in intergovernmental processes that raised the number of ECOSOC-accredited NGOs to almost 4,000 in 2013. Jim Paul observes that "many NGOs saw the UN as an alternative space, especially open when compared to the undemocratic, financially-driven Bretton Woods Institutions and the G-8 meetings with their great-power exclusivity and neo-liberal orthodoxy."[3]

The UN's definition of NGOs, however, has some strict conditions. To be recognized by the United Nations, NGOs must be formalized entities with clear responsibilities, legally defined in the countries where they have their headquarters. They have to be formally established as non-profit making (a definition that allows the International Chamber of Commerce to be recognized, standing for the collective interests of its profit-making members), and until the mid-1990s they had to have an intercontinental membership. This used to mean that an organization with 20 offices in as many African countries was only "regional," while an entity with offices in only Geneva and New York was recognized as "global."

In the process leading to the 1992 Earth Summit, that last condition was dropped, which permitted a massive expansion of the number of NGOs officially listed by ECOSOC as "in consultative status." Agenda 21, one of the major outcomes of the Rio conference, underscored the need to gather expertise and build on the capacity of all groupings of society. It formalized this concept by recognizing nine sectors as the main channels through which citizens could organize and participate in international efforts to achieve sustainable development through the UN.[4] Officially known as "major groups," they include business and industry, children and youth, farmers, indigenous peoples, local authorities, NGOs, scientific and technological communities, women, workers, and trade unions. The nature of the groups is disparate and overlapping. Half of humanity is included in one of them (women), whereas others are defined by their place in the productive cycle (representing workers or farmers) or their role in governance (local authorities). In the follow-up to the Earth Summit, for the first time for-profit businesses were allowed to participate in intergovernmental deliberations.

This grouping made sense in the context of "sustainable development," narrowly understood by some as a synonym of "environmental management"—although the official "three pillars" of sustainable development are social, economic, and environmental. The use of "major groups" was not applied to international summits that followed; and in 1994, the International Conference on Population and Development (ICPD) emphasized that "all members of and groups in society have the right, and indeed the responsibility, to play an active part" in the program of action decided by the conference. When it comes to defining "partnerships," they were referred to by ICPD as "between government, business, non-governmental organizations and community groups."

The term "civil society" was introduced to UN language by the World Summit on Social Development (Copenhagen, 1995).[5] At that time, "civil society" was defined in paragraph 86 as a space implied by the reiteration of the phrases "institutions of civil society" or "actors of civil society" when the reference was to organizations or groups and not to the whole. The usual usage implied that "civil society" included both profit and non-profit groups, as evidenced by the language on "civil society, including the private sector." Nevertheless, paragraph 17 of the Copenhagen Declaration also refers to "Governments, the private sector and civil society." Thus, in the same document we can trace references to Hegel's dualist theory of state versus civil society, including the economy, and to Gramsci's triangular view of the state, economy, and civil society as three distinct domains.[6]

This coexistence of contradictory views persists today; the ambiguity about the roles of "civil society" and the for-profit sector in the UN causes confusion and allows some resolutions to be interpreted beyond their original intent. The term "civil society" has been reiterated in all major UN resolutions since, even when not properly defined. Ambiguity is problematic for implementation but is favored by negotiators because divergent views can be featured in a common text—a consensus made possible because opponents can claim that their views were accommodated.

Language economy further complicates meanings by substituting the expression "civil society" for what used to be formulated as "actors of civil society" or "civil society organizations," thus replacing the part with a whole. Civil society as an arena of interactions cannot have voice or agency, except in very broad ways, but civil society actors have both.

These actors currently relate to the United Nations in a variety of ways: as advocates at global conferences, ECOSOC and its commissions, and special sessions of the UN General Assembly; as bridges to constituencies who favor the UN, especially through annual DPI conferences, to which the Millennium Campaign was added in order specifically to promote the MDGs and views from the UNDG (Development Group) and the UNDP in particular; as service providers, subcontracted by UN agencies to contribute to implementing their programs at the national, regional, and occasionally global level; as advisors to implementing agencies, through specific committees more or less formalized, such as the Civil Society Advisory Committee to the UNDP administrator; as victims or advocates of victims, bringing their complaints to the Human Rights Council through the Universal Periodic Review or other mechanisms, a role that might expand with the entry into force in 2013 of the Optional Protocol to the Covenant on Economic, Social and Cultural Rights that allows individuals or groups to communicate their complaints directly; and as monitoring mechanisms for the implementation of projects and policies, promoting accountability of governments to their citizens and of multilateral institutions toward their members and the public at large.

Different organizations fulfill one or more of these roles, and different UN bodies expect NGOs to operate in one or more of them. While all these roles are necessary and contribute to the world organization's work, the same language is often used to connote different expectations at different moments. The UN secretary-general recognizes in his *Dignity for All* report that "the monitoring and accountability framework can be strengthened through the direct engagement of citizens."[7] Nevertheless, UN agencies accustomed to NGOs as campaigners for the MDGs might be surprised to have aspects of their work criticized by that same NGO exercising its monitoring role.

Between a hammer and an arena

NGOs that regularly attend the DPI's yearly conferences, those that follow the deliberations of ECOSOC and its commissions, and those that implement development projects have different functions, even if there is some overlap in membership. Since the 1980s, the role of NGOs in service delivery has expanded, as a result of the changing role of the state. After World War II, the traditional welfare state provided national and municipal services almost exclusively through government ministries or local authorities. In this model, government bodies determined which services were offered to citizens, who was eligible to receive them, provided funding, set out the conditions for supply, and oversaw delivery.

This arrangement has been replaced in many developed and developing countries by one in which the actual delivery of those services is carried out by NGOs, while governments define the services and provide funding and supervision. In developing countries, a third arrangement is common in which NGOs, with little interference from governmental authorities, provide services that are not available from the government or which duplicate (or complement) services offered by the authorities. The funding often comes from foreign donors.[8] These models have become so common in development practice that UN agencies tend to forget that service delivery was a rather exceptional NGO role when the United Nations was created.

However, while the Secretariat (second UN) and diplomats (first UN) often praise the value of NGOs (third UN) to UN negotiations in providing expertise that informs the debate and even helps build consensus, the diversity of views and opinions expressed by civil society is often annoying. The pressure on civil society to "speak with a single voice" in UN consultations entails a substantial risk: suffocating the inherent diversity of social organizations. "Although Major Groups can sometimes find consensus on some issues, they represent diverse interests," write Barbara Adams and Lou Pingeot. "For some organizations, voicing alternative perspectives and policies is part of their mission. This diversity is not recognized if Major Groups are systematically required to speak in one voice as 'civil society' or as 'Major Groups.'"[9]

An unintended consequence of this demand for a single voice is that Northern organizations are strengthened and Southern civil society voices are weakened. It is much easier for organizations based in industrialized countries to find common ground among themselves (and then attract others to join that "consensus") than for organizations based in Africa, Asia, and Latin America to coordinate within and between their regions and, ultimately, with their Northern colleagues. The efforts (and budget) required are clearly bigger in the latter case and yet the resources for "global networking" tend to be concentrated in the North.

Mark Poster says that the Internet's effects

> are more like those of Germany than those of hammers: the effect
> of Germany upon the people within it is not to make them Ger-
> mans (at least for the most part); the effect of hammers is not to
> make people hammers ... but to force metal spikes into wood. As
> long as we understand the internet as a hammer, we fail to discern
> the way it is like Germany.[10]

The same metaphor can apply to civil society. The UN and particularly its development organizations tend to view civil society in instrumental terms, as a "hammer" or a well-adapted tool to implement
policies, to advocate for them, and perhaps to provide useful feedback.
But civil society is not understood as it should be, namely resembling
"Germany," or a political arena and space without which citizenship
and consequently economic and social development is infeasible.

If civil society is understood as a political space and not as a tool,
the frequently expressed desire for it to speak at UN conferences with
"a single voice" becomes meaningless. Politicians interpret what society
wants. A diversity of voices, representing a variety of views and opinions, frequently conflicting, of different social sectors is a condition
for democracy.

Yet even when "good governance" is among the objectives of projects
of the UN Development Programme (UNDP) little attention is paid by
UN development organizations or the World Bank to the promotion of
a vibrant civil society. In 2011 both the World Bank's "Doing Business" index and the UNDP's Human Development Index classified
Egypt and Tunisia among the best performers in Africa. The diag-
nostic tools used are "blind" to civil society and its enabling conditions
(democracy) and thus did not help actually understand what was hap-
pening in two of the countries receiving substantial development aid,
and thus supposedly most scrutinized by development agencies.

After the Arab Spring, then World Bank president Robert Zoellick
"saw the light" and started a program to support civil society.
Addressing an audience at the Peterson Institute for International
Economics in Washington, DC, in April 2011, he said that the wave of
unrest engulfing the Arab region had shown governments that "you
cannot have successful development without good governance and
without the participation of your citizens." "Now it may be time to
invest in the private, not-for-profit sector—civil society—to help
strengthen the capacity of organizations working on transparency,
accountability, and service delivery," Zoellick added.[11]

The Global Partnership for Social Accountability was organized and launched in record time and the first grants ($9 million in 10 countries) were already disbursed by October 2013. Yet instead of looking at the "enabling environment" in which different civil society initiatives may prosper, the World Bank opted for making grants to selected organizations that provided "social auditing" of public services. To avoid potential accusations of undue interference in national affairs by a multilateral agency, this initiative is limited to countries that explicitly "opt in." This "partnership" departs from the notion of NGOs as service providers and recognizes an "auditing" function, but it still views civil society as a "hammer." In this case, it is a tool for "governance services" and does not address strengthening civil society as a value in itself, essential for democracy and not just for the efficiency of service delivery.

What "data revolution"?

A Life of Dignity for All recognizes that in monitoring and accountability "governments, especially parliaments, will play a central role." That role "can be strengthened" through the "direct engagement of citizens and responsible businesses making use of new technologies to expand coverage, to disaggregate data and to reduce costs."[12] This formulation is ambiguous and raises more questions than it answers.

The role of citizens in monitoring and accountability is well established. The 1789 French *Déclaration des Droits de l'Homme et du Citoyen* already established in its Article 14 that "citizens have a right to decide, either personally or by their representatives, as to the necessity of the public contribution; to grant this freely; to know to what uses it is put; and to fix the proportion, the mode of assessment and of collection and the duration of the taxes." Article 15 explicitly establishes "the right to require of every public agent an account of his administration."[13] The secretary-general's 2013 report falls behind this standard of more than two centuries by converting a "right" into a "strengthening role," on the one hand, and by giving that same role to "responsible business" without any definition as to what that could be, on the other hand. Further, it is not clear if the use of new technologies is for business, for citizens, or both, or whether it is suggested as a way of improving the old role of holding pubic agents to account, or as a precondition to asserting that right.

In fact, the availability of information and the opportunities provided by the "data revolution" are discussed in the subsequent paragraphs of the report more extensively than the role of citizens and their organizations, which are implicit, but not explicitly mentioned, in this context. The phrase "responsible business and civil society" appears also in the report. In order to "galvanize greater efforts" the secretary-general argues, "we will need enlightened and courageous leadership in the halls of government and the engagement of responsible businesses and civil society the world over."[14]

This new association of "civil society" with "responsible business" is even more difficult to pin down, because "business" seems to refer to specific companies as opposed to "private sector," which clearly refers to the whole. But that does not explain which businesses are "responsible" and which are irresponsible.

The secretary-general describes the report from his high-level panel (HLP) on the post-2015 development agenda[15] as "illuminating," referring in particular to the call for "major transformative shifts, a new global partnership and a data revolution for monitoring progress and strengthening accountability." The tool of accountability (enhanced data access) is emphasized here over the actors (parliaments or civil society) that have the right and responsibility to hold governments accountable.

Redefining partnerships

These conceptual shifts away from the traditional actors to new partners are evident in the HLP recommendations that the secretary-general quotes. In the HLP report, there are 30 occurrences of the terms "civil society" or "CSOs" against 120 of the words "business," "corporations," or "companies." "Trade unions" and "workers" are mentioned only three times each, and even "governments" rank lower than "business," being mentioned 80 times. The document is titled "A New Global Partnership" and the panel claims that, in preparing it, "we heard voices ... from over 5,000 civil society organizations working in about 120 countries," and "we also consulted the chief executive officers of 250 companies in 30 countries, with annual revenues exceeding $8 trillion."

The focus on global partnerships is emphasized by the secretary-general's report in its summary, "harnessing the power of multi-stake-holder partnerships." By definition those partnerships should involve civil society organizations. Existing partnerships are offered as models, such as Every Woman, Every Child; Sustainable Energy for All; and Education First. Yet in most cases, the evidence of success refers to monetary commitments by the partners in those initiatives, an approach where the contributions of civil society will always be

dwarfed by those of governments, private foundations, and big corporations. Testimonies gathered by the author from experienced civil
society campaigners in some of those partnerships refer to a sense of
inadequacy in an environment dominated by managerial language, an
obsession for showing results, and a careful avoidance of the language
of rights.

The UN General Assembly decided in September 2013 that the
negotiations on a "new development agenda" to replace the Millennium Development Goals (MDGs) should begin in September 2014 in
order to give countries time to study the issue. However, the creation of
a "partnership facility," which is a key point of the new development
agenda, was already included in the budget proposal for 2014. The
proposed United Nations Partnership Facility (UNPF) would have an
annual regular budget of $1.5 million, 90 percent of which will pay five
senior officials, led by an under-secretary-general. "Extra-budgetary
resources" are estimated at more than $12 million a year. The blueprint
for the new office mandates it to coordinate existing partnerships with
the private sector (corporations, private foundations, and civil society
organizations) and encourage new ones to "significantly increase existing resources and expand the effectiveness of their use," globally and in
developing countries.

The initiatives to be formalized as part of the UNPF include Every
Woman, Every Child; Sustainable Energy for All; Education First, and
several more. The official press releases are optimistic. Every Woman,
Every Child has supposedly "delivered" $10 billion and Sustainable
Energy for All, an initiative launched just a year ago, "has seen pledges"
of $50 billion. These are impressive amounts because total official
development assistance (ODA) is about $130 billion a year and is fall-
ing. However, what these numbers actually mean is not easy to figure
out, as they represent "commitments" that in most cases extend over
several years if not decades. These grants (and sometimes loans) are
not received or controlled by any UN organization or developing
country governments. They may not be additional to current ODA and
other financial commitments made in intergovernmental fora, nor is
there any proof that those resources add to what the foundations would
have disbursed anyhow.

These partnerships are not a new idea. In 1998 the UNDP launched
a Global Sustainable Development Facility that aimed to "create
sustainable economic growth and allow the private sector to prosper
through the inclusion of two billion new people in the global economy."[16] The UNDP administrator at the time, Gus Speth, used to
describe it with the formula "2B4M:2020" (two billion for the market

by 2020). Fifteen multinationals paid $50,000 each to be listed as sponsors. More than a hundred NGOs signed a public letter to Speth and then secretary-general Kofi Annan arguing that "the growing concentration of wealth and power in the hands of fundamentally undemocratic global corporations and other institutions of globalization clashes with the overriding purpose of the United Nations to enhance human dignity and the capacity for self-governance."[17] Mark Malloch-Brown succeeded Speth in 1999 in the middle of this debate; but the new head immediately dropped the initiative and appointed many of the signatories of the letter to serve in the first Civil Society Advisory Committee to the UNDP administrator.[18]

Now, at a time when many developed countries suffer recession and have cut their ODA budgets, the idea of a UN-related facility based on corporate contributions has resurfaced. Using private philanthropy seems obvious and reasonable. However, in 2013 an alliance of civil society networks warned diplomats about the possibility of creating a perverse result:

> Contrary to the perception that leveraging actually draws in private resources to available public funds, increasingly it is about using public money (ODA) to cover the risks of private investment. Losses will be socialized while profits continue to be private—and too often untaxed. Recent experience in many countries shows that these "innovative" mechanisms are often ineffective, poorly regulated, and can lead to corruption in borrowing and lending countries.[19]

By joining these initiatives, corporations may be winning direct access to ODA, with the argument of "leveraging," and indirectly benefit from access to the procurement budgets in ODA recipient countries to the detriment of local small and medium-sized enterprises. Similarly, protagonists from local civil society might suffer, as only big global NGOs specializing in service delivery may have access to these "initiatives."

In December 2013, the UN General Assembly adopted by consensus a budget for the UN of $5.5 billion for the biennium 2014–15. This amount is a reduction from the previous biennium, reflecting the global crisis and "our shared wish for a fiscally responsible secretariat," as Secretary-General Ban Ki-Moon commented. In spite of the financial constraints, the General Assembly did not approve the proposed partnership facility and deferred its consideration.

Consultation or "crowd-sourcing"?

The explicit reference to human rights, a permanent demand by NGOs, made its way into the secretary-general's report: "No person should go hungry, lack shelter or clean water and sanitation, face social and economic exclusion or live without access to basic health services and education. These are human rights, and form the foundations for a decent life."[20] But a right is not really such without concrete mechanisms to enforce it or to seek remedy when violated. The human rights architecture of the UN provides those mechanisms. They exist already and do not need to be created, but they would benefit from further strengthening and from recognition by UN development agencies that basically ignore their existence. The secretary-general's report does not mention them. It does call for "rigorous accountability mechanisms" and for "robust accountability mechanisms."[21]

In both cases, the accountability issue is linked to the request for a "data revolution" instead of referring to it as an established right, and the locus of such accountability is implicitly situated at the national level since "governments, especially parliaments, will play a central role." Thus the debate is left open as to what the global accountability mechanisms should be to assess global efforts, such as the results of the proposed global partnerships. It is also unclear what role civil society can play.

In the process leading to the secretary-general's report, a "global conversation" was launched, including national consultations led by the UNDP in many countries and 11 thematic consultations. Those processes were largely conceived as an "outreach" mechanism and the different thematic efforts at times seemed like an attempt by the different UN organizations to build a constituency for the inclusion of their goals on the list. Global networks and large, Northern NGOs and their partners actively participated, but actual reach beyond that circle was limited.

In parallel to the consultations, the United Nations and "outreach partners" set up a website called "MY World"[22] in an attempt to "crowd-source" the voice of the public. MY World claims to have gathered views from over 1 million people. Visitors to the page were asked to click on six "priorities" out of a list of 16 options as diverse as "Equality between men and women," "Phone and Internet access," "A good education," and "Action taken on climate change."

The results from MY World were presented to world leaders with much fanfare during the 68th session of the General Assembly through a report and an exhibit called "Listening to ONE MILLION Voices."[23] And the exercise was highlighted in the secretary-general's report as an example of openness to public opinion.

Yet the very design of MY World makes it impossible for its results to be taken seriously. The National Council on Public Polls, an association of polling organizations that includes the major US networks and several universities as members, explains on its website that "unscientific pseudo-polls are widespread and sometimes entertaining, but they never provide the kind of information that belongs in a serious report."[24] In a scientific poll, "the pollster identifies and seeks out the people to be interviewed. In an unscientific poll, the respondents usually 'volunteer' their opinions, selecting themselves for the poll." This is precisely the case of MY World.

The British Polling Council includes this question on its site: "'But surely a phone-in or write-in poll in which, say, one million people take part is likely to be more accurate than an opinion poll sample of 1,000?'" The answer is clear: "Not so. A biased sample is a biased sample, however large it is."

It is surprising that a publicity gimmick that could not possibly pass a basic credibility test is quoted by the UN secretary-general in an official report among the sources of his claim that "I sought the views of people around the world." The use of such Internet polls to back policy proposals undermines the validity of consultation exercises. It is misleading for the public and frustrating for civil society activists when opinions formulated after lengthy consultation processes with their constituencies and across networks are so easily equated with the "entertaining" results of a pseudo-poll.

A more credible consultation exercise was launched simultaneously in September 2013 by the UN Non-Governmental Liaison Service (NGLS), an inter-agency service that has actively sought civil society involvement during several decades and is trusted by NGOs, particularly in the South, as an honest broker. The NGLS report, titled "Advancing Regional Recommendations for the Post-2015 Agenda,"[25] includes many voices that had not been heard before in the consultation process. NGLS was brought at a late stage into the consultation process, but with a limited budget and time (four months), it managed to include via conference calls in different languages more than 100 regional networks with 3,000 organizational affiliates that had largely not been heard before.

The recommendations emerging from this consultation go beyond the narrow MDG agenda, focused on ODA and service delivery, and include calls to reform the international financial architecture, to review international trade and investment agreements when they collide with development needs, and "address the problem of excessive concentration of corporate power." The agenda emerging from nationally and

regionally organized civil society groups, mainly but not exclusively
from the global South, covers the following four major areas:

- Rebalance power relations for justice: "The post-2015 agenda must
  focus not only on goals, but also on structural and root causes of rising
  inequality, impoverishment, social exclusion, environmental degradation and conflict. It must address the barriers to meaningful structural
  transformation and incorporate strong means of implementation and
  accountability mechanisms."
- Fulfill human rights and overcome exclusion: "the post-2015 development agenda must be fully aligned with the existing human rights
  framework, reflecting its fundamental principles of universality,
  equality and nondiscrimination, as well as progressive realization
  and non-regression. Human rights are indivisible, interrelated and
  interdependent. Economic, social, cultural, civil, and political rights
  must be fully realized for all; it is critical to focus support for fulfilling
  the rights of vulnerable and marginalized people, particularly those
  who face intersecting inequalities based on gender, age, class, ethnicity,
  indigeneity, sexual orientation, gender identity, (dis)abilities, and/or
  status as a migrant, asylum-seeker or refugee, many of whom have
  been systematically, historically and continually excluded."
- Ensure equitable distribution and safe use of natural resources:
  "Large-scale agriculture is a significant cause of environmental
  stress, and large agri-business has been responsible for extensive
  human rights violations, particularly with regard to land and water
  grabbing. In numerous countries, extractive industries are displacing
  millions of people and destroying land, water and sacred sites, dis-
  proportionately affecting Indigenous peoples. In the face of accelerated climate change—including devastating environmental damage
  and economic loss—the extraction and use of fossil fuels must be dramatically reduced. The transition away from fossil fuels must not lead
  to increased use of other hazardous sources of energy, such as nuclear
  power—often misleadingly positioned as a clean source. Poor and
  marginalized communities are most at risk, and most severely
  harmed, by these activities and climate change impacts."
- Establish participatory governance, accountability, and transparency: "Meaningful implementation of any post-2015 agenda
  requires a strong framework for participatory governance, accountability and transparency [...] anchored in existing international
  human rights agreements and instruments. Human rights standards
  and norms provide a comprehensive framework to guide policy and
  to assess impacts and monitor progress. Democratization and

reform of global governance bodies, especially those dealing with economic and financial affairs [is required]. Accountability in the post-2015 agenda will remain meaningless unless strong means of implementation are put in place. [...] Credible partnership initiatives with the private sector should be subject to binding accountability mechanisms."

At the crossroads

As civil society voices from the South started to raise alternative views on the issues, the chair of the Group of 77 and China vigorously defended balanced civil society representation during the inaugural meeting of the High-level Political Forum on Sustainable Development in September 2013: "Multi-stakeholder dialogues should reflect geographical balance, including think tanks and research institutions from the South, such as the South Centre and the Third World Network, or newly established regional organizations from the developing world such as the Pacific Islands Development Forum."[26] In a dramatic departure from traditional G77 reluctance to enhance civil society participation (largely motivated by the geographic imbalances he complains about, which are not new), he argued that "this participatory and inclusive approach to the implementation of sustainable development will make the Forum more effective in advancing the sustainable development agenda."

Thus, all major negotiating blocs, including the G77 and China, now declare themselves aware of the relevance of civil society participation. But the reverse question also needs to be posed: why is the UN important for civil society? And the question should not be restricted to the development system, but to the entire United Nations. The answer to this question, in brief, is that the UN is a norm- and standard-setting body, which can influence the behavior and perceptions of countries in ways that sustainably address the concerns dear to civil society groups: peace, security, and disarmament; development and poverty eradication; protecting our common environment; and human rights, democracy, and good governance.

Conclusion

There seems to be a high degree of consensus that the traditional notion of development as delivery is in need of profound transformation, but what this transformation will look like is far from clear. On the one hand, the UN is pressured to shift from "business as usual" to just "business," promoting uncritically all kinds of associations with the private sector, and big corporations in particular. On the other hand, many civil society groups are highly critical of such "partnerships" and urge the UN to seek inspiration in the ambitious promises that gave birth to the institution by putting human rights at the center and embarking on genuinely transformative approaches.

A vibrant civil society is essential to development, an issue that is present in the Millennium Declaration but got lost in a narrow implementation of the MDGs that at times seemed to meet "production quotas" instead of genuine development. A clearer understanding of the UN's approach to partnerships is critical. Civil society cannot simply be lumped together with the private sector. Nor should Northern and Southern NGOs always be considered an undifferentiated category.

Small and medium-sized enterprises are also key to development as they generate more jobs and strengthen the social fabric. Yet instead of looking at normative approaches that would promote and enable a development-friendly environment, the UN development system prioritizes "partnerships" with gigantic corporations, emphasizing the promise of external resource mobilization over the very real contributions of domestic entrepreneurship.

In this regard, the recently created High-level Political Forum should formulate transparent rules for NGO participation and adequately support a balanced representation from the South. Moreover, the proposed UNPF should not be approved until the monitoring mechanisms and accountability framework for corporate involvement are discussed and agreed.

Notes

1 "UN System and Civil Society—An Inventory and Analysis of Practices," Background Paper for the secretary-general's Panel of Eminent Persons on United Nations Relations with Civil Society, United Nations Non-Governmental Liaison Service, May 2003. www.un-ngls.org/orf/ecosoc%20HL%20Panel%20-%20Background%20paper%20by%20Secretariat.doc
2 Ibid.
3 James Paul, "Civil Society and the United Nations," in Heidi Moksnes and Mia Melin, ed., *Global Civil Society: Shifting Powers in a Shifting World* (Uppsala, Sweden: Uppsala University, 2012).
4 Barbara Adams and Lou Pingeot, "Strengthening Public Participation at the United Nations for Sustainable Development: Dialogue, Debate, Dissent, Deliberation," Study for UN DESA/DSD Major Groups Programme, June 2013. http://sustainabledevelopment.un.org/content/documents/1926desareport.pdf

210   *Roberto Bissio*

5 Copenhagen Declaration on Social Development, 1995, http://daccess-dds-ny.un.org/doc/UNDOC/GEN/N95/116/51/PDF/N9511651.pdf?OpenElement (accessed on 17 January 2014).
6 Jean L. Cohen and Andrew Arato, *Civil Society and Political Theory* (Cambridge, Mass.: MIT Press, 1994).
7 *A Life of Dignity for All: Accelerating Progress towards the Millennium Development Goals and Advancing the United Nations Development Agenda beyond 2015, Report of the Secretary-General*, UN document A/68/202, 26 July 2013, para. 105.
8 Jason L. Powell and John Hendricks, *The Welfare State in Post-Industrial Society: A Global Perspective* (New York: Springer, 2009).
9 Adams and Pingeot, "Strengthening Public Participation at the United Nations for Sustainable Development."
10 Mark Poster, *What's the Matter with the Internet?* (Minneapolis: University of Minnesota Press, 2001), 177.
11 "Zoellick Prepares Ground for Increased World Bank Support for Civil Society," *Alliance Magazine*, 13 April 2011.
12 *A Life of Dignity for All*, para. 105.
13 The Avalon Project, *Declaration of the Rights of Man – 1789*, http://avalon.law.yale.edu/18th_century/rightsof.asp
14 *A Life of Dignity for All*, para. 13.
15 *A New Global Partnership: Eradicate Poverty and Transform Economies through Sustainable Development: The Report of the High-Level Panel of Eminent Persons on the Post-2015 Development Agenda* (New York: UN, 2013).
16 "The Global Sustainable Development Facility: 2B2M," internal UNDP document, July 1998, quoted by Joshua Karliner, "Co-opting the UN," *The Ecologist* 29, no. 5 (1999): 318.
17 Ibid.
18 The author was a member.
19 "Misdirecting Finance—Who Benefits?" Civil Society Reflection Group on Global Development Perspectives, 24 September 2013, www.reflectiongroup.org/
20 *A Life of Dignity for All*, para. 11.
21 Ibid., para. 16.
22 See www.myworld2015.org/
23 See http://blog.myworld2015.org/category/special-event/
24 Sheldon R. Gawiser and G. Evans Witt, "20 Questions a Journalist Should Ask About Poll Results," *National Council on Public Polls*, 4 August 2006. www.ncpp.org/
25 UN Non-Governmental Liaison Service, *Advancing Regional Recommendations for the Post-2015 Development Agenda*, 22 September 2013, www.un-ngls.org/IMG/pdf/UN-NGLS_Post-2015_Regional_Consultation_September_2013.pdf
26 "Statement on behalf of the Group of 77 and China by H. E. Mr. J. V. Bainimarama, prime minister of the Republic of Fiji, chairman of the Group of 77, at the inaugural meeting of the High-level Political Forum on Sustainable Development," G77, 24 September 2013, www.g77.org/statement/getstatement.php?id=130924

12 Revisiting UN development

The prospects for reform

Stephen Browne and Cécile Molinier

From the outset, coordination has been a fundamental problem within the UN system. Already as early as 1948, Lord Boyd Orr, the first director-general of the Food and Agriculture Organization (FAO), wrote in a letter to Robert Jackson (then assistant secretary-general for UN coordination): "I earnestly hope that you will be able to do what I have been clamoring for in the last two years – bring the heads of the specialized agencies together, and try to get a coordinated drive."[1] We do not know how Jackson responded at the time, but 20 years later he produced his own comprehensive blueprint for UN reform (commonly called *The Capacity Study*), in which he referred to this comment. He, like many others, was fully aware that better coordination in the UN's emerging development system was a missed opportunity from the earliest days: "the UN development system has tried to wage a war on want for many years with very little organized 'brain' to guide it. Its absence may well be the greatest constraint of all on capacity."[2]

The need has only grown with the increasing atomization of this family of organizations: already a "jungle of proliferating agencies" in the 1960s according to Paul Hoffman, the first head of the UN Development Programme (UNDP).[3] Each part of the system has sought to adapt to changing circumstances. But when those constituent parts are competing with each other and with other development organizations for limited resources from finite donor sources, these individual programs of change are focused on parochial interests at the expense of larger questions of development roles within the UN system, let alone the broader development landscape.

Even the UNDP, conceived as the system's coordinator and a serial reformer, has been overwhelmingly preoccupied in its change initiatives with maximizing its own revenues.[4] These intra-organizational transitions have had their value, but they are side-shows to the systemic reforms which UN development organizations must undertake to remain relevant, not just as another player in the well-patronized technical assistance field, but as a system that could still offer an unusually valuable brand of human development.

This chapter describes the long saga of attempted reforms and the reasons for their failure. The most recent attempt was in 2006 by a very senior panel of experts led by three serving heads of government. Its proposals are now widely known under the rubric of "Delivering as One" (or DaO), which helped to initiate the latest phase of reform and whose contribution is assessed. Other processes, such as the ambitiously titled Quadrennial Comprehensive Policy Review (QCPR), have sought to hasten procedural changes and foster harmonization. The outcomes will be part of the necessary process of change, but even the partial results of several recent surveys have underlined the importance of more fundamental reform and the need for Jackson's central "brain."

A brief history of UN reform

In its Article 55, the UN Charter called for "higher standards of living, full employment, and conditions of economic and social progress and development; solutions of international economic, social, health, and related problems; and international cultural and educational cooperation; and universal respect for, and observance of, human rights and fundamental freedoms for all without distinction as to race, sex, language, or religion." The Charter, however, was a statement of intent, and while this article comes closest to defining the scope of the future "development system," the institutional arrangements for managing it were left deliberately vague, apart from references to the Economic and Social Council (ECOSOC) as a "coordinator of activities" (Article 64). No arrangements were made to establish an overarching authority to manage the differentiated institutional system of funds, programs, and other entities of the United Nations development system (UNDS) that were to evolve in the coming decades.[5] Each functional organization was deeply rooted in its own constituencies and had its own governance arrangements, and they were only very loosely coordinated.[6] The Expanded Programme for Technical Assistance (EPTA), set up in 1949, and the UN Special Fund (1959) were merged in 1964 to create the UNDP, designed to act as a central body for the planning, financing, and coordinating of UN aid activities, with the specialized agencies as implementation agencies.[7]

This centrally planned and funded, but functionally decentralized, model evolved significantly with the birth of numerous independent countries and the strong affirmation of the principle of state sovereignty. The concept of service to member states became central, with a shift to country-level programming and funding allocations according to criteria of eligibility. The UNDS became more and more fragmented, with new agencies being established in response to new mandates, delivering a multitude of interventions in response to numerous and diverse government priorities. In an increasingly polarized Cold War context, which saw the emergence of the Group of 77 (G77) developing countries and the Non-Aligned Movement (NAM) as powerful voices for the priorities of developing countries, aid allocations were seen as an integral component of donor governments' foreign policy and increased steadily.

With the end of the Cold War, the acceleration of globalization, and the failure of the "peace dividend" to materialize, a new rationale was sought to justify development cooperation. Many observers, from all parts of the global political compass, believed that the new millennium should signal a clean break with the "lost" decades of the 1980s and 1990s, which had achieved poor results in terms of reducing poverty and meeting human development goals, in spite of numerous international development conferences under UN auspices. The conferences had set and reset many international development goals, but clearer targets and measurable indicators were required. The Millennium Declaration of 2000 and its Millennium Development Goals (MDGs) were the response, providing the UNDS with a meaningful agenda.

Donor aid budgets needed to be justified to increasingly demanding and well-informed publics; and in a highly competitive environment, donors became more concerned about retaining visibility and influence. These concerns translated into a marked increase in non-core, or earmarked, funding for the UN, at the relative expense of core resources. Between 1995 and 2010, while core resources for the UN's development activities (more than 90 percent coming from traditional Northern donors) increased by 8 percent in real terms, non-core resources grew by 350 percent.[8] The dramatic increase in vertical funding for specific development goals, notably in the health and environment sectors, pushed the development agencies to chase after "fashionable" issues in order to mobilize resources, thereby increasing the competition between agencies and the fragmentation of the UNDS.

As the UNDS evolved, three successive reform initiatives addressed the laundry list of problems. In 1969, *The Capacity Study* addressed the issue of extreme fragmentation by recommending that all UNDS inputs be packaged comprehensively in a program tailored to the needs of each country's national development plan, and that UN development funding be channeled through one central organization, namely the UNDP. The subsequent Consensus Resolution (1970–71) formalized country-based programming and a funding entitlement based on an Indicative Planning Figure (IPF), but failed to endorse organizational reforms designed to integrate the components of the UNDS more closely, inter alia by strengthening the authority of the UNDP resident representative, thereby reinforcing centrifugal forces already at work at the headquarters level and contributing to increased fragmentation and dispersion at the country level.[9]

In 1997, Secretary-General Kofi Annan advanced reforms that led to the strengthening of the resident coordinator (RC) system, the establishment of UN houses, the coordination of UN planning and programming at the country level through the United Nations Development Assistance Framework (UNDAF), and the establishment of the UN Development Group (UNDG). The latter is chaired by the UNDP administrator; it initially was made up of only UN funds and programs but now comprises a wider range of some 32 entities. Annan's reform package also included the establishment of coordination mechanisms in the peace and security, humanitarian, and economic and social areas.

Then in 2006, the High-level Panel on System-wide Coherence in the Areas of Development, Humanitarian Assistance and the Environment (HLP), published its report containing many practical proposals liable to contribute to significantly greater cohesion. The best known was the recommendation that the UN "Deliver as One" at the country level, with one leader, one program, one budget and, where appropriate, one office. It also recommended the establishment of a UN Sustainable Development Board "to drive coordination and joint planning between all funds, programs and agencies to monitor overlaps and gaps."[10] The board was envisioned as an intergovernmental body under ECOSOC's auspices, with heads of UN organizations serving ex-officio. One of its functions would have been to oversee and approve DaO programs and funding at the country level. The HLP also proposed the establishment of an MDG-funding mechanism to provide multi-year funding for the one-country programs; the strengthening of international environmental governance; and the establishment of a UN entity focused on gender equality and women's empowerment.

The above indicates that the UNDS has evolved in response to changing demands from member states. However, internal efforts to reform it, led by successive secretaries-general, have been stymied by a "coalition of the unwilling," namely member states (the first UN) and the leadership of individual organizations (the second UN).[11]

Why continuing reforms are so important

The same logic that has driven all past reform efforts has not gone away. Indeed, it has become even more urgent as the UN development system faces at least three kinds of growing challenges; these concern structure, substance, and self-interest.[12]

Structurally, the UNDS is already highly complex and growing more so, in terms of both organization and procedure. Notwithstanding the recent merger of four entities into UN Women, each part of the system guards its independence jealously. Turf is enhanced not diminished by the increasing competition for scarce funds. Meanwhile in the field, new regional and country offices continue to open with little reference to the desirability of sharing or clustering. The complexity of the UNDS is the driving force behind new mechanisms of coordination. But they are falling short. At the intergovernmental level, ECOSOC was always intended to be the point of reference for development, but as "the UN's most unwieldy and least significant deliberative body" its impact on coherence is limited.[13] Within the second UN (the secretariats), coordination is an expensive and slow-moving process, having limited consequences for either structure or policy coherence.

As a substantive partner, the UNDS is increasingly marginalized by existing and new development partners. The World Bank—whose relationship with the UN is consistently raised as a concern by FUNDS surveys—is not just a bank but a knowledge center of impressive amplitude. Unlike the United Nations, it captures, manages, and communicates its knowledge and experience coherently and has become an important reference for a range of development challenges almost as broad as those of the world organization. The research and operations of the well-funded regional development banks outshine the UN's regional commissions.[14] There are also many new publicly and privately financed institutions providing many of the same services as the UNDS, particularly in the areas of research and technical assistance. And global organizations such as the World Economic Forum and the G20 have come to the fore, particularly during the recent years of financial crisis, at the direct expense of economic deliberations in UN forums.[15]

Self-interest and complacency by the UN's governors is a third challenge. The UNDS has been described as too friendly to fail for governments who either patronize it or benefit from its resources. Donor governments (and to a growing extent the private sector) like to exert influence through selective funding. For the governments of "program" (recipient) countries—essentially the developing countries of the G77—the UNDS provides jobs, training, and hardware. There is, therefore, not a strong constituency of interest in favor of reform, since these might circumscribe patronage through and from the UN. And when the UN deliberates on change, the consensus system usually yields proposals of least resistance. There is scope within the second UN to lead reform, but there is rarely a sense of urgency or crisis since funding support for each organization tends to roll over annually. Where individual organizations suffer reduced funding—for example, when donors withdraw, as has happened in recent years in the UN Educational, Scientific and Cultural Organization (UNESCO) and the UN Industrial Development Organization (UNIDO)—they rapidly adjust their staffing and operations, but with little reference to their place in the system as a whole. As we discuss below, however, funding is one of the keys to future reform.

The evidence of global opinion

Perhaps surprisingly, rather few surveys have been conducted on the UN's effectiveness. The main exception has been an exclusively donor group, the Multilateral Organization Performance Assessment Network (MOPAN), established in 2002 and now comprising 17 governments. MOPAN uses surveys to assess effectiveness in four dimensions (strategy, operations, partnerships, and knowledge) and assesses several individual multilateral organizations each year. Reviews of the main UN funds and programs and selected specialized agencies are repeated every three years and provide valuable feedback on how each can enhance its organizational effectiveness.

Some individual organizations (such as the UNDP) have also been conducting their own internal surveys of governments, staff, and partners as a guide to senior management. And in 2012 the UN Secretariat conducted a survey of government representatives and UN resident coordinators (repeated in 2013) on aspects of the UN development system as a whole, mainly focusing on procedural aspects of UN field operations.

What have been lacking, however, are "bottom-up" surveys that encompass the intended beneficiaries of UN development. Since 2010 the Future UN Development System (FUNDS) project has been trying to fill that gap with a series of surveys on perceptions of the UNDS, which also compare the relevance and effectiveness of UNDS organizations as a whole, and make comparisons among them. Two global surveys (in 2010 and 2012) received over 6,500 responses from all regions, across six occupational groups. The respondents included those from the public sector and the UN, but the largest cohort by far was a sample of those outside the public sector: the third UN comprising NGOs, the private sector, and academia. Staff from other non-UN intergovernmental organizations were also canvassed. Further FUNDS surveys have been conducted among smaller numbers of UN-watchers and development specialists.

The results—liable to be more objective than from internal surveys—are illuminating, even if intuitively predictable for the most part. A survey of FUNDS global experts reaffirmed the advantages and disadvantages of UN development assistance compared with other multilateral sources. There was broad agreement that the United Nations was different. Respondents stressed the importance of UN neutrality, values, and adaptation to country needs. But there was also broad disagreement over whether or not the UN was better coordinated and—especially—more efficient (see Figure 12.1).

The global surveys reflected a loud clamor for change. Addressing the short term, respondents were asked to rank six organizational challenges. The data in Figure 12.2 show the ratio of the numbers of those who agreed to those who disagreed. The ratios were strongly positive (i.e., greater than 1). Taken as a whole the top two priorities were lack of financial resources and organizational structures, ahead of emergence of alternative mechanisms to the UN, lack of adaptability, ineffectiveness, and access to competences.

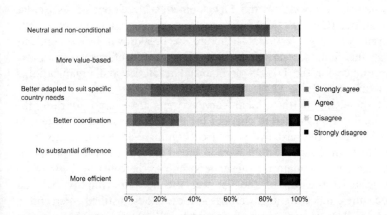

Figure 12.1 Comparing the UN with other multilateral development assistance
Source: FUNDS Global Expert Survey 2013

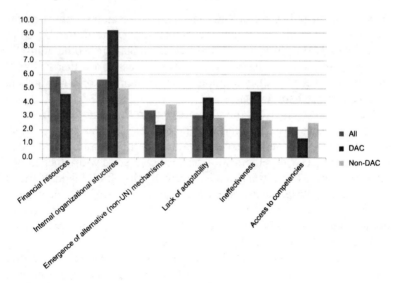

Figure 12.2 Six main challenges faced by the UNDS: ratio of "agreed" to
        "disagreed"
Source: FUNDS Global Survey 2012

There were contrasts between North and South, however. For respondents from the North—in the countries of the Organisation for Economic Co-operation and Development's Development Assistance Committee (OECD/DAC)—the most outstanding challenge by a wide margin was organizational structure. A breakdown by respondents from the first, second, and third UNs also confirms the primary importance for the UNDS of financial resources and organizational structures (see Table 12.1).

Respondents in the global surveys were also asked to rank the desirability of 14 different changes for the UN development system to consider over the next five years (see Figure 12.3). Respondents from the North and global South were in broad agreement on the priorities, and there was a majority (never less than 65 percent) in favor of all changes. At the top of the list was the need to simplify business procedures, reflecting a prevailing—if not wholly justified—perception that the UN is excessively bureaucratic. While it probably appears more so when compared with the private sector, with which it is more frequently in partnership, many respondents were unhappy about UN management and efficiency. Partnerships, more funding from

Table 12.1 UNDS challenges viewed by first, second, and third UNs

	1st UN	2nd UN	3rd UN			
	Governments	UN	International organizations	Nongovernmental organizations	Private sector	Academia
Priorities	Financial resources	Financial resources	Organizational structures	Organizational structures	Financial resources	Financial resources
	Organizational structures	Organizational structures	Financial resources	Financial resources	Organizational structures	Organizational structures
	Emergence of alternative (non-UN) mechanisms	Ineffectiveness	Ineffectiveness	Ineffectiveness	Emergence of alternative (non-UN) mechanisms	Emergence of alternative (non-UN) mechanisms

Source: FUNDS Global Survey 2012

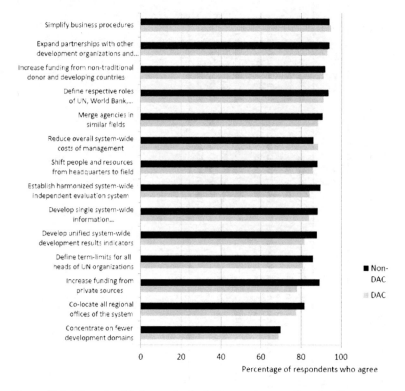

Figure 12.3 What should change in the UN over the next five years?
Source: FUNDS Global Survey 2012

non-traditional donors (but not necessarily from private donors), and a clearer demarcation between the UN and the Bretton Woods institutions were also popular reforms.

On structures and mandates, respondents attached more importance to organizational consolidation ("merge agencies") than to a reduction in the scope of the system ("fewer development domains"). However, there was substantial variation in the popularity of the 20 different domains of work of the UNDS (see Figure 12.4). In order to control for varying communication capacities across the system, only the responses of those "familiar with the area" were taken into account. Health, human rights, and education were clearly considered the most effective UN development domains by the full sample and by the respondents from developing countries. At the other end of the scale were services and tourism, drug control, and transportation.

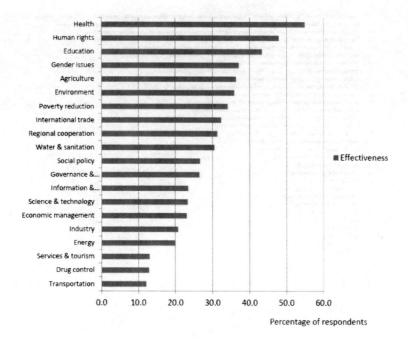

Figure 12.4 FUNDS survey respondents: favored UNDS domains
Source: FUNDS Global Survey 2012

Respondents from the South were more strongly in favor of agriculture, trade, and economic management. Those from the North were more positive about gender issues, water and sanitation, social policy, energy, and governance.

The preferences by domain are reflected in assessments of individual UN organizations, since the World Health Organization (WHO) and UNICEF were also ranked highest for effectiveness and relevance (in both the 2010 and 2012 surveys). Interestingly, it was the cohort of UN staff members who proved to be highly self-critical, displaying the widest range of organizational relevance (see Figure 12.5). In the 2012 survey, they also ranked UNICEF and WHO highest by a significant margin. At the other end of the scale, fewer than 20 percent considered 12 UN organizations as relevant, including four of the five UN regional commissions and four of the technical norm-setting agencies. These preferences clearly reflected a strong "field operations" bias. The global surveys also sought opinions on the main DaO principles, revealing strong support for greater in-country convergence (see Figure 12.6), and particularly single offices and UN leaders.

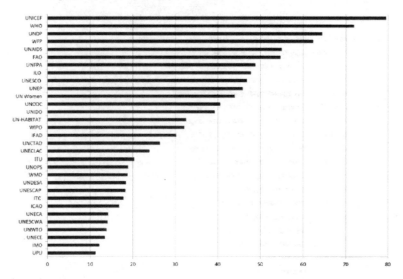

Figure 12.5 FUNDS survey respondents: assessment of organizational relevance
         by UN staff
Source: FUNDS Global Survey 2012

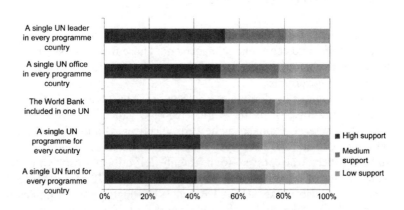

Figure 12.6 FUNDS survey respondents on Delivering as One
Source: FUNDS Global Survey 2012

Where next for reform?

To this point, the reform narrative runs as follows: The parts of the original UN that have become its development system were never organized around a coherent structure. The system has subsequently grown by accretion, becoming increasingly dispersed and atomized. From quite early days, however, the need for more coherence was recognized, and there have been repeated attempts to reform the system, calling for unified oversight and greater convergence. For various reasons, successive reform initiatives have fallen short and the institutions in place have approved only incremental changes. While wholesale reforms have stalled, surveys have confirmed that the UNDS is facing a threefold challenge of coherence, relevance, and complacency. The danger, therefore, is that support for the UNDS from member states will fade faster than effective change can be wrought. The signs of this fading interest can already be seen in falling core and non-core contributions, withdrawals from membership of some development organizations,[16] and a declining interest in positions of UN leadership.

Designing a revamped UNDS can more easily be done on paper than in practice. There is no effective head of the UNDS despite calls for one in 1977 (director-general of development) and 2006 (development coordinator). There is no effective oversight body, which ECOSOC might have been intended to become. There is no single global fund in the style of the EPTA in 1950, arguably the last year in which UN programmatic coherence prevailed.

There are, nevertheless, a few frontiers of change of both a structural and procedural nature that can and should be pursued to prevent the decline of the UNDS. The HLP's 2006 report contains many important and insightful recommendations, most of which remain to be implemented. However, there are two notable exceptions. One was the creation of UN Women in 2010, which demonstrated that it is possible to get agreement on merging related parts of the system. The resulting creation of a wholly new entity (as opposed to the choice of harboring it within an existing organization, such as the UN Population Fund) will be justified if the familiar centrifugal forces of autonomy, competition, and turf can be constrained.

The second initiative has been the concerted attempt, driven by the UNDG, to deliver as one at the country level. The timetable envisaged by the 2006 HLP has faltered, but significant progress has been achieved in and beyond the original eight pilot countries (Pakistan, Viet Nam, Tanzania, Rwanda, Mozambique, Cape Verde, Uruguay, and Albania). And the principle has been adopted in a growing number of "self-starters" (32 to date, with 70 countries implementing elements of DaO).

The overall evaluation of the DaO approach has been generally positive, as evidenced by the stock-taking exercises in seven of the eight pilots, the declarations of governments in annual review meetings, and the 2012 independent evaluation commissioned by the General Assembly.[17] As early as 2009, all the pilot and self-starter countries agreed at a meeting in Kigali that there is "no way back."[18] That assessment was reiterated in stronger terms at subsequent meetings in Hanoi, Montevideo, and Tirana.[19]

The evaluation determined that the DaO approach has resulted in a number of benefits. Joint programming has been better aligned with national priorities and has become more demand- rather than supply-driven. Programming has become more transparent for governments, development partners, civil society, and UN organizations. Within each program document, all stakeholders have a concrete, clear idea what the UN will be doing during the next programming cycle and how. There has also been more predictability, with a clearer overview of activities, expected results, and budgets. Since governments now only need to sign one instead of several documents, joint monitoring and reporting has decreased the burden on implementing partners. Accountability has been enhanced by a better division of labor. UN organizations are working in areas where they have the greatest capacity and comparative advantage and are accountable for the results achieved.

In terms of efficiency, joint programming has increased internal UN transaction costs, with more time and resources being spent on co-ordination, but such cost increases need to be assessed against the expected benefits in terms of improved development impact. Furthermore, transaction costs with external partners, government, and donors have substantially decreased, ensuring more transparent and streamlined communication, decision making, monitoring, and evaluation. There has also been better use of resources, including some savings in operations. In the best example of convergence, in the Joint UN Office in Cape Verde, three international professional posts were saved and the three Rome-based agencies (the FAO, World Food Programme [WFP], and the International Fund for Agricultural Development) have embarked on joint procurement and travel management processes. The WFP has been saving $3 million a year since 2010 through the use of a "connect system" relying on a cloud-based infrastructure used for data processing, email, voice communication, and video conferencing.

Joint procurement is becoming the norm in some of the larger duty stations, where economies of scale can be achieved, and in Mozambique and Tanzania the country teams have also set up joint data communication infrastructures. But as the independent evaluation also records, there also are downsides to the DaO experience. While joint programming has led to larger and more coherent programs with stronger participation from non-resident agencies, it remains difficult to strike the right balance between a strategic focus on a few priority outcomes, involving a few key, high-impact agencies, and inclusiveness, encompassing a large number of UN agencies, whose impact on the priority development challenges of the country may not be very significant. While the use of the single budgetary framework has enhanced transparency of resource requirements, it has been applied in different ways in different countries, making the aggregation of data difficult.

The resident coordinator function has been strengthened, and recruitment procedures have become increasingly competitive, with some 40 percent of RCs now coming from the UN family, outside the UNDP. But the RC still lacks formal authority over the country team, since vertical accountability of agency heads to their parent organization prevails over horizontal and mutual accountability of the RC and the country team members for delivering on the outcomes of the One Programme—in spite of the endorsement of the 2008 Management and Accountability Framework by all UNDG agencies.

Single funds have been touted as a potential contributor to greater coherence, and they have given programming flexibility to governments and country teams, as well as to UN organizations without country representation. However, the size of these funds varies significantly across countries (it represents 33 percent of funding requirements in Viet Nam but only 6 percent in Pakistan),[20] and their sustainability is in question because they are declining in size and dependent on a small group of donors—five donors contribute over 80 percent. Joint programs, therefore, have to rely heavily on non-core resources.

The single office is perhaps where the greatest challenges remain. Progress has been slow, and few costs have been saved. It is here that the General Assembly, through the 2012 resolution 67/226 on the Quadrennial Comprehensive Policy Review (QCPR; a periodic deliberation on the operations of the UNDS) has been most explicit in urging more harmonization. The resolution requests UN organizations to reduce the duplication of functions as well as administrative and transaction costs, through the consolidation of support services at the country level and the establishment of common services at the country, regional, and headquarters levels; the harmonization of procurement practices; and system-wide interoperability of enterprise resource planning systems, with the objective of harmonizing the electronic processing of internal and external management information.

Has the DaO process reached its limits?[21] While the principles of a common UN have spread to more countries, securing the full benefits of the DaO initiative will require several objectives to be met. One is the complete alignment of procedures and business practices with the support of the headquarters of the respective parts of the UNDS. The other is a move toward genuine integration (as has been demonstrated in Cape Verde, see Box 12.1) as opposed to convergence.

Box 12.1 The joint office in Cape Verde: a model to be replicated?

The first, and so far only, joint office was established in Cape Verde in 2006, responding to concerns that separate UN offices in smaller countries ran up excessively high management costs in relation to the value of the programs being delivered. The office is headed by a single representative of the UNDP, UNICEF, and UNFPA, who is supported by an integrated program unit, a common operations unit, and a single administrative platform. The government and other development partners have seen clear advantages in a single UN interlocutor and integration has facilitated the design and implementation of several joint programs, supported by a single results framework and a common budget.

However, the ambition of having a common business platform has been thwarted by the inability of the organizations' enterprise resource planning (ERP) systems to communicate. And the lack of access by the staff to the three organizations' administrative systems and knowledge and expertise platforms has diluted their sense of identity and impacted the office's ability to represent fully the agencies' mandates. Before the joint office model can be replicated in other small program countries, it is essential that the participating agencies renew their ownership of and commitment to the model and fully empower the representative and the staff by giving them full access to their resources. It is also essential that the joint office be mainstreamed into DaO, allowing the UN to respond better to the needs of small program countries.

Neither objective will be easy to reach. Greater harmonization of procedures and platforms has been urged for many years, but the progress has been halting. A particularly startling example is the failure of individual UN organizations to agree on a single enterprise resource planning (ERP) platform. The antecedents for integration are not promising either. More than two decades ago, following the break-up of the Soviet Union, "unified" UN offices were established in 12 of the new republics. These offices were well ahead of the current DaO examples. They were headed by a single UN representative and began to pursue unified funding and programming arrangements. By 1994, however, after only two years, the experiment collapsed in the face of intra-UN rivalry and the insistence of some organizations on their own representative offices in the same former Soviet countries.

The General Assembly resolution requests that progress on the QCPR recommendations be monitored and reported. However, the problem, as ever, is the flimsiness of the mandate from the first UN. The General Assembly and ECOSOC can "request" the UN funds and programs to take action, but only "encourage" the specialized agencies, which recognize the primacy of their own governing bodies. Within the system itself, implementation by the second UN is subject to the authority of the secretary-general in the Chief Executives Board (CEB), which he chairs, and the UNDG, which the UNDP administrator chairs. But neither has the formal authority to impose any obligations on the specialized agencies.

The evaluations of DaO and the QCPR processes show a cautious way forward, underlining the operational role of the UN in helping countries to achieve better development outcomes, while reaffirming universal standards, norms, and values. The HLP report also continues to be relevant as a realistic basis for reform, and there is continuing scope for the second UN to take up its remaining proposals. There are also mandates from other intergovernmental processes. The outcome document of the UN Conference on Sustainable Development (Rio +20) of June 2012 proposed the creation of a High-level Political Forum to "provide political leadership, guidance and recommendations for sustainable development," as well as consultation and oversight of sustainable development activities. On the plus side, the "high-level political" composition suggests that it could become a body with some authority. However, there has to be a consensus within UN circles about a broader definition of sustainable development, which hitherto has been synonymous with energy and environmental management.

228   *Stephen Browne and Cécile Molinier*

Conclusion

Whether they are considered crises, or merely challenges, the circumstances that confront the UNDS today are a clarion call for accelerated reform, loudly echoed by global opinion. Without change, the coziness of the status quo will condemn the UN's development activities to growing irrelevance in a world of rapid transformation. Nothing short of a strategic repositioning is required for the UN to rediscover its role in a changing global environment. Yet progress so far has amounted mainly to tinkering with procedures, as opposed to more comprehensive structural change.

Where will the needed reforms come from? The hermetic and procedure-bound nature of UN intergovernmental processes is not propitious for reform. Even when the debating chambers let some light in from specially appointed commissions, or from parallel civil society meetings, the proposals are watered down through compromise and the retreat into voting blocs. Rio+20 in 2012 provides just one more recent example.

The introverted nature of UN discussions has been blamed on the permanent representative system. Senior diplomats in the main UN headquarters are expected to have positions on the entire gamut of UN interests. Partly in consequence, diplomatic representation in UN development forums is spread thinly and "has led to the neglect of substantive issues in interactions between governments and these bodies, and to an almost exclusive concern with administration and personnel rather than specific normative, policy, and operational questions."[22]

Extending its external partnerships, the UN has strengthened its links to nongovernmental organizations and can benefit from closer partnerships with the private sector. Relations with business can be mutually beneficial and also have their perils,[23] but on the UN side, responsive and un-bureaucratic business practices should be emulated. Other sources of outside influence can be opinion surveys on the impact of the UNDS's activities and overall approaches. These have helped to expose a very sheltered system to the opinions of those whom it purports to assist and hold a mirror up to the current shortcomings of UN development, underlining the need for reform.

While the first UN of member states needs more exposure to the development world outside, there is also considerable scope for the second UN of secretariats to modernize the system. Champions of change are required in all parts of the system. Also critical is a sense of commitment by the organizational heads of the UNDS, acting more as generals than secretaries, with the communication skills to match. Vision is not easily contrived, but it can be stimulated by a heightened perception of looming crisis. Funding can be a big part of the equation. In 2014, a funding drought threatens, and for the reform process shrinking resources could help to raise the sense of urgency. Diminished funding could force harder choices that have been postponed for too long.

The picture is not entirely gloomy. Taking some inspiration from the creation of UN Women through consolidation, there is an ongoing attempt to bring together seven UN training and research institutions, which all fall under the direct authority of the secretary-general,[24] in order to create a UN knowledge management and networking center. A closer look inside the UN also reveals a strong sense of innovation in many places. At the country level, where UN teams often work closely together, there are many examples of successful (albeit partial) UN convergence with gains in reduced costs, programming coherence, and development effectiveness. Successful innovations emanating from any part of the system should be recognized and replicated.

These changes are positive, but they still do not meet the structural needs of the UN's development system that those within it recognized many decades ago. Now, more than ever, there is a need for a "brainy" center, which could only be guaranteed by two conditions, each of which has been proposed at different times.[25] One is the appointment of an authoritative and globally renowned development specialist as the head of UN development, with the seniority not merely to convene but also to advise and direct the different parts of the system. The second condition is intimately connected to the first and has growing pertinence as the United Nations faces new budgetary strains: increased funding for the priorities of the agreed UN development agenda, combined with pooled funding at the country level. Both proposals would substantially reduce duplication, obviate wasteful competitive soliciting of resources, and ensure more strategic UNDS responses.

As a consequence, the UN could reposition itself strategically. It is imperative that it adapt its presence and interventions to the requirements of a radically changed world, which implies a reduced and differentiated presence, better quality strategic advice, and more coherent facilitation of access to and management of knowledge and expertise.

Notes

1 Robert Gillman Allen Jackson, *The Capacity of the United Nations Development System*, vol. I (Geneva: UN, 1969), 33 (hereafter *The Capacity Study*).
2 Ibid., para. 31.

3 Quoted in Craig N. Murphy, *The United Nations Development Programme: A Better Way?* (Cambridge: Cambridge University Press, 2006), 142.
4 Craig N. Murphy and Stephen Browne, "UNDP: Reviving a Practical Human Development Organization," FUNDS Briefing no. 6, June 2013. www.futureun.org/en/Publications-Surveys/Article?newsid=12
5 John Burley and Stephen Browne, forthcoming chapter in Dan Plesch and Thomas G. Weiss, eds, *Wartime History and the Future United Nations: Past as Prelude?* (London: Routledge, 2014); Timo Mahn, "Country-level Aid Coordination at the United Nations: Taking the Resident Coordinator System Forward," German Development Institute, June 2013, 19. www.die-gdi.de/uploads/media/Studies_77.pdf
6 Bruce Jenks, "Emerging Issues in Development Operations," UN Department of Economic and Social Affairs, April 2012, 19. www.un.org/esa/coordination/pdf/desa_emerging_issues_2012.pdf
7 Silke Weinlich, "Reforming Development Cooperation at the United Nations: An Analysis of Policy Position and Actions of Key States on Reform Options," German Development Institute, March 2011, 25. http://acuns.org/wp-content/uploads/2012/06/ReformingDevelopmentCooperation.pdf
8 United Nations, "Analysis of Funding of Operational Activities for Development of the United Nations System for the Year 2010," UN Department of Economic and Social Affairs, July 2012, 14.
9 Stephen Browne, *The United Nations Development Programme and System* (London: Routledge, 2011), Chapter 1.
10 *Delivering as One: Report of the Secretary-General's High-level Panel on UN System-wide Coherence in the areas of development, humanitarian assistance and the environment* (New York: UN, 2007), 44.
11 Thomas G. Weiss, Tatiana Carayannis, and Richard Jolly, "The 'Third' United Nations," *Global Governance* 15, no. 1 (2009): 123–42.
12 Stephen Browne and Thomas G. Weiss, *Making Change Happen: Enhancing the UN's Contributions to Development* (New York: World Federation of United Nations Associations, 2012).
13 Thomas G. Weiss, "ECOSOC Is Dead, Long Live ECOSOC," *Perspectives*, Friedrich Ebert Stiftung, December 2010, 1.
14 Stephen Browne and Thomas G. Weiss, "How Relevant Are the Regional Commissions?" FUNDS Briefing no. 1, February 2013, www.futureun.org/media/archive1/briefings/FUNDS_Brief1.pdf.
15 Ramesh Thakur, "The G20 Versus the UN: Rival Development Forums?" FUNDS Briefing no. 3, April 2013. www.futureun.org/en/Publications-Surveys/Article?newsid=9
16 For example, following the withdrawal of the United Kingdom from the UN Industrial Development Organization in 2012, France has announced its departure in 2014.
17 *Independent Evaluation of Delivering as One* (New York: UN, 2012), 74–75.
18 Weinlich, "Reforming Development Cooperation," 27.
19 "Delivering as One: The United Nations We Want—Our Commitment to the Way Forward," United Nations Development Group, June 2012, www.undg.org/docs/12604/Tirana%20Outcome%20Document.pdf
20 *Independent Evaluation of Delivering as One*, 307.
21 Silke Weinlich and Urs Zollinger, "Lessons from Delivering as One: Options for UN Member States," German Development Institute Briefing

Paper 13/2012, November 2012. www.die-gdi.de/en/briefing-paper/article/lessons-from-delivering-as-one-options-for-un-member-states/
22 Leelananda de Silva, "The UN Development System: Taking it Local," FUNDS Briefing no. 9, August 2013, www.futureun.org/media/archive1/briefings/FUNDS_Brief9_August2013.pdf
23 Asmita Naik, "Can the UN Adjust to the Changing Funding Landscape?" FUNDS Briefing no. 2, March 2013, www.futureun.org/media/archive1/briefings/Briefing-2-FINAL.pdf
24 The Dag Hammarskjöld Library (DHL), Library of the United Nations Office at Geneva (UNOGL), United Nations Institute for Training and Research (UNITAR), United Nations Institute for Disarmament Research (UNIDIR), United Nations Interregional Crime and Justice Research Institute (UNICRI), United Nations Research Institute for Social Development (UNRISD), United Nations System Staff College (UNSSC).
25 In 1977 the UN agreed to the designation of a "director general for development and international economic cooperation" to head the development system. However, as in most senior UN appointments, then and now, the two successive incumbents of the post were not international development specialists. The director general had no control over funding. Well before that, in the 1950s, the UN also had a central funding mechanism, the EPTA, but it allocated funds by a system of entitlement rather than development need.

13 Conclusion

Post-2015, can change happen?

Stephen Browne and Thomas G. Weiss

This book is about the crying need for comprehensive and radical reform of the United Nations development system (UNDS) and of the individual organizations within it. This final chapter reviews the reasons for change, followed by a list of recommendations suggested by the analyses in the preceding chapters. While contributors undoubtedly would agree to most of our suggestions, what follows reflects the editors' views.

This chapter departs from the realization that the UN's emphasis on technical assistance is outmoded while global public goods remain woefully under-provided. The globe looks very different than it did in 1945. If the UN is to remain a relevant rather than an anachronistic actor in the development arena, it must adjust its strategy to meet twenty-first-century challenges; alter its in-country operations to enhance effectiveness and reduce waste; generate greater collaboration to further ideas and advocacy; expand participation of civil society; and create more robust compliance mechanisms for agreed norms and conventions.

Elsewhere we have made the case and pleaded for a dramatic and complete overhaul of the UNDS, but here the recommendations aim at the first five years of the post-2015 era. They are hardly pie-in-the-sky proposals but rather well-grounded and doable for those interested in anything except inertia and maintaining the status quo. Indeed, they are either based on a best-practice experience that merits consideration and replication more widely, or they are already under discussion within intergovernmental or administrative forums. Some in fact are inspired by former UN secretary-general Kofi Annan's last comprehensive reform agenda, which has only partially been implemented.

Shifting strategy to address twenty-first-century challenges

The foregoing pages have largely begged two obvious questions: Why change? Should the United Nations continue to have a role in supporting development? The short answer to both is "yes," but the logic is different for each.

The world organization was founded on principles of multilateral cooperation. Before "development" was defined and refined, the UN Charter referred to the need for "international economic and social cooperation." During the UN's early years, cooperation had been translated into a transfer of expertise and resources from richer to poorer countries, with the UN itself and its system of organizations playing a leading role in the transmission.

The world has changed but the UN has not. After almost seven decades, development has succeeded, to the extent that there are three times as many people on the planet and more of them are leading better lives. While there are still stubborn areas of impoverishment, the number of poor countries has declined markedly and many are graduating to middle- and upper-income status. What Kishore Mahbubani calls the "great convergence"[1] had long been anticipated by such economists as Simon Kuznets.[2]

With globalization has come international convergence but accompanied by exacerbated income inequalities within countries. Notwithstanding the existence of a bottom billion in more fragile states,[3] the largest concentrations of the world's poor now are in large and well-resourced middle-income countries, suggesting that solutions to poverty are more likely to be found in domestic policy decisions than in improving traditional aid disbursements and practices.[4]

At the same time, "problems without passports" that transcend borders have proliferated. Global cooperation should emphasize the generation of global public goods. In the health domain, for example, progress would mean developing vaccines and managing global pandemics rather than building clinics. The context of cooperation is thus changing from ODA (official development assistance) version 1.0, based on international resource transfers from the North to the global South, to ODA 2.0, heralding a new era of global development cooperation in which responsibility is more widely shared.[5] In some ways, we could consider that we are returning to the original intention of the Charter and redefining "cooperation."

Of prime concern today is thus whether the world organization actually has the capacity to adjust to the new era of cooperation necessitated by the globalization of development challenges. This book has outlined five future domains of change. But the UN and its individual organizations are still looking inward and taking a very self-interested and short-term perspective. It is by no means clear that the United Nations has yet begun to anticipate the consequences of change-drivers—the ones figuring prominently here are migration and mobility; political economy; security; the physical environment; and science and technology—or indeed from where such consideration would come. In light of the absence of a strategic center of deliberation—what Robert Jackson referred to as a "brain"[6]—our first recommendation, therefore, is a plea for forward-looking strategic thinking.

Recommendation 1

Under the auspices of the Chief Executives' Board (CEB), a high-level panel should be appointed to examine the implications for the system of the new era of global development cooperation.

Changing the implementation and focus of country operations

The findings from the previous chapters suggest that in order to improve its performance the United Nations should develop more robust evaluation mechanisms; better allocate resources by developing more in-country coherence to its programming, including through a single budget; withdraw from emerging economies; and concentrate on war-torn societies.

In brief, the new context that confronts the UNDS lies beyond aid as we and the world organization and its partners have known it.[7] In most developing and in all emerging countries, the main impediments to accelerated development no longer are a lack of expertise and resources, which once was the case and provided the justification for a huge transmission effort. Thus, the UN's perennial pursuit of resources to fund technical assistance should be a fading priority, especially since the world organization's record is less than exemplary in many domains.

In a workshop to consider the draft chapters of this book, one of the authors aptly observed, "The UN has failed as an aid delivery mechanism. It has lost the race to others." Then he added, "But it doesn't matter!" We think it does, however, because there is no alternative for the legitimacy and leverage that comes from the world organization and its universal membership. While the need for traditional forms of assistance is receding, the UNDS soldiers on even though it often performs poorly, or at least less effectively than many other competitors—ranging from nongovernmental organizations to transnational corporations, from regional organizations and banks to bilateral aid agencies—as sources of assistance and expertise that have emerged over the UN's lifetime.

This perception is confirmed by the global surveys conducted by the Future UN Development System (FUNDS) Project.[8] Indeed, the range of perceived relevance or effectiveness of the UN, whether across development domains or among individual organizations, is startling. Consistently at the top end of the scale are health, education, and human rights. Correspondingly, the World Health Organization (WHO) and UNICEF are also considered most relevant by some 60 percent of respondents. But at the other end of the scale, there are areas where the world body is judged to be ineffective. Almost half of the UN development organizations are considered of "low relevance" by 40 percent or more of respondents who claim to know of the organizations. And among the least well-rated activities is economic management.[9] While these are only perceptions, they are significant because they mainly (over 90 percent) emanate from precisely those respondents in the global South whom the UN is purporting to help and to work with.

Other responses confirm that the UN development system is perceived to be slow, hidebound by procedures, uncoordinated, and wasteful. A large part of the UN's operations on the ground are perceived by global surveys to be poorly targeted and uncoordinated and therefore ineffective. Moreover, some budgets are heavily absorbed by generous staff salaries and benefits and diminished by the purchase of vehicles and other hardware, which means fewer resources for intended beneficiaries.

Hence, the most visible of the UN's development roles is the target of these negative perceptions, namely its field operations; and some of the most vociferous critics are among UN staff. Impatience with the world organization's inability to change its operating style significantly is one of the reasons why traditional (and non-traditional) donors have so generously supported new experiments with vertical funds in health and environment outside of the UN system, which are capable of quicker disbursements and have better reputations for delivering results.

But does the UN's marginalization matter? "No" and "yes" are the answers. "No" because, in fact, the United Nations is becoming less crucial in relationship to growing competition as other sources are picking up the slack and performing better, and economic growth and trade become far more essential than outside assistance. At the same time, an affirmative answer suggests why a marginalized world organization constitutes a loss for a more just and fair world order. First, to a growing degree, UN field operations have become examples of what has been described as "Trojan multilateralism."[10] They are funded by external sources, casting UN organizations in the role of implementing agencies on behalf of individual donor governments, or such major multilateral and vertical funds as the European Commission agencies and the Global Fund. These "non-core" sources take advantage of the extensive field networks of UN organizations and their working relationships with counterparts in governments. While these non-core resources have helped to keep many UN organizations and their staffs afloat, heavy patronage from the global North has altered perceptions of the United Nations as an objective and neutral source of assistance. "Cooptation" most often describes this evolution. These new sources of funding, in other words, detract from the unusual advantages of UN operations, namely a reputation for impartiality and neutrality.

How can we assess the UN's track record? Perceptions through surveys tend to be negative. Comparative analyses rank the world organization lower than many other multilateral and bilateral sources. And the emergence of large parallel funding mechanisms suggests a loss of confidence in UN operations—even if some of these alternative funds are channeled back into the United Nations. However, project evaluations undertaken by individual UN organizations are mostly positive. Who should we believe?

As this book has highlighted, there are serious shortcomings in the UN's evaluation practices; credible and common independent systems have yet to be established. The fact that seven decades after its founding we are still struggling to implement "common" evaluations is a microcosm of larger problems. To obtain a more accurate reading of performance, meaningful evaluation within the UN needs to come from at least three different directions: reliable and comparable metrics to assess performance; much greater independence of evaluation offices from senior UN management; and system-wide evaluations to identify relative organizational strengths and weakness as well as duplication. To its credit, the General Assembly in its 2012 resolution 67/226 emphasized improving evaluation in its Quadrennial Comprehensive Policy Review (QCPR), stressing "the need to strengthen independent and impartial system-wide evaluation of operational activities for development." We support that emphasis.

Recommendation 2

Independent system-wide evaluation of the UN's operational activities should be undertaken at the global, regional, and especially country levels, not merely to have information and comparison but in order to determine the development performance of the system. It is essential to highlight strengths and weaknesses, areas of duplication, and opportunities for more cost-effective outcomes. At the country level, UN development assistance frameworks (UNDAFs) intended to encompass all UN activities should be evaluated for their impact.

To ensure comprehensive oversight of the UN, consideration should also be given to setting up system-wide services of auditing and investigation. All forms of oversight should not only be agreed, but also implemented and acted upon.

More positively, UN projects still represent helpful resources flowing to the global South and rarely harm the development process. We have argued elsewhere that the first UN of member states—whether donors, emerging powers, or recipients—considers the world organization "too friendly to fail."[11] It follows therefore that for many with a stake in the organization, the more UN, the better. Politically, that may be an acceptable maxim. But when resources are finite, it is managerially as well as fiscally indefensible. Hence, the United Nations (especially the second UN of secretariats) should use funds where it has genuine comparative advantages and avoid those where it has comparative disadvantages even if resources are available.

One participant in the 2012 FUNDS global survey summarized: "Given better capabilities in other parts of the international development system, the UN should exit from all activities that these agencies undertake. The UN should then focus on what it can do best: building consensus, keeping peace, raising visibility on global issues and the like. [It should] get out of other areas of direct operations."[12] Thus, a salutary aspect to the UN's cutting back on marginal operations would be redeploying to areas where it can make a difference.

Irrespective of quality, UN technical assistance is increasingly superfluous in countries advancing to middle- and upper-income status. Even the physical presence of most partners in the UN development system may be questioned. In another 2013 FUNDS survey, this time of a panel of invited global experts, 20 percent of respondents thought that the UN should have no presence at all in emerging economies. And of those who thought that a presence was still desirable, 80 percent recommended a unified office with a higher priority accorded to human rights, partnership building, information, and advocacy than to technical assistance.[13]

Unified offices were proposed by the 2006 High-level Panel on UN System-wide Coherence,[14] and a modest congruence of UN organizations has resulted. Although there have been benefits for host governments in dealing with fewer UN interlocutors, the 2012 evaluation of the initiative found that attempts to "deliver as one" (DaO) had driven up transaction costs—certainly for UN organizations and for some governments—precisely the opposite of the desired outcome from the point of view of efficiency and cost-effectiveness.[15] The best example of One UN (apart from the fully unified offices temporarily established in the countries of the former Soviet Union in the early 1990s) has been in Cape Verde, a small African country that has recently graduated from least-developed status. Here a UN representative was formally accredited to several organizations, obviating the need for the United Nations to appoint separate representatives for each organization and truncating the costly processes of coordinating programs driven from headquarters. It is still the best demonstration of how the system can be more cost-effective.

Recommendation 3

The UN development system should accelerate the process of consolidation at the country level, if necessary setting cost-reduction targets to ensure a more economical use of resources. Since One UN works best when there is integration rather than convergence, its presence in the upper-middle- and higher-income countries should be confined to a single integrated office which, while acting as a mouthpiece of the UN as a whole, manages a diminishing portfolio of technical assistance operations.

The UN's operational activities are still, and even especially, pertinent in conflict-prone and fragile states because the world organization has a unique capability of pulling together the various components—security, humanitarian, human rights, transition, and development—of outside efforts in such countries. The challenges, of course, are complex and delicate. The transition from the economics of war to the economics of peace and then to the economics of sustained development require the gamut of political, security, humanitarian, and development-related expertise and resources available from the UN system. The RAND Corporation judged the UN's record superior to US bilateral efforts in peacekeeping and transition in war-torn societies.[16] But the world organization's record in transitions has left much to be desired, again in large part because of a failure of integration, not just of the development system, but especially of the UN as a whole. On one side of New York's First Avenue, the UN Secretariat harbors peacekeeping and political affairs but lacks a global operational presence. On the other side, the UNDP and UNICEF provide operational and humanitarian services but steer clear of political and security concerns. The political and non-political UNs operate in parallel universes. At the instance of the Security Council, missions are designated and deployed drawing on staff from different organizations, but they rarely achieve the cohesion or versatility demanded in conflict-prone states. The problem is similar to that of One UN countries: each senior official reports to a different headquarters. Until recently, even the employment conditions and pay-scales of UN officials reporting to different parts of the UN, but with identical seniority, were different. Peacebuilding missions should also be provided with sufficient financial resources to ensure that their activities can be fully sustained until peaceful circumstances prevail. This entire arena is generally regarded as an important and growing area of UN comparative advantage.

Recommendation 4

In conflict-prone and otherwise fragile states, the UN has the capacity to support peacebuilding, all under the sole authority of the secretary-general. Yet its performance is less cohesive and coordinated than it should be. The UN should constitute integrated missions that are tailored to the needs of each situation and adequately resourced, providing a single reference point to which all parts of the mission respond and report.

For effective country operations, at least two other considerations are paramount. One is under active consideration while the other has been ignored.

Business practices are in the first category. A converging system is under pressure to make its procedures more compatible, not merely among the funds and programs under the authority of the secretary-general but across the specialized agencies as well. The 2012 General Assembly's resolution about the QCPR aims at the long-overdue rationalization and harmonization of their business practices and operations. It "requests" the funds and programs (i.e., the UNDP, UNICEF, World Food Programme, and UN Population Fund) and "encourages" the specialized agencies to do so; and it expects progress by 2016.

Central to this process will be encouraging electronic compatibility, an area where the absence of harmonization has entailed substantial additional costs. Lacking central guidance, and with no thought for their role within the system, each organization has made an independent choice of its enterprise resource planning (ERP) system amounting to investments in the tens of millions of dollars. In addition to the higher costs of each organization's going it alone, the UN is now making substantial additional investments to ensure that the different ERP systems can actually communicate with one another. Greater harmonization would greatly facilitate the pooling of administrative services in each country and also result in significant cost savings. If the UN were conscious of a bottom line, harmonization undoubtedly would have occurred long ago. Unfortunately we are not pushing on an open door, although such standardization seems an obvious first step in the direction of necessary integration.

Another recommendation of the 2006 high-level panel was to have a single budget for a composite UN program in each country. Moreover, there is no question that one funding source for the system under the authority of each UN resident coordinator would do more than anything else to promote unity. In the first flush of enthusiasm, several One UN Funds were established. But in each country, they covered only a small part of the total UN program, attracted few donors, and have since begun to dry up. There should be a renewed attempt at consolidation pursued by the UN Development Group and supported by donors.

Recommendation 5

In each One UN country, a single program framework should be drawn up to encompass the activities of all UN organizations, and it should be supported by a single multi-year budget framework to which donors willing to support the UN in that country should contribute exclusively.

Enhancing collaboration to advance ideas and advocacy

If the regular and long-standing operational activities of the United Nations should be better managed for purposes of cost-effectiveness in some poorer countries, and scaled back in middle-income ones in order to free-up resources to concentrate on conflict-prone countries where the UN has a comparative advantage, there will remain essential functions for the organizations of the UN development system to pursue in all countries. First and foremost, the UN has been a fount of ideas: the right to development itself, fairer international economic relations, women's empowerment, environmental sustainability, and human development. It is no exaggeration to claim that these ideas have "changed the world."[17] It is certain that UN thinking has been influential and could have been more so had international power politics been more propitious. Alternative development paths have often been followed—or rather pressed on developing countries—impelled more by banking strictures than human development goals and with a scale of financial backing (mainly from sources such as the Bretton Woods institutions) that was unavailable to the United Nations.

That the Washington Consensus prevailed over the UN's agenda illustrates the golden rule—the organization with the gold rules. It also suggests that the UNDS was unable to get fully behind an influential paradigm of its own. The most original and also the most comprehensive example was human development, expounded since 1990 by the UNDP in more than 20 annual reports (and 700 regional and country reports). But because of atomization and rivalry within the system, without central leadership or pooled resources to guide it, development ideas have been strictly identified with one or another organization. Hence, human development itself remained largely a UNDP monopoly, while other UN organizations promulgated their own versions of social, sustainable, and other development guises.

From the human development story, there are two obvious conclusions. First, that the United Nations is an important source of value-driven development research. Research capacity resides in several organizations, including the International Labour Organization (ILO), the UN Conference on Trade and Development (UNCTAD), the UN Department of Economic and Social Affairs (DESA), the UN Educational, Social and Cultural Organization (UNESCO), and UNICEF, not to mention a clutch of research and training organizations such as the UN Research Institute for Social Development (UNRISD), and the UN University (UNU) and its many affiliated centers of excellence. Even within some of these entities, there are teams working on different aspects of development. A prime example is DESA, which has separate divisions for "development policy and analysis," "social policy and development," "public administration and development management," and "sustainable development."

The second conclusion is that a more concerted and collaborative approach to research by the system as a whole would give the UN a more influential voice in shaping development agendas. And of course partnerships with centers of excellence worldwide should be routine, not exceptional. The award of the Nobel Peace Prize to the Intergovernmental Panel on Climate Change (IPCC) provides a "model" of sorts for the kind of interagency effort (in this case, of the UN

Environment Programme and World Meteorological Organization) that pulls together world-class scientists and thinkers to address a problem and change the way that it is framed and perceived by policymakers.

DESA's convoluted and redundant divisional structure has deep historical roots. Most divisions were designed to be the secretariat of specialized commissions established early in the UN's existence, bringing together experts on key aspects of development research. These included commissions on social development, sustainable development, statistics, and population and development. They still exist today, and the Commission on Sustainable Development has been upgraded to a "high-level political forum" in the wake of the Rio+20 Conference in 2012. The worthy intentions of these commissions were to establish, at the heart of the UN, forums of deliberation on critical development issues.

Two of these commissions—on statistics, and on population and development—have remained among the most authoritative sources in their respective fields: national accounting systems and global demographic data, respectively.[18] But in other areas, the UN development system—not to mention the World Bank and many other competing development organizations—has moved on from the 1950s and 1960s. There has been, since then, substantial parallel growth of capacity for research to service other forums. The failure of the system to recognize and adjust to this evolution results in some unfortunate anomalies. One of the most obvious is the heavy overlap of the research activities among DESA, UNCTAD, and the five regional commissions. They all persist, for example, in producing international trade statistics, alongside the International Trade Centre (ITC), the World Trade Organization (WTO), the World Bank, and the International Monetary Fund (IMF). DESA, UNCTAD, and the ILO produce annual reports on a range of global (but not actually "human development") issues. And the list goes on.

Alternative sources of research would be less of a problem if there were not duplication of effort (and resources), and crucially if the UN system as a whole had a means of managing its knowledge, another priority highlighted but ignored by Robert Jackson's *Capacity Report* 45 years ago, but which today would be greatly facilitated by the existence of almost limitless electronic communication platforms.

Recommendation 6

The UN University should become a global hub for training and research for the UN system, assisting in communication, exchange, and dissemination among the extensive network of existing institutions. The UN should establish a smart electronic portal providing easy access to all past and ongoing research undertaken throughout the UN system.

The Millennium Declaration of 2000 and its Millennium Development Goals (MDGs) offspring helped to illustrate the importance of greater unity in the system. The MDGs provided a focus for virtually every organization, even if some only belatedly signed on to the goals. Consequently, the UN had a powerful basis for development advocacy, providing additional arguments for the system to concert its wide-ranging research efforts.

Recommendation 7

With consolidation would come the opportunity for stronger advocacy by the UN across a range of policies. Its positions on gender equality, income equality, human rights, international economic justice, environmental management, and other areas—based on original research inspired by UN ideals—should be backed by an enhanced communications role at the center of the system (e.g., by the UN Department of Public Information).

Promoting norms and compliance

Internationally agreed norms impart rationality to the process of decision making and are translated into national rules and standards, beginning with ratification by parliaments. Because the UN is fundamentally a normative forum, the same Chapter IX of the Charter and its Article 55, from which its activities of "international economic and social cooperation" are derived, is also one of the most significant. Warfare had defined the functions of international peace and security, while genocide had prompted the corollary inclusion of human worth: "universal respect for, and observance of, human rights and fundamental freedoms for all without distinction as to race, sex, language, or religion."[19] Charter Article 56 enjoins member states to take action to address these aims. Concerns of national sovereignty inhibited a more explicit formulation (as compared, for example, with the Charter's chapters on international peace and security), but these articles served to imbue the UN with the value-system that, in fact, is its hallmark. In the spirit of Article 55, many UN-agreed norms and conventions have followed, starting with the 1948 Universal Declaration of Human Rights and two subsequent agreements in 1966, the International Covenant on Economic, Social and Cultural Rights, and the International Covenant on Civil and Political Rights.

International norms pertaining to what we might call the "human condition" are invariably controversial. They may clash with national, regional, or other (e.g., religious) values. Given the timing of its formulation after World War II and prior to decolonization, the Universal Declaration was driven mainly by US and European interests, and there has been subsequent debate that "Asian values," for instance, are somehow different. As the frontiers of social norms are advanced, most often by societies in developed countries, these clashes become more acute, for example over issues such as contraception or sexual orientation. However, the character of a global debate, even when inconclusive, can help to draw attention to issues that are crucial for human well-being and can begin to change national policies.

The UN's deliberations have traditionally showcased the governments of its member states, and only governments can approve conventions and resolutions. In 2003, the UN secretary-general established a panel on UN–civil society relations, which a year later recommended that the UN "should engage more systematically with world public opinion to become more responsive" and "to help shape public attitudes."[20] While much remains to be done, to an important degree the UN has become more representative of world opinion, which has helped to widen the agenda for debate on issues pertaining to human well-being.

The UN's global conferences, beginning in the 1970s but particularly from the 1990s onward, have provided opportunities for civil society representatives to contribute to global debates and help influence the texts of intergovernmental outcomes.[21] This process has advanced furthest in the UN deliberations on human rights, gender, and the environment.[22] In the first Rio summit on sustainable development in 1992, the UN recognized nine sectors of society ("major groups") within which civil society organizations (CSOs) were encouraged to participate, carrying the idea forward to the annual commissions on sustainable development.

Recommendation 8

The UN should build on its experience in interacting with CSOs. It should establish processes to formalize their participation in intergovernmental deliberations, and mechanisms to guarantee more interaction with senior UN officials for purposes of advice, advocacy, implementation of programs, and monitoring.

The UN is an irreplaceable source of norms, whether in the form of soft law (declarations and resolutions) or hard law (conventions and treaties). But along with other intergovernmental organizations, it suffers from compliance gaps.[23] In the development arena, there is no Security Council or even the equivalent of the Human Rights Council's Universal Periodic Review (UPR) that seeks to monitor country performance in human rights. While monitoring is part of compliance, there are no sanctions tied to a monitored and verified noncompliance anywhere within the development arena. The anodyne wording of most declarations and resolutions reflects the course of least resistance and the lowest common denominator among the many disparate voices of the UN's membership. More meaningful and path-breaking resolutions are agreed by consensus—a prime example being the Millennium Declaration of 2000—because government representatives can sign up knowing that there are no consequences for noncompliance.

However, sanctions are not the only way to foster greater compliance. There is a lot that senior officials and secretariats of the second UN can do once the first UN of member states has come to an agreement. Following the signing of the Millennium Declaration in September 2000, the UN Secretariat could have launched a major communications campaign distributing the text to parliaments and civil society organizations around the world in local languages. Had it done so, the United Nations might not have spent at least the next decade trying to retail the MDGs to beneficiaries, with limited success. The key is in the nature of the monitoring and the conclusions that are drawn from it. Both processes need to be reliable and objective. Over the MDGs, there was much debate about the responsibility for producing country monitoring reports. In the end, it was decided that this should be the joint responsibility of the UN and the governments concerned. Consequently, these reports rarely apportioned blame or responsibility to governments when they were found to be falling short of the goals.[24]

Norm-setting in all its guises is a fundamental UN function and comparative advantage—there is, in fact, no competitor. But to have a greater impact on actual development processes, it needs to be linked to more meaningful compliance mechanisms.

> **Recommendation 9**
>
> Key normative instruments agreed by the UN, in whatever form, should be associated with compliance mechanisms that involve objective monitoring and are capable of identifying the explanations and causes of noncompliance. The role of the second UN should be not only to facilitate agreement but also to apportion responsibility for meeting agreed norms. This is another area in which the UN should work more closely with civil society organizations.

Technical standards are a special case of normative advance, and the preserve of many of the lesser-known specialized agencies, including those with the longest pedigrees. The International Telecommunication Union (ITU, established in 1865) and the Universal Postal Union (UPU, 1874) are two examples of public institutions established to facilitate international communications through universal standards. Other prominent standard-setters are the International Civil Aviation Organization (ICAO), International Maritime Organization (IMO), World Meteorological Organization (WMO), and World Intellectual Property Organization (WIPO).

But is intergovernmental standard-setting under UN auspices inevitable, or even desirable, particularly as private interests are the primary drivers of globalization? The example of the International Organization for Standardization (ISO), which uses "voluntary consensus standard-setting,"[25] suggests an alternative. Over more than 60 years, the ISO has established technical standards that affect a multitude of industrial products, as well as environmental, managerial and other quality norms. These standards have been agreed through elaborate consultations that include enterprises, consumers, and civil society organizations, in addition to governments and national standards organizations. Another nongovernmental organization, the Internet Corporation for Assigned Names and Numbers (ICANN), is responsible for assigning domain names, an essential aspect of Internet governance. After its founding in the 1990s, it quickly grew to take on a global dimension. Although individual governments have urged that ICANN's responsibilities be taken over by the ITU, this possibility has been opposed by user-groups who have access to ICANN and are evidently satisfied by the services that it provides.

The examples of ISO and ICANN suggest that, even if it is not directly applicable to existing UN organizations, voluntary consensus standard-setting could be applied to areas of negotiating norms and conventions in which there is a wide range of interested parties.

Recommendation 10

In the setting of norms and standards, as well as in other negotiations, voluntary consensus standard-setting could provide a useful model within but also outside the UN.

Appointing a development leader

Moving ahead with substantial change will require strong leadership at the very top of the world organization. But while the UN has a secretary-general who takes primary responsibility for international peace and security, the UN development system, which comprises the vast bulk of expenditures and employs the majority of professional staff, tends to get ignored in the press of high politics and diplomacy. Even those secretaries-general like Dag Hammarskjöld who wished to emphasize development became enmeshed in the high politics of international peace and security. The deputy secretary-general may or may not focus on this pillar of activities when he is not replacing the UN's chief diplomat. The absence of an authoritative head is a serious lacuna, which has long been recognized but never fully resolved.

Anyone taking a dispassionate look at the complex structure and labyrinthine processes of the UN development system would be astonished to find that it is expected to address and manage a new far-reaching, post-2015 development agenda without a leader. Our final recommendation, therefore, is a reprise of a proposal, codified in General Assembly resolution 32/197 of December 1977.

Recommendation 11

The General Assembly should ask the secretary-general to designate the administrator of the UNDP as director-general to lead the United Nations development system, exercise overall coordination within that system, and ensure the coherence, coordination, and efficient management of all activities in the economic and social fields financed by the regular budget or by extra-budgetary resources.

Final thoughts

Our conclusions and recommendations have been inspired by reflections about UN reform set out in the preceding chapters. However, much of what we are proposing here is based on existing recommendations from several sources. Some are under partial implementation. The door to reform is partially ajar, but it needs a far firmer push.

We nevertheless have few illusions about the difficulty of changing significantly the UN development system in order to make it fit for purpose in the post-2015 era. The most comprehensive agenda for change remains that of the 2006 high-level panel, but most of its recommendations have yet to be taken up. The contributors to this book, as well as the large constituency of interested parties whom we consult through periodic FUNDS surveys, believe that much more still needs to be done to give competitiveness, capacity, and coherence to the UNDS. But crucially, the first UN of governments and the second UN of staff must also overcome its greatest single obstacle: complacency. Business-as-usual is the default setting, but it cannot be if the United Nations is not to continue sliding toward being a marginal anachronism rather than the universal convener that is so desperately required.

Notes

1 Kishore Mahbubani, *The Great Convergence: Asia, the West and the Logic of One World* (New York: Public Affairs, 2013).
2 Simon Kuznets, "Economic Growth and Income Inequality," *American Economic Review* 45, no. 1 (1955): 1–28.
3 Paul Collier, *The Bottom Billion* (Oxford: Oxford University Press, 2007).
4 Andy Sumner, "Global Poverty and the New Bottom Billion," IDS Working Paper 349 (Brighton: IDS, 2010); Gilles Carbonnier and Andy Sumner, "Reframing Aid in a World Where the Poor Live in Emerging Economies," *International Development Policy*, special issue, no. 3 (2012): 3–18.
5 Andy Sumner and Richard Mallett, *The Future of Foreign Aid* (London: Palgrave Macmillan, 2013), 61.
6 United Nations, *A Study of the Capacity of the United Nations Development System (Capacity Study)* (Geneva: UN, 1969), UN document DP/5, 12–13.

7 Stephen Browne, *Beyond Aid: From Patronage to Partnership* (Aldershot: Ashgate, 1999); Olav Stokke, *The UN and Development: From Aid to Cooperation* (Bloomington: Indiana University Press, 2009).
8 Available at www.futureun.org/Surveys. A third global survey will take place in spring 2014 and be published later in 2014.
9 Stephen Browne, Thomas G. Weiss, and Vikas Nath, *How Relevant Is the Development UN* (FUNDS report based on 2012 global survey, 2012), available at www.futureun.org/media/archive1/reports/How-Relevant-Is-the-Development-UN.pdf
10 Devi Sridhar and Ngaire Woods, "Trojan Multilateralism: Global Co-operation in Health," *Global Policy* 4, no. 4 (2013): 325–35
11 Stephen Browne and Thomas G. Weiss, *Making Change Happen: Enhancing the UN's Contributions to Development* (New York: WFUNA, 2012), 11.
12 www.futureun.org/en/Publications-Surveys/Article?newsid=19
13 www.futureun.org/en/Publications-Surveys/Article?newsid=25
14 High-level Panel on UN System-wide Coherence, *Delivering as One* (New York: UN, 2007).
15 United Nations, *Independent Evaluation of Delivering as One, Main Report* (New York: UN, September 2012).
16 James Dobbins, *The UN's Role in Nation-Building: From the Congo to Iraq* (Santa Monica, Calif.: Rand Corporation, 2005).
17 Richard Jolly, Louis Emmerij, and Thomas G. Weiss, *UN Ideas That Changed the World* (Bloomington: Indiana University Press, 2009).
18 Michael Ward, *Quantifying the World: UN Ideas and Statistics* (Bloomington: Indiana University Press, 2004).
19 Peter R. Baehr and Leon Gordenker, *The United Nations: Reality and Ideal* (New York: Palgrave Macmillan, 2005).
20 Panel of Eminent Persons on UN–Civil Society Relationships, "We the Peoples: Civil Society, the UN and Global Governance," UN document A/58/817, 11 June 2004, 29.
21 Michael G. Schechter, *United Nations Global Conferences* (London: Routledge, 2005).
22 For discussions, see Roger Normand and Sarah Zaidi, *Human Rights at the UN: The Political History of Universal Justice* (Bloomington: Indiana University Press, 2008); Devaki Jain, *Women, Development, and the UN: A Sixty-Year Quest for Equality and Justice* (Bloomington: Indiana University Press, 2005); and Nico Schrijver, *Development without Destruction: The UN and Global Resource Management* (Bloomington: Indiana University Press, 2010).
23 Thomas G. Weiss and Ramesh Thakur, *Global Governance and the UN: An Unfinished Journey* (Bloomington: Indiana University Press, 2010).
24 During the ECOSOC's annual session in Geneva in July 2013, the UNDP administrator stated: "We don't monitor countries, we only monitor our own performance" (Author note).
25 Craig N. Murphy and JoAnne Yates, *The International Organization for Standardization* (London: Routledge, 2009).

Index

climate change 21, 24, 69, 185;
climate change migration 62–63,
70; developed country 98;
developing country 62–63, 98;
GPG agenda 28, 29; IPCC 24,
241; Momentum for Change 31;
SDGs 188; *see also* environment;
sustainability
Clinton, Hillary 47
Cold War 95, 97, 162, 164, 167, 213
collective action 65, 66, 70, 99, 107,
166
Collier, Paul 151
Cooper, Frederick 36
cooperation: development
cooperation 21, 22, 97–98, 102,
106, 213, 234; global cooperation
31, 32, 33, 64 (new demands on
global cooperation 11, 70);
inter-agency cooperation 27–28;
intergovernmental cooperation
17–18, 27; multilateral
cooperation 233; regional
cooperation 30–31; South–South
cooperation 9, 18, 30–31; UN as
"nucleus of global international
cooperation" 10, 32; UN Charter
233; *see also* partnership
corruption 25, 149, 151, 204
Cox, Robert 182
crime 69; organized crime 29, 61, 62,
69, 96, 97, 98, 130, 164, 165

DaO (Delivering as One) 3, 28, 89,
141, 191, 212, 214, 221, 223–27,
237; 2006 *Delivering as One* report
13; Annan, Kofi 48, 214;
assessment 100–101, 106, 107,
221, 224–26, 237 (achievements
100, 224–25; shortcomings 101,
225, 226); efficiency 224–25;
funding fragmented nature 85, 93;
One UN 174, 238–39, 240; pilot
countries for DaO 159, 223–24,
226; UN General Assembly 225;
unified office 237–38 (Cape Verde
226, 238); *see also* UNDS reform
DDR (disarmament,
demobilization, and reintegration)
133–36, 137, 139, 148, 169;

coordination 134; DDR fund 137;
demobilization 135; disarmament
134–35; Liberia 134; MDRP 134;
the military 134–35, 136; objective
134, 136; reintegration 134,
135–36; Sierra Leone 169; World
Bank 169; *see also* peacebuilding
Deaton, Angus 7
debt relief/forgiveness 25, 138, 185,
194
Del Castillo, Graciana 12, 144–59
democracy 5, 32, 48, 62;
peacebuilding mission 161, 168;
post-2015 DA 188; UN 19, 25, 44;
UN General Assembly 168
demography 57
developed country 8, 193; climate
change 98; costs of "being green"
62; donor 8, 77, 80, 81, 86–87, 90;
industrialized country 28, 64, 77,
80, 86, 87, 90, 199
developing country 7–8, 98, 193; aid
8, 131; climate change 62–63, 98;
donor 77, 80, 81–82, 131;
environmental damage 62, 98;
GPG agenda 28; IFIs 21;
international migration 58; NGO
199; ODA 46, 47; post-2015 DA
186–87; UN 21, 24, 35, 39, 40;
see also global South
development 20–21, 130, 132;
definition 184; development as
"development and poverty
eradication" 184; development
cooperation 21, 22, 97–98, 102,
106, 213, 234; development/
environmental agendas 24;
economic development 23, 97,
133, 137, 151; economic growth
130, 132; economics of
development 12, 146, 152;
government 19; Millennium
Declaration 184; peacebuilding/
development nexus 130, 134,
140–41, 147, 151, 168–69; pillar of
the UN system 11, 18, 129,
131–32; a second-order goal
96–97; security/development nexus
12, 56, 61, 96, 98, 102, 107, 129;
"third way" development strategy

Routledge Global Institutions Series

International Migration
Khalid Koser (Geneva Centre for Security Policy)

Human Development
Richard Ponzio

The International Monetary Fund (2nd edition)
Politics of conditional lending
James Raymond Vreeland (Georgetown University)

The UN Global Compact
Catia Gregoratti (Lund University)

Institutions for Women's Rights
Charlotte Patton (York College, CUNY) and
Carolyn Stephenson (University of Hawaii)

International Aid
Paul Mosley (University of Sheffield)

Global Consumer Policy
Karsten Ronit (University of Copenhagen)

The Changing Political Map of Global Governance
Anthony Payne (University of Sheffield) and
Stephen Robert Buzdugan (Manchester Metropolitan University)

Coping with Nuclear Weapons
W. Pal Sidhu

Twenty-First-Century Democracy Promotion in the Americas
Jorge Heine (The Centre for International Governance Innovation) and
Brigitte Weiffen (University of Konstanz)

EU Environmental Policy and Climate Change
Henrik Selin (Boston University) and
Stacy VanDeveer (University of New Hampshire)

Making Global Institutions Work
Power, accountability and change
Edited by Kate Brennan

Global Governance and China
The dragon's learning curve
Edited by Scott Kennedy (Indiana University)

The Politics of Global Economic Surveillance
Martin S. Edwards (Seton Hall University)

Mercy and Mercenaries
Humanitarian agencies and private security companies
Peter Hoffman

Regional Organizations in the Middle East
James Worrall (University of Leeds)

Reforming the UN Development System
The politics of incrementalism
Silke Weinlich (Duisburg-Essen University)

The United Nations as a Knowledge Organization
Nanette Svenson (Tulane University)

United Nations Centre on Transnational Corporations (UNCTC)
Khalil Hamdani and Lorraine Ruffing

The International Criminal Court
The politics and practice of prosecuting atrocity crimes
Martin Mennecke (University of Copenhagen)

Past as Prelude?
Wartime history and the future United Nations
*Edited by Dan Plesch (SOAS, University of London) and
Thomas G. Weiss (CUNY Graduate Center)*

Expert Knowledge in Global Trade
*Edited by Erin Hannah (University of Western Ontario), James Scott
(University of Manchester), and Silke Trommer (Murdoch University)*

The European Union (2nd edition)
Clive Archer (Manchester Metropolitan University)

The African Union (2nd edition)
*Samuel Makinda (Murdoch University), Wafula Okuma (The African
Union), and David Mickler (University of Western Australia)*

The Politics of International Organizations
Views from insiders
Patrick Weller (Griffith University) and
Xu Yu-chong (Griffith University)

BRICS
João Pontes Nogueira (Catholic University, Rio de Janeiro)
and Monica Herz (Catholic University, Rio de Janeiro)

Governing Climate Change (2nd edition)
Peter Newell (University of East Anglia) and
Harriet A. Bulkeley (Durham University)

Contemporary Human Rights Ideas (2nd edition)
Betrand Ramcharan (Geneva Graduate Institute of International and
Development Studies)

Protecting the Internally Displaced
Rhetoric and reality
Phil Orchard (University of Queensland)

The Arctic Council
Within the far north
Douglas C. Nord (Umea University)

For further information regarding the series, please contact:

Taylor & Francis
2 Park Square, Milton Park, Abingdon
Oxford OX14 4RN, UK
+44 (0)207 842 2057 Tel
+44 (0)207 842 2302 Fax
Craig.Fowlie@tandf.co.uk
www.routledge.com

Lightning Source UK Ltd.
Milton Keynes UK
UKOW05f1307311014

240922UK00001B/26/P

9 780415 856638